Changing Churches

The Local Church and the Structures of Change

Changing Churches

The Local Church and the Structures of Change

Michael Warren, editor

ISBN 1-56929-033-4

Pastoral Press
A Division of OCP Publications
5536 N.E. Hassalo
Portland, OR 97213
Phone: 800-LITURGY (548-8749)
Email: liturgy@ocp.org
Web site: www.pastoralpress.com
Web site: www.ocp.org

Printed in the United States of America

Library of Congress Cataloging-in-Publication Data

Changing Churches : the local church and the structures of change / Michael Warren, editor.
p. cm.
Includes bibliographical references.
ISBN 1-56929-033-4 (pbk.)
1. Church. 2. Sociology, Christian. 3. Christianity and culture. I. Warren, Michael, 1935-

BV625 .C48 2000
262'.2--dc21 00-028559

To Ellis Nelson

Contents

Introduction What Led to This Book 1

1 Writing the Gospel into the Structures of the Local Church 11
Michael Warren

2 Culture and History as the Material Condition of the Genesis of the Local Church 49
Joseph A. Komonchak

3 Congregational Reorientation 67
C. Ellis Nelson

4 Tracks into a New Civilization: A View of the Irish Roman Catholic Church 91
Martin Kennedy

5 Going to Church: Parish Geography 111
Marianne Sawicki

6 Local Learning: A Congregational Inquiry. 139
Edward Farley

7 Raising Lay Consciousness: The Liberation of the Church 163
Paul Lakeland

8 What Does a Local Church Look Like? 185
Rosemary Luling Haughton

9 In Defense of Cultural Christianity: Reflections on Going to Church 207
Stanley Hauerwas

10 The Liturgy, Preaching and Justice 231
John Barrett

11 Christian Practices and Congregational Education in Faith 247
Dorothy C. Bass
Craig Dykstra

Introduction

What Led to This Book

In the mid-1980s I came to the conclusion that the major influence in the lives of most persons was not education or religious education or Christian education, but culture. I set out to study culture in hopes of finding a working theory of culture by which to guide my own work in theology and education. One of the published results of that study was *Communications and Cultural Analysis* (1992), now revised and retitled *Seeing through the Media* (1997).

Those familiar with the book know that I approached culture, not by way of anthropology but via sociology and semiotics, with special attention to the writings of the late British scholar Raymond Williams. His writings highlight the way a social order's signifying system is able to shape the consciousness and behavior of all within it. To be adequate in a time of electronic communications, educators had to begin with attention to the prior and pervasive influences of culture. Religious educators and, even more so, Christian educators could not be effective without pondering the effects of modern communications, not just on students but on themselves.

In these studies of culture my concern focused on churches. If culture — and especially the economic system at the heart of a social order — shapes the attitudes of all, then it shapes those who enter the sacred space of worship, most often, in ways outside their awareness. When they walk into a church, the culture's assumptions about reality tend to walk in with them in the same way that the louse observed by Robert Burns on the hat of a woman in the next pew had walked in with her.[1]

Culture's unavoidable influence became the theme of my writing about the local congregation as the key bearer of the possibility of gospel practice. Could the local church locate itself firmly enough in the signifying system of its own sacred texts so it could see what in the wider culture was not acceptable to it? Or was the local church doomed to shrivel its own zone of meaning to fit neatly and comfortably within the wider culture, no questions asked? Does the church — can it — drink from its own wells?

Foreground

Exploring these questions I followed some hunches about the conditions under which the church might engage in a critical dialogue with culture. The task was difficult. There did not seem to be much literature dealing with the actual practices of the local church. There were, however, various persons — including all in this collection — whose writing indicated sympathy with my own questions and hunches. Reading what they wrote encouraged me to think I might be on the right track. I wondered what might happen if a group of these persons gathered to reflect together on the dilemma of the local church today, each from his or her unique angle. This book is the result.

St. John's University awarded me a summer study stipend to research recent writings on the contemporary problems of the local church. The Lilly Endowment funded a conference on the local church to be held in New York City. One goal was that women theologians comprise at least half of those invited to take part, in consideration of the character of scholarship today and the important questions raised by women. Among those whose writings about the church caught my attention were some of the most sophisticated women theologians working in the United States today. All those contacted were interested in the project; most of them either declined from the beginning or initially accepted and later declined, all for the same single reason: the press of other commitments. Their affirmation of the project was heartening, though I remain disappointed more women are not represented here.

Seedlings

Each person invited to the conference was sent a specific question on the local church based on a passage in his or her published writing. Each was asked to expand on something already written, in order to get at "the specifics of the particulars of the local church." These particulars I called "the material conditions of the local church." The following is the description of that term, which each participant received.

The "material conditions of the local church" is a way of expressing the specifics that go to shape a local community. A local church is shaped by implicit meanings, explicit meanings and concrete embodiments. Each community embodies many things:

- not only a set of sacred texts and a written set of official doctrines [explicit meanings] but also a social location based on the class and social identifications of its people [implicit meanings];
- underlying assumptions about life in general and religious living in particular, assumptions that can be found in directive metaphors [implicit meanings];
- a corporate life structure formed by the network of decisions that have over time become institutionally embedded in buildings, policies, programs, the succession of particular kinds of leaders, various polities and management of financial resources [concrete embodiments].

The local church is a text open to analysis and critique, able to be reshaped by dealing with various "textual" elements.

There are difficulties in dealing with specifics such as those cited here. The details of corporate life may seem trivial and non-disclosing, like shards of pottery from some distant culture revealing a feature of that life but little of the overall ethos that had been lived or the procedures by which it had been realized. Yet if only general principles are dealt with, these may not be able to be applied in a helpful way to specific situations. This symposium seeks to overcome the disconnection between meaning and action and to unite the details of local corporate life with the vision of living found in our sacred texts.

The symposium is to examine in a systematic way the question of how local communities of religious people actually live out their purpose, and to suggest lines of thought helpful for reconfiguring life in these communities.

> The symposium seeks to re-connect espoused meanings and the practice of these meanings through a hermeneutic of life practice.

I was looking to see what scholars with these interests had to say about this general problem. I wanted them to function creatively as artists, not technicians.

The Harvest

The eleven essays here represent the originality and scholarship of those who agreed to be part of this project on the local church. From the open-ended "seedling" invitation offered these scholars, what sorts of flowering bounty for understanding the practices of the local church emerged out of their own skills of cultivation? What common themes emerged that may guide those who wish to study and reflect further on the conditions of local church practice? If a wider literature on the local church is to develop, what issues, based on the clues found in these essays, can we expect to surface in that literature? The following are themes worth studying in these essays: culture, maintenance of meaning, embodiments and specificity in localness. These themes are clearly interconnected.

1. Culture. Though culture was not mentioned in the focus statement sent participants, it emerges as an issue in most of the essays. The most helpful description of culture for me has been Raymond Williams's: "Culture is the signifying system through which necessarily . . . a social order is communicated, experienced, explored and reproduced."[2] This description fits the wider social order, which in most parts of the world is defined by consumer capitalism. It also effectively describes the signifying system of the churches serving not consumer capitalism but what Jesus announced as the Kingdom of God. Almost every essay here deals with aspects of the following problem of culture: How can the church maintain itself as a distinctive signifying system when it dwells in another, wider sign system of great power, backed by the electronic amplification needed by an intrusive economic order?

Martin Kennedy [Chapter 4] examines the crisis that can erupt when a small nation officially adopts the ethos of a single denomination, Roman Catholicism, and finds many of its people moving suddenly and seemingly decisively away from the traditional faith. By his manner of being alerted to but not alarmed by the problem, Kennedy offers local churches a thoughtful and active way of probing what is going on at the corner of X Avenue and Y Street. Implicit in Kennedy's essay, and every other essay here, is a conviction that religious meaning is not self-maintaining but is a continual achievement of intentionality. This same intentionality underlies the Bass and Dykstra work [Chapter 11] on the concrete practices indispensable for a local church.

Joseph Komonchak [Chapter 2] looks at the church struggle with questions of culture and history from the angle of nationalism and ethnic allegiances. He is convinced that a key to resolving such struggles lies with the local churches. Jesus' teachings are about communion, not only among his followers but also among all children of God. This perspective raises troubling questions about the behavior of Christians today and in the last century. Ellis Nelson, whose foundational writings on culture and faith have influenced so many, looks [Chapter 3] to the double formation system of the church and the wider culture, especially as it affects children. His essay shows the cultural formation / ecclesial formation polarity to be a theme in congregational studies done over the past twenty years.

Edward Farley [Chapter 6] calls for "ordered learning" toward disciplined skills of interpretation as necessary for fidelity in the face of cultural forces. Ironically, these forces make resistance to church learning almost inevitable. The result is religious childishness.

2. Maintenance of Meaning. The need to nurture religious conviction is another theme in the chapters of this book. Understanding cannot be vague and characterized by whimsy. To repeat Farley, that way leads to religious childishness.

Religiousness, if it is to endure, needs a web-like structure for its coherence. Not a rigid structure, the web is flexible in wind and rain but able to maintain its basic pattern. Neither is a web untethered; its flexibility is anchored in reality. Webs sometimes need to be repaired, and many have marveled at a spider's nimble working of such repairs, faithfully reproducing the basic pattern and re-attaching its anchors.

One might say the reason so many of these scholars have stressed this theme is that they are Christian educators specializing in helping people understand. I would put it the other way around. The reason they are Christian educators is that they recognize religion is not self-maintaining: once instilled it will not automatically endure, as Kennedy so clearly shows [Chapter 4]. The maintenance of religious understanding is an achievement of intentionality, especially of communal intention. My own essay and its survey of the lapses of the twentieth century [Chapter 1] are all about this matter. Meaning today is not set in the form of logical syllogisms but in the form of images and narratives with latent, implicit messages, most of them communicated to us over electronic networks.

Here, Barrett [Chapter 10] examines preaching in the context of worship, especially as it affects issues of justice. Sawicki [Chapter 5] reminds us that people who gather in churches arrive there by multiple paths whose ways and intersections are all potentially significant to a lived faith. Hauerwas [Chapter 9] simply describes what going to church is like for him in helping him remain religiously focused. Nelson's and Farley's essays [Chapters 3 and 6] are perhaps the ones with the greatest attention to this theme. Bass and Dykstra [Chapter 11] examine not so much the pattern of the web as the actual, endless making of the web.

3. Embodiment. This third theme is found in all the writings here. The Christian church is not a theory so much as a practice. Its results are not so much a theoretical structure

of thought as a local group whose way of living is tangible and accessible for all to see — for well or ill. Their way of living can actively deny or validate the faith they proclaim. What they live can be a vital witness to the goodness and value of their faith or it can be a counterwitness to that faith. Embodied faith offers compelling evidence of faith's goodness that is beyond propositions and arguments. Whatever arguments may be put forth are already affirmed or denied by the unavoidable evidence of a way of living. Put in positive terms: there is no religious argument as convincing as a faithful life.

The theme of embodiment, therefore, represents a central focus of this book of essays and is perhaps set forth most cohesively in the final chapter by Dykstra and Bass. It is the issue behind Lakeland's analysis of clericalism [Chapter 7] and Haughton's survey of ways of being local [Chapter 8]. It could be summed up in the sacramental principle [a central assumption in Chapter 2] of Roman Catholicism: As seen in Jesus, God's tendency is to take visible form both in faith-filled individuals and communities. Like the "shook foil" of Gerard Manley Hopkins' poem, God's presence tends to shimmer. Indeed this is the issue left us as an unwelcome legacy of the twentieth century: the dilemma of living what we name instead of merely intoning what we dare not live.

4. Localness and Specificity. The fourth theme connecting these chapters is the nature of religious assembly as a communal body in a particular time and place. It either responds to local conditions and needs, or it ignores them. Its particularity — these people in this place and this time gathering around these particular ways of looking at the world and of living in the world — is a gift and a challenge. Unfortunately, that challenge can be avoided when a local church becomes abstracted from its own concrete existence and untethered from the needs erupting all around it.

Of all the issues that surfaced in the first drafts written for our face-to-face symposium, this one appeared in powerful and unexpected ways. Readers will surely find their own surprise and pleasure in exploring this theme. Marianne Sawicki's elegantly written proposal of prizing path over place [Chapter 5] offered a new way of considering localness, but so did Rosemary Haughton's [Chapter 8] exploration of "localness," Kennedy's metaphor of laying flexible tracks to meet ever-new needs and Komonchak's reflections on the local church's genesis.

John Barrett's study of preaching focuses on the issues that are allowed or disallowed in a particular assembly, a matter Hauerwas describes in a simple and direct narrative way. Lakeland's concern with lay agency — in particular, congregations — gets at the same matter. Those familiar with Nelson's and Farley's writings know that this issue is central in their other published works: Farley's *Ecclesial Reflection* and Nelson's *Where Faith Begins*. Their essays here carry the matter forward. The last chapter written for this collection caps the importance of local practice and challenges all local congregations to ponder what their actual practices have written into their lives.

The Feast

The metaphor of "feast" seems most accurate for those two days of affirmation, critique, questions and struggle when we gathered in New York. Who would not have been "filled" by such a gathering on such an issue? Who could be with such a group of scholars and not be deeply pleased by both the challenges and the delightful surprises of such a gathering? Although it was indeed a metaphoric feast of fellowship, insight and challenge, it was also, literally, a wonderful time of eating and drinking together.

These essays make the intellectual side of our symposium feast accessible to many others. My hope is that eventually many in local churches may be able to partake of the solid nourishment offered by these scholars.

Acknowledging Those Who Served

A group of others participated in the symposium, although not as writers. Chief among them was Pamela Kirk of the St. John's University theology faculty, who chaired the discussions and kept them on track with her careful and subtle attention to particulars. Her competence proved crucial, as did Connie Loos's ability to remember the sequence and content of various comments made around the table. Jim Daniels, a recent graduate of the B.A. and M.A. theology program at St. John's, helped by taking care of every detail of the conference rooms and the surroundings.

Of indispensable help in carrying through the original inspiration for the conference were two persons who have not met each other, one from the staff of St. John's theology department, the other a professor from Texas. The first was Fran Fico. Had she not been on our theology staff, I would not, as I have truthfully told her, have attempted the project at all. Before and after the symposium, she knew what to do and did it. The second was C. Ellis Nelson of Austin Presbyterian Theological Seminary, whose advice and encouragement included the patient exchange of dozens of letters and more dozens of phone calls needed for the Lilly Endowment grant that made the conference possible. This is as perhaps it should be, since my reading of his work *Where Faith Begins* as a graduate student in the late Sixties has indelibly marked my own subsequent work.

A word about the authors. Though four have been ordained in various denominations, only one, John Barrett, is a full-time practicing priest. For the most part, then, this book represents, like Robert Burns's poem, a view from the pew, from members of the worshiping assembly.

Endnotes

1 "To seeing Louse, On a lady's bonnet at church," *The Complete Works of Robert Burns*, vol. 1 (New York: Bigelow Brown and Co., 1909), 259–61.

2 Raymond Williams, *The Sociology of Culture* (New York: Schocken Books, 1982), 13.

Chapter 1

Writing the Gospel into the Structures of the Local Church

Michael Warren

The essay deals first with the record of Christian practice in our own century and then moves on to diagnoses of the problem before finally considering remedies. Accurate diagnosis is the basis for a proper remedy. Christian denominations invited at the end of a millennium to peer predictively into the future would also do well to look back on the specifics of the past century and their role in resisting and assisting its calamities.

Some readers may find this essay overly theoretical and may want to move on to more specific essays. I encourage such moves in a book like this. Actually this piece could have been a final essay to this collection. Readers wanting to read more along these lines may want to read the author's earlier Faith, Culture and the Worshiping Community (Portland OR: Pastoral Press, A Division of OCP Publications, 1993) or At This Time and in This Place: The Spirit Liberating the Local Church (Valley Forge PA: Trinity Press International, 1999).

This essay is about Christian living in the future. Jesus' followers do not face the future with a clean slate. Scribbled all over our slate are inscriptions, devout and blasphemous, from our recent past that cannot be wiped away. Like the unstanchable blood dripping from Bluebeard's tiny key, these inscriptions demand our attention.[1] They scream to us to judge our past as we look to the future. This essay is partly about what is on that slate and partly about what future churches might do to avoid the worst lapses written there. Those lapses open the claims of Christian discipleship to ridicule, as much as they summon followers of the Jesus Way to pay attention to what they actually do. Though these matters sound grim, my essay is written from a deep gospel hope that the Spirit of Jesus will perdure.

While most of the essay is about practice, its first section is grounded in the questions our past century's social evil puts to followers of Jesus. The next three sections are diagnostic. They look at religious groups as involved in two kinds of production processes. One is the active production of gospel living; the other, the passive ingesting of socially produced attitudes and perceptions that need to be judged in the light of the Spirit of Jesus. Unless this passive ingesting is recognized and faced, it becomes the more influential of these processes. These diagnostic sections deal with 1) the production of meaning itself in its most concrete and "material" forms; 2) perception in a time of electronic communication; and 3) the role of decisions, explicit and unconscious, in shaping life. The final two sections are prescriptive but not in the sense of offering a formula for discipleship. They move toward the remedial by reconsidering the art of practice and by looking at how some communities have been able to achieve a gospel focus.

Centennial–Millennial Questions

Persons examining the historical record left by those who lived in the 20th century will have the right to ask what significance local Christian congregations had in that record. Christians, concerned for their tradition, may have a duty to ask this question. Whatever the social and cultural achievements of that century, they are overridden by the social and cultural horrors it produced. The number of those who died violently by calculated human intent in wars, massacres of civilian populations and attempts to erase entire peoples from the face of the earth has surely been summed up somewhere. My own count hovers near 200 million, a number fattened by end-of-century horrors in the Balkans, where the religious convictions of Roman Catholic Croats, Russian Orthodox Serbs and Bosnian Muslims did not check the slaughter of hundreds of thousands and in Rwanda, where the Roman Catholicism of Hutus seems to have had little influence in stemming bestial behavior. This 200 million does not include those killed by institutionalized social systems that starved and maimed human beings in the specially cruel ways that go with structural injustice. The enormity of the evil here seems to make blasphemous any attempt to do such a count, as if quantifying somehow allows our minds to deal with the evil done. Were we capable of imagining the particulars of these horrors — the children, the families, the terror — we would be in danger of going mad.

My question above focuses not so much on the significance of these deaths *for* groups of Christians looking back on them, but on the significance *of* those gospel-oriented groups that lived at the time or in the places where the horrors occurred and the significance such Christian groups may have in the future when similar horrors threaten. In the past century, did the group-life of those pledging fidelity to the words and deeds of the Galilean Jew of the first century make, or attempt to make, any difference when victims were being singled out for killing? How many churchgoing Christians in Poland risked their lives to save Jews from the horrors awaiting them?[2] How much hatred of Jews existed in Roman Catholic Poland or Christian Germany long before the Nazis took over those lands, and what forms did that hatred take? If that hatred was widespread, how did it happen that the sacred texts announced in weekly assemblies had such little hold on the hearts of the assembled? Worse, how did those texts, in their way of being interpreted and applied, provide the context for hatred? [Modras, 1996][3]

These questions are neither novel nor insightful. They are the standard sorts of questions asked in the face of our century. They need to be pressed on Christian assemblies concerned for the challenges ahead. What are the conditions required for "recognizing the Risen Lord?"[4] Asking such questions, local churches can examine the adequacy of their current procedures. Cultural shifts in the past forty years call for a studied appraisal of the forms of communication and decision-making currently in use in local churches. If a starting place for re-appraisal is the condition of misery and suffering, I can turn to the questions of German theologian Johannes Metz about that condition.

Metz asks why the horrors and suffering of our times show up so little in theology. Is theology itself, as written by the learned or practiced by the "faithful," a conspicuous practice of apathy, i.e., a way of ignoring the unjust suffering there in plain sight in our midst? How can theology reclaim its political version as action for the salvation of those who suffer unjustly here and now, or its prophetic version as speech about the victims and the beaten-down of history? In Auschwitz, specifically, Metz finds "a horror that makes . . . [all] noncontextual talk about God appear empty and blind," in the face of which he asks, "Is there . . . a God whom one can worship with back turned to such a catastrophe?" At issue here is "the question of how one can speak of God at all in the face of the abysmal history of suffering in the world." [Metz, 1994: 611, 612; Soelle, 1975, 1984][5] How indeed? How, now, in various of the more than three hundred thousand local religious assemblies in the U.S. today?[6] Can we speak of God (or of the groups pledging fidelity to God) without pretending there is no human collusion in the creation of suffering?

Metz's question of how to connect God and suffering not only deserves to be asked; he claims it is prompted from within the Judeo-Christian tradition itself, a landscape of cries to God, lamenting and objecting to God about unjust suffering. The talent for God, the capacity for God, found in Israel is marked by an incapacity to be consoled by neat ways of explaining away evil. "The language of [Israel's] God-mysticism is not primarily one of providing consoling answers to experiences of suffering; rather, it is much more a language of passionate requestioning that arises out of suffering, a requestioning of God, full of highly charged expectation." [Metz, 621] Tied to this mysticism is what Metz calls "anamnetic reason," reason that resists forgetfulness and, instead, attends carefully to the silence of those who have disappeared, as a way of being attentive to "Godself."

Metz's question sparks further questions — about the conditions under which a refusal to ignore or forget unjust suffering can become part of a local church. Considering the limitations of each person's attentiveness, how will a local assembly be able to maintain attentiveness to unjust suffering in our world as a condition necessary for the ecclesial landscape of cries and lament? By maintaining its communal landscape of cries and lament, the assembly may over time maintain both attentiveness as a mindset and action as a habit.

Diagnostic 1: Religious Production as a Discernable Process

If attentiveness to unjust suffering is called for by our tradition, along with an action-stance on behalf of victims, how is this "God mysticism" to be achieved? Another, jarring way of asking this question is, How will it be produced? Can such a religious attitude or frame of reference be produced, or is it a gift of God's own self beyond human production? The question is important because it directs us to the specifics of the particulars of being Christians.

Religious sociologist Robert Wuthnow invites us to consider the important matter of religious production: the intentional production of religious insights, convictions, commitments, rituals and patterns of response. With his invitation, however, comes a warning that the very idea of religious production may rub most of us the wrong way. [Wuthnow, 1994][7] We have been taught to think of revelation as a gift of God, an epiphany disclosing God in God's way and at God's moment, not as a human product. Indeed, the New Testament emphasizes God's free intervention in Jesus' double birth: through Mary at Bethlehem and in the resurrection at Jerusalem; yet Wuthnow presses on us our teaching that God reveals "Godself" through human words and deeds — in a fully accessible human way, through very human processes.[8] This teaching is bolstered by current religious sociology.

Most sociologists of religion today make a distinction between religion and the sacred, with religion being a network of humanly devised procedures and with the sacred being religion's inner core, which is of God. Sociologists have not always made this distinction. Like some of today's believers, many nineteenth-century sociologists dismissed this distinction, but from an opposite direction. They held the sacred to be a confidence trick produced by religion as a way of making capitalism seem willed by God. In their view, religion takes humanly produced procedures and makes them seem to be made by God, that is, sacred. Thus religion produces a false consciousness, a basic misunderstanding of how the world actually works. The human hands behind various social procedures are disguised and the procedures themselves made to appear sacred and unquestionable.

As noted above, current sociology of religion honors the distinction between the human processes of religion and the sacred mediated by these processes. However, I find the oversimplifications of nineteenth-century sociology to have important lessons for religious professionals today. As a religious believer I find, even in this perspective's most unnuanced version, a useful reminder of the possible distortions of humanly constructed religious forms. One such distortion is a sort of "institutional blindness" of some believers to the arbitrary character of many of religion's own procedures.

Though not actually named as sacred, procedures of the group come gradually and quietly to be awarded an unwarranted sacral character. The way a chemical or mineral can bleed from one substance into another, the sacred can bleed unwittingly into this-worldly decisions and arrangements, rendering them unexaminable, unquestionable and uncontestable. My essay seeks to unlock the door keeping procedures untouched and instead invite examination, questioning and, if needed, contestation and reform.

Social science's more recent appreciation of religion's relation to the sacred can be helpful for religionists in their task of renewal, as Wuthnow's book shows. Current social science sees culture as a signifying system communicating a social order, that is, a humanly constructed system of meaning communicated by particular processes: gestures, language, rituals, laws, customs, even ways of cooking and eating. What is true of culture in general is also true of the cultural form called a religious tradition. In such a tradition the sacred is carried by "symbolic frameworks . . . set apart from everyday life, giving a sense of transcendent, holistic meaning." [Wuthnow, 3][9] The sacred gives us access to realities not so evident to human perception, but does so only by means of individuals, communities and organizations and the particular procedures they use to communicate.[10] While God may be unfathomable, a religious culture's "ways" can be measured and charted — and examined for appropriateness.

A friend tells of his first deep sense of the sacred when he was fourteen years old. His memory of what happened may illustrate the concrete decisions and actions that led to his profound insight. In a large church near his all-boys' high school, he was at a worship service opening the school year. Hearing hundreds of male voices singing a particular hymn, he found himself caught up in such a tingling sense of the presence of God that he never forgot the power of that moment, that place, that start to a new period of his life. The reality of God for him then was intense and ecstatic, seeming to lift him out of his own body. To recognize that that sense of God was made possible by human procedures in a space constructed by human ingenuity to lend a special quality to the human voice denies none of its reality. I do not claim that such a life-orienting insight defines the sacred, only that it was mediated by a human event. Neither was that sense of God, in all likelihood, exclusive to my friend but was available at various levels of insight to many others present in that group.

On reflection many recognize that in their own lives the sacred has become accessible and real — produced — through human agents or events that were channels of God's gifts. Some can name those agents and vividly describe places, events and procedures many years after they occurred. However, the matter is not clear to all. Some think the sacred is communicated only by way of startling interventions of God, in acts that disrupt the laws of nature. Those who have taught the bible have heard from students this complaint: the God who did marvels centuries ago as a means of communicating with mortals seems to have lost interest in them today. Students' evidence for this assertion is that God currently produces no similar marvels as a way of communicating with them. This misunderstanding, a stubborn one, can be corrected, not necessarily easily, through a more adequate theology, through insight into the interpretation of texts and through more attention to the role of individuals, communities and organizations in the communication of religious insight.

Even a quick reflection on the conditions under which my friend had his presence-of-God insight shows how ordinary activities of individuals, communities and organizations helped shape that moment. He himself did not come into that church devoid of previous influences; he, his brother and sisters came from a devout family, whose life was marked by regular times of worship and prayer, both within their home and in their local church. When he entered that church with his fellow students, his previous religious formation walked in with him, accompanied by his religious struggles. He was questioning whether he wanted to accept as his own his family's religious commitments.

I have already mentioned the fact that the space of that church where he and so many others were gathered had been constructed to enhance a sense of God's presence by means of space, light, color and sound. Further, he was with others, hundreds of them, whose presence was organized by teachers and administrators who awarded worship a significant part of the first day of school. The hymns sung had been taught those students and the words said in unison were either memorized or available to be read off printed sheets. The orderly sequence of the ritual itself was also planned. What happened to him that day was no accident but an achievement of human intentionality backed by the gift of God.

Robert Wuthnow claims that a useful avenue for systematic reflection on these procedures is the "recent 'production of culture' literature in sociology that emphasizes the role of organizations, professionals, power arrangements and other social resources in generating cultural artifacts, such as music, books and art." [Wuthnow, 6] As a method of studying how cultural artifacts are produced in social contexts by communities and organizations, this perspective can be used also to examine how religious communities and organizations function in relation to the sacred.

Wuthnow illustrates this approach in an examination of how a particular person became an artist, specifically a painter. As I did above, he initiates a series of questions about the social conditions under which the crafting of a particular artwork was possible. Was there special training, and if so, what kind of financing made it possible? In the place where any actual painting was done, what was the physical space like: its dimensions, location and any other conditions helpful to an artist? Who provided the space? What materials and technologies were used? How were they acquired? Was a particular work commissioned, by whom, at what cost? How did the one commissioning come to know the artist or the artist's work? How did any or all these factors influence the content of a particular painting?

But there is also the question of the artist's own self. How does one come to internalize for oneself the social role of the artist? Who were the mentors who influenced that role for a particular person? Did these mentors operate out of a particular model of an artist? Was a social process operating by which funding was made available or by which talent was recognized? Such questions can easily be applied to the cultural artifact we call religion. [Wuthnow, 25–27] For example, how did the administrators of my friend's high school come to see that a large group worship service might beneficially displace the religious instruction given in a classroom that opening day of school?

Applied to a local church or congregation, these sorts of specific questions get at what I call the material conditions of the local church. They do not always produce exactly what the local assembly wishes; sometimes they produce unexpected results. Wuthnow warns of this two-sided character of the results produced by these material conditions:

> The important issue for our purposes is simply that cultural production results in both products and by-products, that is, intended results and unintended results. . . . Some of what they [public religious organizations] produce is deliberate and some is unplanned and unexpected. In both cases resources are expended, and social circumstances influence what happens. [27]

I think this warning has to be expanded, especially to meet the centennial or millennial critique of actual religious functioning.

Sometimes religious groups or organizations produce results that disaffirm or deny the very realities they claim to affirm. Such communities can become radical living disconfirmations of their own sacred texts, official positions and the very religious rituals in which they themselves engage. Our own century offers numberless examples of religious groupings being unable to break through socially and culturally constructed walls of ethnicity, nationalism, class, regionalism and religion to encounter the human beings of other religions, ethnicities and so forth, as temples of the living God. Religion's focus on God as unifier would seem to crack these walls of separateness; however, group decisions based on domination or superiority can subvert the religious perceptions meant to guide those decisions and be guided instead by hate. Those who deny that possibility are far more susceptible to this subversion than those consciously alarmed by it. Where this denial is in place, a community in a sense hides from its own self.

Diagnostic 2: Patterning Perception Electronically

To repeat: these questions are not new. However, the situation in which they are asked is relatively new, because of the new power of communications to shape people's perceptions and interpretations of their world.[11] Every culture represents a way of imagining the shape of the *humanum*. This imagination is so encoded in the culture's signifying system that people ordinarily do not think about it. Culture, then, is a system of signs that successfully imprints in people the implicit and explicit codes undergirding a social order and its economic system. Of central importance to religious persons is that these codes tend to function as norms for behavior and for ordinary judgments. In Ireland, driving a young woman to her home, I honk at a balky, uncertain driver. My passenger slouches down in her seat so no one will see her presence with one who impolitely honks from impatience. Her behavior puzzles me, and she explains that *my* behavior violates an unspoken code of road courtesy: honk not, except to avoid an accident. New York's code is not acceptable in Cork.

In an unprecedented way, codes today can be quickly constructed, communicated, shifted and re-focused by means of electronically communicated images and narratives. The unprecedented character of electronically communicated meaning lies not in its newness: Because of the way this chain of meaning continues to evolve (or metathesize) exponentially, it is best termed as not just new but endlessly or progressively new. The social order's signifying system is "in our faces" so incessantly it takes on the taken-for-grantedness of social codes themselves. As George Gerbner says, "Children used to grow up in a home where parents told most of the stories. Today television tells most of the stories to most of the people most of the time." [Gerbner: 8] Ironically, the most effective of these stories are not the main narratives that fill an hour of teletime but the fifteen- and thirty-second mini-tales that spike into the main narrative during commercial breaks. In the face of this electronically maintained world of meaning, one might ask what possibilities assemblies gathering weekly around the altar have of maintaining their alternate view of the world?[12]

Codes are norms; norms fuel judgment — like my passenger's judgment about my rude behavior on an Irish road. But there is a further side to this matter. Religions themselves are true cultures, though they exist within a wider culture. They represent special ways of imagining the shape of the human. They are signifying systems by which a social order is communicated, but a social order called for by God's self, a social order that is more than an idea because of its being implemented via religious action, though not yet fully actual. Like the wider culture's, a religion's codes are also normative and also communicated through signs: narratives, patterns of ordinary action and ritual actions like sharing bread and drinking from a common cup. Some of these religious codes offer cautionary judgments on the codes of the wider culture. Religion's "Your neighbor's misery is God's call to you," or, as Emmanuel Levinas puts it, "The material needs of my neighbor are my spiritual needs,"[13] would be one such example of a commentary on the wider culture's codes. Notice that a consumerist culture does not say, "Your neighbor is of no concern to you." Its message is more subtle and nuanced than that. It might rather say, "When your neighbor's misery and your wants are in conflict, your wants take priority." Religion's imagination of the *humanum* contests that conclusion.

An important feature of the wider culture's coded norms is that they tend to be implicit. Silently, claimlessly, they work their way into our behavior and "ways." However, religion's norms, coming as they do from a tradition and inscribed in texts, tend to be explicit. Coming from God, they add to their normativeness the edge of ultimacy. With ultimacy bestowed by God, these norms are worth living for and dying for. Here we encounter an irony worth the attention of all who follow religious traditions: the implicit norms can have greater power than the explicit ones. Implicit norms, ordinarily unspoken, are more difficult to contest than explicit ones with their open claims. Once the implicit norms have been internalized, explicit religious norms may be so used as to rarely intersect with, let alone contest, the norms of the wider culture.

In a time of electronic communications, the incessantly but implicitly communicated norms of consumerist culture seem to overwhelm the explicit, seemingly ultimate, not often articulated norms of religion. Inert norms, announced but not embraced, known but not applied, are in fact no norms at all. They are the idea of a norm. Norms, when embraced, configure a stance, a positioning of the self or of the community in the face of situations judged by the norms. In this sense a norm is very much like a belief, as described by Charles Sanders Peirce: "The essence of belief is the establishment of a habit, and different beliefs are distinguished by the different modes of action to which they give rise." [Peirce: 263–64]

When some in an audience stand and boo a poor opera performance in noisy, impolite protest to bad singing, the norm they honor is that of good singing. In application, however, norms are not rigid because, seeking benchmarks or standards, they plot possibility along a line of more or less. Norms are matters for discussion, whether applying them is an art or a science. Norms are sharpened by being applied, by attention to the specifics and nuance [the materiality] of what is being judged, by remembering conditions under which some past stunning achievement came about, and by maintaining a sense of what "the more" could be. Lacking these efforts, the normative eye, with its sense of what is right and its ability to make a nuanced evaluation, can be lost through disuse.

If norms fuel judgment and judgment fuels action, the question seems to be: Under what conditions can religious groups embrace their norms, consciously use them in judgments, and opt for forms of action consistent with those judgments? Norms are not only accepted and applied individually. Their chief form is found in the communal dimension of judgment, where persons are invited into the circle of norms and to grapple with the problem of application to concrete situations. An individual or a group cannot decide for others or apply norms for others, because deciding, norming and judging require full human agency and, for a group, result from an interactive process. There is no group stance without the struggle to see how norms apply or to discern the difference they make. Today, deciding or "decisioning" is a key religious act, and its absence represents a yawning religious void. Without decisioning, true religious action is replaced with rote repetition.[14] My purpose here is to foster reflection on decisions and action taken after gospel-based judgments are made. At the start of this essay I alluded to the Bluebeard folktale. The cautionary element in that story is not about Bluebeard himself or how he became a monster; it is the question of how and why the naive young sister came to choose him as her life partner, despite warning clues. But first I want to reflect briefly on the consequences of decisions.

Diagnostic 3: Judgment, Decision, Behavior, Exclusions

Social philosopher Albert Borgmann seeks to question the modern segregation of doing from making, of decisions about conduct from decisions about technology. As a result of this split, morality becomes the realm of conduct, presumed to be unconnected to the realm of production. This segregation of doing from producing "fails to see that a technological accomplishment, the development and adoption of a technological device always and already constitutes a moral decision." [Borgmann, 110] Products, the material results of production, have profound power to shape our conduct, all the greater when that power is not recognized. Borgmann finds badly flawed and unhelpful any moral theory that dismisses as basically neutral the material setting of society, especially its connection to technology. The materiality of our world has important moral implications for the very specific kinds of decisions we make. Here I will recount some of Borgmann's analysis of decision-making as being of potential help to the local church.

Understanding the character of decisions sheds light on the significance of particular decisions for behavior and the overall patterning of our lives. All of us "entrust" our aspirations to various kinds of decisions that anchor our spirits in specific deeds that are the marks of that self in the world. Borgmann makes helpful distinctions. A daily personal decision is different from a fundamental decision, the daily decision being made on a particular day for that day only. A fundamental personal decision, however, is an action marked by a different character of intention, one that binds us to a whole pattern of action over many days into the future. A desire to become more familiar with Shakespeare's plays can lead to either a daily or a fundamental decision. If the desire leads to a daily decision to read some play of Shakespeare's or even something about his plays, that decision must be remade day after day. A fundamental decision is different; it looks ahead and binds one to a chain of actions over many days to come, like enrolling in a course on Shakespeare at a local college, and carrying out corollary actions: paying tuition, buying books, setting aside time for class and study and so forth. For a fundamental personal decision to be suitable, it must have some promise of being carried out. Records will show that not all who sign up for Shakespeare have made a decision suited to being carried out.[15]

Borgmann makes a further distinction about our decisions. A decision that shapes the material environment he at first calls a fundamental *moral* decision, but quickly shifts to naming it as a fundamental *material* decision, calling attention thereby to the moral implications of material decisions. When such a decision is made without responsible insight, that shaping of our environment can be harmful or at least can have unforeseen consequences. Parents whose home is hooked up to a cable network decide their nine-year-old daughter may have a TV in her bedroom at the top of the house. They have decided to allow her, once in that room alone, unsupervised access at any hour to a range of televisual "entertainment," some of it unsuitable to one her age. In Borgmann's view the decision to allow the TV in the bedroom is moral not so much because there may be unseemly programming on it but because the decision shifts the relational patterns between child and parents, among others in the home, and ultimately, the pattern of influences. The child of nine may now find herself in the electronic hands of persons who imagine for her the shape of the human, persons her parents might never have allowed into their home had they met them first.

Borgmann himself uses an astute example, also involving electronic communications, that discloses the importance of material decisions.

> Gary Larsen has pictured his father and his family "in the days before television." Dad is sitting on the couch, son and daughter lying on the floor, the dog between them, all four staring at the same blank wall. Once the situation that was tacitly assumed is rendered explicit, it becomes a cartoon and reveals *the absurdity of the assumption that life has empty slots that can be filled without needing to*

> *rearrange the order of life.* [emphasis added] Life is always and already full; it is a total fabric. It may contain empty spaces for inconsequential additions. But if anything is added to life that takes time, the web of life is torn and rewoven; a hole is made by the new device. Saving and taking time come down to the same thing here. A timesaving device creates a hole in traditional practices no less than does a device that devours time.
>
> Once a television set is in the house, the daily decision whether to read a book, or write a letter, or play a game, or tell stories, or go for a walk, or sit down to dinner, or watch television no longer really ranges over seven possibilities. The presence of television had compressed all alternatives to one whose subalternatives are contained in the question: What are we going to watch tonight? [Borgmann, 111]

What Borgmann has described here is a "material decision," in this case a decision to purchase something that patterned a group's behavior and interaction — the fabric of group life.

Fundamental and material decisions made at a personal or family level can also be made at the collective level, which proves to be the key level in Borgmann's analysis. When made at the collective level, decisions tend to coax along or "pre-form" the decisions made at the individual and family level. For example, when a collective decision leaves TV signals too weak for good reception in some areas, residents may be pushed to rely on a cable system. What Borgmann is sorting out here is a chain of influences in decision making. In his schema then, 1) fundamental personal and material personal decisions preform the daily decisions by shaping the context of those daily decisions. The fundamental personal decision to study for a degree or the material decision not to own an automobile affects many daily decisions. 2) Collective material decisions pre-form the personal fundamental and material decisions. Collective decisions about public transportation and about the non-importance of sidewalks also shape decisions at the individual level, like the purchase of an automobile. The already constructed patterns of cable TV fare preforms or shapes the results of a decision to allow a TV in a child's bedroom.

Borgmann's point is that decisions are particular and affect behavior. His chief concern is to direct more attention to material decisions, both personal and collective. Churches would do well to consider the implications of this point for their own group life. By naming these categories of decision he helps us attend to them more thoughtfully and intentionally They shift the particularities of our lives. Such attention is important: "The moral fabric of family life is typically patterned not so much by practices as by acquisitions, by material decisions, as I will call them, rather than by practical decisions." [Borgmann, 112]

Borgmann's analysis of modernity also provides an interesting way of looking at judgment, of some importance to religious persons. He notices that modern common sense distinguishes between private and public, with the private seen as the sphere of individual discretion and the public the sphere of collective regimentation. Admittedly this polarity has ancient roots in seeing family life as the zone of intimacy and seclusion as opposed to the open, inclusive life of civic engagement. Today, however, the realm of the private has come to be seen as place where "commodious individualism" can be pursued — but protected by "privacy," a word that designates the essence of the private realm. Increasingly in our time privacy has been defined as *"freedom from intrusions that can lead to an unwarranted judgment* [emphasis added] on the person whose sphere of intimacy has been invaded." [Borgmann, 42] Family members who comprise our private circle and those friends allowed into that circle may make judgments, but no one else is entitled to. What is being protected here from judgment is "the unencumbered enjoyment of consumption goods or commodities. . . , the collective affirmation of consumption as an exercise of freedom." [43] Ultimately no judgments about consumption are to be made by any person at all, because the ultimate space of privacy is not seen as occupied by a single person but by a single *consumer*.

Borgmann's analysis is cited here in detail for its way of getting at a little noticed but important exclusion of a whole area of life from reflection in religious congregations. Obviously the entire private realm is not excluded, since congregations give attention to kindness toward one's loved ones and to sexual fidelity. Excluded is reflection on how we think about and use money and leisure, the closely guarded commodities of privacy. A kind of silent, even unwitting collusion has agreed that this vital area is out of bounds for religious discourse — and with it the whole question of public resources. Ironically, what religious discourse dares not discuss, commercial orchestrators of human desire use every conceivable stratagem to manipulate. Once money and leisure are agreed to be out of bounds for discussion, no gospel norms are allowed and no judgments, even tentative ones, can be made about them. The use of an assembly's common funds might provoke vigorous discussion, but the discussion dares not spill over to how members deal with their own personal, private finances. Roman Catholic preaching rarely attends to the use of money as a religious question, except in the case of tithing for the local church. Under what conditions might a community's members agree to examine their attitudes toward their own individual use of money?

This matter is not settled by mathematical formulas but by a communal grappling with scriptural texts and with the various ways the tradition has met the question. Norms are not be imposed from outside, any more than religious convictions are. Are there conditions under which a worshiping assembly can begin to ponder this question and respond to it? Religious texts raise important questions about our responsibilities to others and the use of resources, including money, in meeting those responsibilities.

I am aware that thus far I have intentionally sketched in bold strokes outlines that need to be filled in. Attention to human misery of our time, recognition of the materiality of religious living, facing the problem of the two cultures and of religious judgment, and understanding how decisions shape our private and collective lives — these tasks provide important lines of ecclesial self-reflection. I now proceed to another broad area that may help us reflect on the materiality of the church.

Prescriptive 1: *Phronesis* as skill in communal action

How shall the resources of a committed religious group actually move toward living the gospel? Joseph Dunne's detailed examination of *phronesis* (knowledge of practice) in the writings of Aristotle provides further insight into the nature of communal action. Dunne's study is founded in the same dissatisfaction with instrumental, technical rationality that is behind many current efforts to break free of the hegemony of the Enlightenment. These efforts seek to reconceive an alternative way of guiding practical activity. Instead of prizing detachment, conceptual control, universality and objectivity, these revisionist thinkers have sought to move past the theory-practice split to a better-differentiated, alternative account of human reason itself.[16]

Aristotle distinguished between kinds of knowledge, with practical knowledge differentiated from theoretical knowledge. He recognized in practical knowledge two modes, each of which governs a particular kind of activity. The first — and my chief concern here — is *phronesis,* or practical, non-technical knowledge which guides the activity of *praxis*. The second mode of practical knowledge is *techne*, a productive knowledge geared to products. *Techne* is the knowledge that guides *poiesis*, the activity of producing crafted products or artifacts. *Praxis*, the name given the activity guided by *phronesis*, is the effort to work out with others humanizing ways of acting together for the common good. Confusing these two modes of knowledge, i.e., *techne,* or knowledge about how to produce products, and *phronesis,* or knowledge about coordinating practice, and their appropriate activities, can lead to disaster. For example, to conceive of action for the common good as a product instead of as a practice might lead us to misapply activities suited to products to "produce" communal practices, which are not products in that sense at all.

Basically Aristotle's distinction is between products and practices, with each using its own specific kind of practical knowledge in different kinds of activities. Both *techne* and *phronesis* are embodied kinds of knowledge, verified only in the activities that allow them to function, or better, to flourish. Each represents a particular kind of practical wisdom that, if pursued, becomes a virtue of doing — in *poiesis*, a productive doing and in *praxis,* a practical doing.[17]

Though well aware of the stumbling blocks in these distinctions and their unfamiliar phraseology, I find that mastering them offers a helpful way for conceiving the kind of activity we actually engage in when we seek with others to create a religious assembly. The activity of praxis using the knowledge of phronesis calls for a true agency, not just of leaders but of all in the community. The goal of praxis, as we will see, is self-implicating self-direction, not of an individual self, but of a community. I use the analogy of an orchestra that has a conductor: the conductor's role is to coordinate, not create, the true agency of every artist in the ensemble. The conductor helps provide the conditions that release the artistry of the group.

The problem Dunne deals with in his book is that of giving an adequate enough account, first of phronesis and then of its activity, praxis. Unless techne and poiesis are grasped in their own particularity, phronesis and praxis cannot be seen for the specific kinds of wisdom and activity they actually are. Today, in a time dominated by the machine metaphor, we conceive of any kind of crafting in mechanistic terms. The kind of knowledge techne represents is far from mechanistic but rather marked by art and craft. Phronesis, on the other hand, represents a kind of wisdom-in-doing — in creating communal practice — not much considered, let alone prized, in our time. The best of the thinking about practical theology, especially as found in the work of Don S. Browning and Edward Farley, is grounded in Aristotle's important distinctions. I now pursue these distinctions further in the light of Dunne's study.

In making or production (poiesis), the maker is able beforehand to specify precisely the outcome of the making, which represents a purpose or end (telos) of the activity. To make a boat, one must have beforehand at least an idea of what the boat will be like. The goal is outside or beyond the activity; when the boat is finally made, the activity ceases. "Techne then is the kind of knowledge possessed by an expert maker; it gives the maker a clear conception of the why and wherefore, the how and the with-what of the making process and enables the maker, through the capacity to offer a rational account of it, to preside over the activity with secure mastery." [Dunne, 9] These characteristics are significantly different from those of praxis.

Aristotle's genius was his refusal to give poiesis, or productive action, an unlimited jurisdiction in human affairs and in his seeing the need for another type of activity, praxis, which represents a quite different relationship between the doer and the activity done. Praxis is "conduct in a public space with others in which a person, without ulterior purpose and with a view to no object detachable from the self, acts in such a way as to realize excellences that one has come to appreciate in one's community as constitutive of a worthwhile way of life." [Dunne, 10] This kind of activity involves a more intimate, more self-involving and self-realizing form of action than poiesis. In praxis one does not have the kind of sovereignty or distance the maker has in producing an object in poiesis. When the crafted object is completed, the activity stops, its focused goal achieved.

The activity of praxis, however, is open-ended, ceaseless, and the knowledge behind it more supple and less formulable. Communal excellences are not objectifiable the way a well-crafted vase, a boat or an electric swizzle stick is. Underlying the knowledge called phronesis is an awareness of how dependent it is on various circumstances. The end of praxis is not outside the activity as in poiesis where once the boat is completed, the productive activity stops. Praxis is its own end, and it is always in process of being achieved. For this reason, praxis is more emotionally self-involving than poiesis. The activity forms and reveals the practitioner's character.[18] Students come to a marriage course looking for the right information and useful techniques to make relationships work; only slowly do they come to see that relationships do not work out as a product. A relationship is a self-involving and other-involving process of never-ending communication. If there is any key to it, it is not the right information but on-going transformation of two selves. In this sense it falls under praxis rather than under poiesis. It gains more from thoughtful silence than from lists of rules.

Dunne points out how the knowledge of phronesis implemented in praxis fundamentally modifies the means-ends framework. The skills of praxis are "more elusive to our conceptual net than poiesis." [Dunne, 263] For its importance in religious praxis, this point bears emphasis. As stated above, the maker of a product can stand outside the materials used and allow the production process to be guided by a pre-conceived model, resting when it is achieved. The agent-of-practice, however, does not have the comfort of such precision. The achievements (and comforts) of praxis are of a different sort. This agent in praxis is constituted through the actions which disclose her both to others and to herself as the person that she is. She can never possess an idea of herself in the way that the craftsperson possesses the form of her product; rather than her having any definite 'what' as blueprint for her action or her life, she becomes and discovers 'who' she is through these actions. The medium for this becoming through action is not one over which she is ever sovereign master; it is, rather, *a network of other people who are also agents and with whom she is bound up in relationships of interdependency.* [emphasis added, 263]

For this reason, if someone asks me how to repair a broken pipe, I say, "Get a good handbook and follow it carefully." If someone asks me how to do youth ministry in a local church, I say, "Keep a journal" and form a youth ministry circle.[19]

The self-involving aspect of praxis deserves more explanation. At the heart of it is a particular kind of desire, of animation, and commitment. In praxis one is not a technician, ready to pick up one's tools and apply one's skills when summoned. Instead one is already engaged, drawn into a situation out of care for its possibilities of engaging others in a fruitful human interaction. If a class on marriage is to be more than a transfer of information, the group will have to discover its proper forms of interaction. "Is this going to be on a test?" is a question that subverts the commitments of praxis. At the heart of praxis and the knowledge behind it is a desire for excellence in the form of excellent performance. This desire does not have to be "worked up." It is always present. As with kindness (an excellence), the attitude and its practice cannot be distinguished; if they were in fact distinct, the virtue would not exist. All this is to say there exists a dynamism in phronesis-and-praxis that transcends any single act. "[P]hronesis is not a cognitive capacity that one has at one's disposal but is very closely bound up in the kind of person one is." [Dunne, 273]

A characteristic of the working wisdom of phronesis with particular importance for pastoral practice is attentiveness to the specific features of emerging situations. Via attentiveness, the present situation is allowed to "unconceal" its specific meaning. Here readers may see why this matter is of such importance to me, worth being re-connected with Aristotle's categories. The situations of most local churches form a kind of murky cloud of concealment: unseen, uncared-about and unpondered. These situations continue to conceal their meaning because we do not approach them in a praxis mode, which opens them to reflection and action. Dunne dwells on the Greek idea of *nous,* the perceptiveness found in particulars, to get at the way phronesis carries the agent of praxis to specifics and then to discern their significance. Such specifics are what is meant by the material conditions of the local church. If a church is not a ministry to attentiveness, it is a ministry to nothing. In the end the effectiveness of praxis is found in moments "not of manipulation but of inter-*play*." Interplay seems to be the character of the phronetic mode.

In my study of Dunne's book, the following image of a person I have known and loved kept recurring to me, as a psychic reminder that phronesis and praxis are not primarily abstractions but only exist as embodied in persons and communities.

My grandmother's cousin, Nell Burns, who lived all her life in the same house in a town in the southwest of Ireland, became known to me only in her old age. She was an extraordinarily frail woman, who, hardly able to make her way to the door to welcome guests, left the key in the lock as the sign of their welcome. Her face was partially paralyzed and her hands trembled with palsy. In her nineties, she continually, as I myself often witnessed, had a stream of callers flooding through her doors, many of them for advice and comfort. Homebound, she seemed to me to be engaged in praxis, the practice of enlivening the community. What was particularly noticeable about her was her attentiveness, her keen capacity to read a face, a tone of voice or a posture, and her wit and quick sense of humor. She was clearly enchanted by "the human thing." A few months before her death a photographer asked to take a series of photographs of her. These photos are all remarkable, but one in particular shows the countenance of joyful attentiveness that Dunne finds so much a characteristic of phronesis. The photographer has named that photo "The triumph of old age." In the aliveness of that face, frail with old age, one finds the dynamism of phronesis-in-praxis that Dunne recovers for us out of Aristotle.

Phronesis–praxis in the Church

As already hinted, Dunne comes to his study of phronesis via his concern for teaching, about which he has extraordinarily illuminating things to say, many of them with implications for the renewal of praxis in the church. In our time, he is convinced, many more engage in teaching as a product-related activity than as a practical, self-involving and other-involving process of coming to know and be. There is a kind of deadness one finds in rote-teaching — in its dispensing of information with little regard to the questions or stumbling points in students, in its determined retrieval of that same information via objective tests and in its final product of a grade recorded on a document. That same deadness can be found in ministry.

We could profitably puzzle over the fact that, the many studies of congregations notwithstanding, very little writing about the life of congregations has been done by those leading them or those actually engaged in them. Why? Are those who lead congregations uninterested in the life there and the possibilities of new life? Are they using handbooks suitable for fixing broken pipes when they might be wiser to keep a journal of the ebb and flow, the progress or regress of communal life itself? Is pastoral attentiveness to praxis stifled by a conviction that things keep going on but nothing much is happening? When I read Dunne's account of the self-involving, dynamic character of praxis, I think to myself, Some in ministry seem to find more self-involvement and "inter-play" in their golf game than in their ministry.

The problem is not even so much one of leadership. All churches have their named leaders. The problem is that not many of these leaders are able to invite their fellows into the circle of reflection on their own practices. Dunne implies that the true teacher becomes the student of her co-teachers, who are her assigned students. Something happens in the inter-*play* which draws learners into the circle of learning where all became teachers. In too many churches the "way" of the community does not succeed in drawing the people into the circle of ministry, using more fully the resources of their own baptism. The problem is not leadership in the sense of managerial, bureaucratic leadership; it is that leadership keeps power to itself and is unwilling to take the form of servanthood. [See Hinsdale, 1990.]

These last sentences might seem idealistic to some. However, in the framework of praxis they are not. Praxis is a process and is always in process. There are norms, visions, goals and hopes working in all this but the activity itself is a process of finding the right practices, not just now or once-for-all, but continually. That is why the youth minister's journal is so important as a way of reflecting and developing a habit of reflecting, on practice.

Prescriptive 2: Practice Guided by Vision

In the preparation of this essay I found myself studying various proposals for Christian living, and in this last section I share what I found there. Apparently, the living of Jesus' vision of the human never ceases to be a problem, with the most difficult task being "reformulating the assumptions, rules, forms and practices" of the congregation. [Chopp, 86] The project tends to go off course, especially from the pulls of culture that are not so responsive to Jesus' vision. Through the ages various strategies have sought to "re-specify" the specifics of the gospel in a way suited for a particular time. A chief form of such re-specifying is the development of "rules" or codes of conduct for monastic groups. The fact that such rules existed at all is instructive, but even more so is that they are still being used by those intent on a community that stands somewhere particular and for something specific. I wonder if such specifying codes are not in fact quite normal, even when unwritten and implicit in the sort of *"geist"* fostered by a local church. Here I will comment on some recent proposals for such rules or codes.

I first started reflecting on such codes in my attention to the "way" of Transfiguration parish in Brooklyn, New York, an extraordinary local church whose very life is its message and its means of formation. In speaking with those who helped re-found this church in its current renewal beginning around 1968, I found they adopted a particular spirituality, as a kind of gospel way within the gospel way. They decided they would follow the spirituality of Charles de Foucauld, an agnostic and libertine French military officer who was converted and eventually went off to North Africa to live and die among those he considered "the poorest of the poor," the Tuareg nomads of the desert.[20] For those who might come to join him, he sketched in writing the way he had set out for himself. This "way" prized solidarity with the poor and a life of poverty, and its spirituality guides this local church in the Williamsburg section of Brooklyn. Such "ways within the Way" are not unusual.[21]

Though a detailed examination of this particular local church is beyond the scope of this paper, a sketch might help anchor my concerns. From a single base community committed to Foucauld's spirituality in 1969, there are now about twenty-five base communities of nearly twenty persons each. These groups meet once a week to reflect on the reading of the coming Sunday in the light of their everyday lives. Representatives of these groups meet on Saturday morning in a kind of assembly to help the pastor prepare his homily. He is enabled to speak both out of the life of the community and into the life of the community. The community has three week-long festivals of learning: in Advent, Lent and Pentecost, each followed by a street festival of eating, drinking and dancing. In a place teeming with immigrants without documents, the parish has a fulltime lawyer advocating for immigration rights and social benefits. In winter, its family shelter cares for about ten families, while up to fifteen undocumented men live in the parish house, originally built for two priests. The parish convent, originally reserved for nuns who taught in the school, houses more than ten undocumented women. Living in this community of reflection and action is its core way of communicating gospel commitments. Education is endemic, that is, located among the people and flowing from the life of a people.

Another example of a communal rule of life or set of guidelines is the following sketch of a proposed rule of life written by the New Zealand poet James K. Baxter for the Jerusalem Community, a Maori settlement on the Wanganui River in New Zealand.[22] Whether it was actually adopted by the community I do not know, but it seems to have been the rule that guided Baxter's last years of life.

A Cast-Iron Programme for Communal Activity

> Feed the hungry
> Give drink to the thirsty
> Give clothes to those who lack them
> Give hospitality to strangers
> Look after the sick
> Bail people out of jail, visit them in jail and look after them when they come out of jail
> Go to neighbors' funerals
> Tell other ignorant people what you in your ignorance think you know
> Help the doubtful to clarify their minds and make their own decisions
> Console the sad
> Reprove sinners, but gently, brother and sister, gently
> Forgive what seems to be harm done to yourself
> Put up with difficult people
> Pray for whatever has life, including the spirits of the dead.
> Where these things are done, Te Wairua Tapu [the Holy Spirit] comes to live in our hearts and doctrinal differences and difficulties begin to vanish like the summer snow. [Baxter, 1971:11–12]

While significant for its brevity, this statement is shocking for its difficult particularity. If the gospel itself is an interpretive lens by which to view all reality, the above plan is an interpretive lens of *action* on the gospel. If followed it would give the gospel an unaccustomed edge in a time of bureaucracy. Rooted in specific words of Jesus, it captures the flavor of the gospel. Baxter calls it a "programme," that is, a plan to be followed. I prefer the term "rule" because it suggests a guiding norm against which to measure actual living.

The history of Christianity is threaded with such rules, set forth as a way of making the following of Jesus more specific in particular circumstances. In fact, every Roman Catholic and Protestant religious order I know lives according to a rule. One of the most famous early ones, the archetype of most that have been written since, is the *Rule of Benedict,* still followed today. Benedict's rule led to numberless variations found today in the rules of religious orders in the various denominations. The Franciscan rule is another famous guide for following Jesus in a particular time. Francis' rule met the rise of a new market economy head on with its own embrace of poverty and the condition of the poor. This latter rule is as instructive in its many revisions as it is in its original insight. Again and again, by becoming gradually accommodated to culture and the comforts proposed by culture, the Franciscan rule lost its radical gospel edge. Endless reforms of Franciscan life — including several breakaway Franciscan orders — were needed to bring the rule back to its original direction. [See Little, 1975.]

To repeat, these rules were ways of bringing sacred texts to bear on very particular social circumstances hostile or at least not open to the words and deeds of Jesus. In effect they proclaimed: having studied our Word of God, this is what we see it means for living in this time and in this place. In our struggle to understand discipleship, we have come to see that these particular ways are how we must strive to live. In such rules, all written after the demise of the catechumenate, the concerns of the ancient catechumenate and the processes of life reform embodied in it were carried on in the church.

Could it be that any gathering of people espousing discipleship would benefit by adopting such a rule for their own local life, if only because such a rule could not be written and accepted except after extended discussion of the character of discipleship today? Here I am thinking of a rule more particular than the ethos of a denomination, which is itself a particularizing and interpreting of the meaning of Jesus words and deeds. What would happen when a congregation of a denomination began to follow its own adopted rule of what its life stood for and what its priorities would be? Would such a step allow a fidelity focused toward the particularities of a congregation's situatedness? A local church is situated in a neighborhood, a city, a state, a nation and a world.

James K. Baxter's "Programme for Communal Activity" is clearly focused on very local sorts of needs, though his attention to those needs connected him to a broader vision beyond the local. A year or two before his death he wrote,

> If I say that contemporary society is unfree, I do not mean simply that one can't do what one feels like. Communal freedom itself is never absolute. To be free from the commercial and technological and military obsessions of modern society would mean only to enter a gap, a limbo, an area of unrelated personal isolation, if there were not also the freedom to cooperate and relate to other human beings.
>
> Certainly in contemporary society our personal freedom is absurdly limited. We can be jailed for example, for swearing in the street or for having no job and no money. But the terrible aspect of our lack of freedom is the fact that we are not free to act communally, when communities are everywhere ceasing to exist, and only a desacralized, depersonalized Goliath remains to demand our collective obedience.
>
> I do not relish the role of David, in confronting that Goliath, who numbs the soul wherever he touches it. But I find myself curiously, perhaps absurdly, cast in that role. And the five water-worn stones I choose from the river, to put in my sling, are five spiritual aspects of Maori communal life:
>
> *arohanui*: the Love of the Many
> *manuhiritanga*: hospitality to the guest and the stranger
> *korero*: speech that begets peace and understanding
> *matewa*: the nightlife of the soul
> *mahi:* work undertaken from communal love.
>
> I do not know what the outcome of the battle will be. My aim may be poor. But I think my weapons are well chosen. [Baxter, 1971:53–54]

A group of priests I know, who meet regularly to discuss their ministry, encourage one another and pray, have adopted "Rule for a New Brother," originally written for use in a Dutch community of brothers. This rule is brief: 58 pages, each no more than 24 lines, with only a few words to a line since the rule is written in verse form. In the genre of a book of advice, this rule sketches the priorities and attitudes needed to be a disciple but also the specific behaviors called for in a community of disciples. A sample:

> The community is the place where you daily share riches and poverty, energy and weakness, joy and sorrow, success and failure, your hope and your doubt. In this kind of community can grow something of Christ's bond with His father: 'All that I have is yours, all that you have is mine.' Live like a poor person without parading your poverty. Stand by the poor wherever they live and work. Your first love must go out to the least of persons. Don't tie yourself down to the rich or powerful of the world. Get rid of the inclination to court the great and influential. Otherwise you would deform the image of the church. [Brakkenstein Community, 24–25]

One of the most imaginative of such rules I have come across is the complete reworking of the text of Benedict's rule so as to apply it to family life, done by Larry Spears, a Quaker husband, father and lawyer. Spears is well aware of the dangers of writing such a rule for family life, but holds that a rule is actually a living tradition, providing "a means of passing on, adapting and concretizing the previous tradition in a new context," a way "to preserve the guidance of the past in establishing the norms of human life now." [Spears, 143] Any culture, but especially a religious culture, needs to find a way in a new context to preserve and pass on the wisdom gained in the past. According to Spears, when what is being preserved and passed on is a way of living basically unconformed to a society's lifestyle and values, then special intentionality and conscious effort are needed. Otherwise, the general lifestyle of a society becomes the norm established for and lived by the family.

Spears sees a rule as a guide to right practice, for the ordering of the patterns that determine our attention and our actions. In the Rule of Benedict, he finds a model of practical wisdom capable of being adapted to life today and to families. How credible is his claim? What sorts of problems may underlie Spears' proposal? Can a monastic rule devised in the sixth century be adapted for family life in the twenty-first century? Will such an adaptation result in children unprepared for life in our time? Will it mean the rejection of all aspects of modernity? How will parental authoritarianism or manipulation be avoided, along with the possibility of children rejecting their entire formation as arbitrarily imposed on them? If parents have opted for this rule, under what conditions will their children make this option, especially when they realize it is not followed by the families of their friends? Is Spears' proposal the equivalent of imposing an Amish lifestyle on all Anabaptists or a monastic lifestyle on all Catholics?

Spears answers these questions, not point by point but in general. He points out that all families tend to follow implicit rules set by the patterns of decisions that haphazardly coalesce into patterns of behavior. In some families, such an implicit rule might be, "You can watch any TV program before dinner (or early in the morning) as long as you do not disturb Mom or Dad preparing dinner (or sleeping late Saturday or Sunday morning)." The operative family "rule" is either clear or hidden. An overt rule may prove unwise, but since its presence is not denied it can be challenged. A covert rule, adopted but not acknowledged, is not open to reconsideration or adaptation. "The hidden rule is passed on hidden to new generations, along with habits and ideas of little importance. Undistinguished from the trivia, its impact can generate serious problems in family life." [Spears, 145–46]

It might be added — though Spears does not advert to the fact — most families have their little library of "how to" guides directing them to specific procedures in children's health care and in shaping children's behavior in matters ranging from eating habits to patterns of preparing children for bed. In many churchgoing families such guides and their specifics are not supplemented by guides to religious specifics. At the outset of his proposal, Spears challenges families that find his rule unacceptable to develop an alternative rule. If parts of his proposal seem improper, families should devise more suitable guidelines.

If Spears were to revise his own proposal, I would suggest more attention to influences beyond the household. One of these is the "ways" of other families on any family's life practice, influencing especially through the children. Since such ways can be negative or positive, they call for being decoded in terms of the family's own code of life. If a family were in touch with other families who had also adapted for their circumstances a rule for Christian living — or even with one family that had done so — its own rule would have more coherence. Perhaps a circle of wise parents would be a needed buttress for such a rule. Lacking this attention, Spears' approach might be seen as individualistic. Other influences to be faced but not mentioned in Spears' rule are those of television, film, or radio. Wise rules about these features of current life will probably not come easily.

Spears' insight is that Christian living is forged from the particularities of everyday life. Though often ignored, that insight, whose roots are in the earliest communities and at all points in the evolving tradition, needs to be reclaimed today by local churches. This insight, further, could ground communal struggle toward a renewed praxis. Another way of making the same point:

> [T]he church's practices impede our ability to faithfully proclaim and hear the Scripture. Our failure to understand what Paul "really meant" is not the problem. Our problem is that we live in churches that have no practice of nonviolence, of reconciliation, no sense of the significance of singleness; so we lack the resources to faithfully preach and hear God's Word. If such an approach means that I risk being "unscholarly," it is a risk well worth taking in order to free theology from its academic captivity. [Hauerwas, 8]

However we respond, the goal is fidelity to Jesus' way and to his quickening Spirit present in communities of disciples. We struggle toward fidelity but we rely on God's promises that in the end all tears shall be wiped away and robust children shall laugh and play. These resources of hope are our gift to those who come after us in the new millennium.

References

Baxter, James K.

1971 *Jerusalem Daybook*. Wellington: Price Milburn.
1972 *Autumn Testament*. Wellington: Price Milburn.
1980 *Collected Poems*. Edited by J.E. Weir. Wellington and New York: Oxford University.
1982 *Selected Poems*. Edited by J.E. Weir. Wellington and New York: Oxford University.

Block, Robert

1994 "The Tragedy of Rwanda." *New York Review of Books* 41:17 (20 October 1994), 3–8.

Borgmann, Albert

1993 *Crossing the Postmodern Divide*. Chicago: University of Chicago.
Brakkenstein Community, Blessed Sacrament Fathers.
1976 *Rule for a New Brother*. Springfield IL: Templegate.

Chopp, Rebecca

1991 "Situating the Structure: Prophetic Feminism and theological Education," 67–89. *Shifting Boundaries: Contextual Approaches to the Structure of Theological Studies*. Edited by Edward Farley and Barbara Wheeler. Louisville: Westminster/John Knox.

Donoghue, Denis

1996 "The Philosopher of Selfless Love." *New York Review of Books* (21 March 1996), 37–40.

Dunne, Joseph

1993 *Back to the Rough Ground: 'Phronesis' and 'Techne' in Modern Philosophy and in Aristotle*. Notre Dame: University of Notre Dame.

Gerbner, George.

no date "The Challenge of Television." Unpublished paper. Annenberg School of Communication, University of Pennsylvania.

Gourevitch, Philip

1995 "Letter from Rwanda: After the Genocide," *The New Yorker* (18 December), 77–94.

1996 "The Poisoned Country." *New York Review of Books* (6 June), 58–64.

Gregorian, Vartan

1986 "A Place Elsewhere: Reading in the Age of the Computer." *Bulletin of the American Academy of Arts and Sciences* 49\4:54.

Hauerwas, Stanley

1993 *Unleashing the Scriptures: Freeing the Bible from Captivity to America*. Nashville: Abingdon.

Hinsdale, Mary Ann

1990 "Power and Participation in the Church: Voices from the Margins." University of Tulsa, Warren Lecture Series in *Catholic Studies,* #13 (8 October 1990).

Jagger, Alison M.

1989 "Love and Knowledge: Emotion in Feminist Epistemology." *Gender/Body/Knowledge: Feminist Reconstructions of Being and Knowing,* 145–71. Edited by Alison M. Jagger and Susan R. Bordo. New Brunswick: Rutgers University.

Kearney, Richard

1995 *Poetics of Modernity: Toward a Hermeneutic Imagination*. New Jersey: Humanities Press.

Lash, Nicholas

1988 *Easter in Ordinary: Reflections on Human Experience and the Knowledge of God.* Notre Dame: University of Notre Dame.

A Little Brother of Jesus

1977 *Silent Pilgrimage to God: The Spirituality of Charles de Foucauld.* Trans. Jeremy Moiser. New York: Orbis.

Little, Lester

1975 "Evangelical Poverty, The New Money Economy and Violence." *Poverty in the Middle Ages,* 11–26. Edited by David Flood. Werl/Westfl.: Dietrich-Coelde-Verlag.

Metz, Johann Baptist

1994 "Suffering unto God." *Critical Inquiry* 20 1994, pp. 611–22.

Modras, Ronald

1996 *The Catholic Church and Anti-Semitism: Poland 1933-39.* Harwood Academic.

Patinkin, Mark

1986 "A Narrow Edge of Life, Death." *The Seattle Times*, 21 May 1986, p. A6.

Peirce, Charles Sanders

1986 "How to Make Our Ideas Clear." *Writings of Charles Sanders Peirce: A Chronological Edition,* vol. 3 [1872–78], 257–75. Bloomington: Indiana University.

Sawicki, Marianne

1988 "Recognizing the Risen Lord." *Theology Today* 44\4: 441–49.
1994 *Seeing the Lord: Resurrection and Early Christian Practices.* Minneapolis: Fortress.

Soelle, Dorothee

1975 *Suffering.* Philadelphia: Fortress.
1984 *The Strength of the Weak: Toward a Christian Feminist Identity. Philadelphia:* Westminster.

Spears, Larry

1989 "A Rule for Families of Faith." *American Benedictine Review* 40/2: 142–69

Tyler, Anne

1991 *Saint Maybe.* NY: Knopf.

Warren, Michael

1992 *Communications and Cultural Analysis: A Religious View.* Westport CT: Bergin and Garvey. Paper Edition: *Seeing through the Media: A Religious View of Communications and Cultural Analysis.* Harrisburg PA: Trinity Press International, 1997.

Wuthnow, Robert

1994 *Producing the Sacred: An Essay on Public Religion.* Chicago: University of Illinois.

Endnotes

1 See Iona and Peter Opie, The Classic Fairy Tales (NY: Oxford University Press, 1974, pp. 103–09).

2 A brief but stirring account of one who did — Maria Bochenek — is Mark Patinkin's "A Narrow Edge of Life, Death," The Seattle Times, 21 May 1986, p. A6. Bochenek was honored and memorialized on Jerusalem's Avenue of the Righteous.

3 See Ronald Modras, The Catholic Church and Anti-Semitism: Poland 1933–39 (Harwood Academic, 1996).

4 This is the provocative phrase probed by Marianne Sawicki, first in "Recognizing the Risen Lord," Theology Today 44:4 (1988), 441–49, and then more comprehensively in Seeing the Lord: Resurrection and Early Christian Practices (Minneapolis MN: Augsburg Fortress, 1994).

5 Johann Baptist Metz, "Suffering unto God," Critical Inquiry 20 (Summer, 1994), 611, 612. Dorothee Soelle's eloquence on this matter is well known in such works as Suffering (Philadelphia: Fortress, 1975) and The Strength of the Weak: Toward a Christian Feminist Identity (Philadelphia: Westminster, 1984).

6 R. Stephen Warner, "The Place of the Congregation in the Contemporary American Religious Configuration," in James P. Wind and James W. Lewis, eds., American Congregations, vol. 2, New Perspectives in the Study of Congregations (London and Chicago: University of Chicago Press, 1994, p. 55).

7 Robert Wuthnow, Producing the Sacred: An Essay on Public Religion Chicago: University of Illinois Press, 1994).

8 For an illuminating examination of these human ways, and especially of language as a key vehicle for encountering God, see Nicholas Lash, Easter in Ordinary: Reflections on Human Experience and the Knowledge of God, 1–70 (Notre Dame IN: University of Notre Dame, 1988).

9 Wuthnow, p. 3.

10 Paul Berman wrote: "The single greatest shift in the history of mass-communication technology occurred in the fifteenth century. . . . It was a cathedral . . . an awesome engine of communication." The cathedral told the history of Creation and of Christianity itself. Quoted in [Gregorian, 1996].

11 For more detail, see Chapters 1 and 2, "The Problem of Popular Culture," and "What Is Culture," of Warren, 1992.

12 This question can be asked about the creation of hate in Rwanda via radio broadcasts by a relatively small group of Hutus bent on genocide. One can ask whether this electronic creation of meaning was countered by a religious proposal of a counter-meaning of love? [Block, 1994; Gourevitch, 1995; and Gourevitch, 1996].

13 Levinas quotes here the Lithuanian rabbi, Israel Salanter. See Donoghue, 38.

14 Of course, a further question, but one I will not deal with here, is: Under what conditions can the best of the norms in each culture enrich the human imagination of the other cultural sector? When each sector is true to the best in its tradition, when each embraces what in its "way" enriches the humanum, then the cross-fertilization of each sector will be fruitful.

15 Of course it is possible to do an action without intending any decision let alone commitment, and still find oneself involved in a network of consequences to which one judges oneself quite unsuited. A casual erotic encounter leading to fatherhood and its cares might be one example. For a stunning narrative of a misdeed unintentionally leading to a lifelong commitment, see Anne Tyler, Saint Maybe.

16 Dunne, 8–9. The problem of reason today is well probed in Jaggar, 1889.

17 Here I stop italicizing the Greek terms.

18 See the whole of Chapter 8: "Theory, Techne, and Phronesis: Distinctions and Relations," 237–74.

19 Marianne Sawicki warned of this example, for the best plumbers engage in their work as a craft, seeing the inner configuration of the home's supply systems as related to the house's outer design. The plumber can approach her craft as an art, and to

suppose she can't might be an example of class prejudice. Indeed Dunne himself at several points in his book eloquently calls readers to note how techne and phronesis intersect. I have since found an account of poiesis that emphasizes its way of shaping the entire imagination and, through it, the entire person. See Kearney, 1995: xi–xii.

20 A very readable life of De Foucauld is, Marion Mill Preminger, The Sands of Tamanrasset: The Story of Charles de Foucauld (NY: Hawthorne Books, 1961); a more scholarly biography is, Philip Hillyer, Charles de Foucauld, vol. 9 of The Way of the Christian Mystics, Gen. Ed., Noel Dermot O'Donoghue (Collegeville MN: The Liturgical Press, 1990).

21 One passage from this Rule for what he named as "The Little Brothers of the Sacred Heart": The Little Brothers will not only gladly welcome the guests, the poor, the sick who ask for hospitality; they will invite in those whom they encounter, begging them, kneeling if necessary like Abraham to the angels, not to "pass your servants by" without accepting their hospitality, their attentions, their marks of brotherly love. Everyone in the neighborhood must know that the Fraternity is the house of God where every poor or sick person is always invited, called, wanted, welcomed with joy and gratitude by brothers who love and cherish them and regard their entry as the discovery of a great treasure. They are in fact the greatest treasure of all, Jesus himself: 'Insofar as you do this to one of the least of these brothers of mine, you do it to me?'" [Little Brother, 43]

22 See James K. Baxter, 1971, 1972, 1980, 1982. Roughly a fourth of Baxter's 2,600 poems appear in the Collected Poems.

Chapter 2

Culture and History as the Material Conditions of the Genesis of the Local Church

Joseph A. Komonchak

The author of this essay, a professor of theology in the Department of Religion and Religious Education at Catholic University of America, is a leading U.S. Roman Catholic ecclesiologist. He has specialized in the sources of the Roman Catholic renewal of the theology of the church before and after Vatican II and draws on this background in his work. Readers should not be misled by Komonchak's own denominational history to expect his use of "Catholic" to be a denominational one, a point he makes clear in his discussion of catholicity.

While acknowledging the new importance given to the local church, he cautions against conceiving the "local" primarily in cultural terms and argues for a more geographical and situational meaning, for which the culturally specific may be one many elements. Catholicity entails the role of the church in the redemptive integration of variety and difference in history.

In the face of ethnic and national hatreds erupting at the end of the millennium, Komonchak's essay opens up hard questions for any local church seeking to embody the Spirit of Jesus in our time. Because of the way these questions can focus ecclesial vision and energies for coming decades, Komonchak's essay finds its place near the beginning of this volume. Readers may want to note how Komonchak's comments on space and localness connect with similar concerns in Sawicki's and Haughton's essays.

The Emergence of a Theology of the Local Church

In Catholic theology since Vatican II there has emerged an ecclesiology that seeks to restore their proper place to the local churches. The ecclesiology dominant before the Council had focused simply on "the church," in the singular, a universalistic perspective that was taken for granted both by an institutionally oriented ecclesiology that stressed the universal primatial role of the bishop of Rome and by the first generations of ecclesiological renewal who insisted on the spiritual and sacramental principles of the church's distinctive life. Vatican II began its work in this context, and its scattered references to and vindications of the local or particular churches significantly nuanced but did not eliminate the universalistic assumptions.

Within a remarkably short time after the Council, some began to speak of a "Copernican revolution" in ecclesiology whereby initial attention is focused on the local churches, on what we might call their cultural distinctiveness and on their right to self-determination. A primary factor leading to this "revolution" was the conciliar affirmation that the one church exists only in and out of the local churches *(Lumen gentium,* 23). This simple sentence made it impossible to think of the one church as existing prior to the many churches and contributed greatly to the discrediting of an idea or image of the church as a transnational religious corporation with central headquarters in Rome, branch offices in major cities and retail shops in parishes.

Another factor was Karl Rahner's proposal that pastoral theology be conceived as the theory for the church's *Selbstvollzug,* its self-realization. While this process can be outlined in general terms, as a sort of heuristics of the church's self-realization, the fact remains that if the one church is realized only in the many particular churches, the many churches are precisely that: *particular*, specific, individual, coming to be in concrete and perhaps even unique circumstances and conditions. There was a need then to include in one's generalized heuristics of the church what we are calling the various "material conditions" of the church's self-realization.

Since the Council these material conditions have often been addressed in terms of inculturation, a word that itself emerged as an element of this new focus on the local churches. Against a perceived Eurocentric bias and against a tendency to conceive unity as uniformity, the need for the church to be *concretely* global, duly respectful and welcoming of cultural variety, was stressed over and over again. The church, like Christ, the Council had said, should not be a stranger to any time or place or culture. And the last two or three decades have seen a massive emphasis on the need for an African, an Asian, a North and South American church, etc.

Elsewhere I have tried to put together an outline of a heuristic ecclesiology that distinguishes two moments in the self-realization of the church.[1] The first rests upon the divine and universal principles that make the church the distinctive social body it is supposed to be. The Council identified them as the call of God, the gospel of Christ, the grace of the Spirit and communion under apostolic ministry. But of themselves these principles do not yet constitute the church.

The church only exists when these principles have generated the human principles of the church: the faith, hope and love by which men and women receive and appropriate the divine principles.

Yves Congar some time ago proposed distinguishing these two moments in terms of the classic difference between "form" and "matter." The formal divine principle of the church's essence is the divine gifts of word and grace; the material human principle is the men and women who receive and appropriate those gifts by and in their active subjectivity of faith, hope and love. The actual church, of course, comes to be only when form and matter, the "essence" of the church, are given concrete existence by the power of the Holy Spirit.[2]

The form-matter analogy has its uses, particularly in opposition to a tendency to reify the formal principles, as, for example, in facile distinctions between the church that is holy and sinless in its distinctive and generative principles and the members of the church who are sinners. In fact, of course, that church, pure in its formal principles, does not exist, at least not on earth; all that exists and can be called "the church" is a community of sinners gathered out of their alienation and division by the gospel and grace of reconciliation, struggling to be faithful to those gifts, and required, as Augustine and Aquinas said, daily to pray, "Forgive us our trespasses." In this respect the analogy is useful in keeping ecclesiology focused on actual communities.

Another value of the metaphysical analogy is its stress upon the differentiating principles of the church. Some people resist referring to these principles as "universal" on the grounds that this adjective threatens the values being recovered in new emphases on regionalism and localism. But if the day ever comes when there are genuinely inculturated forms of Christianity in Asia, Africa, etc., and it is still possible to say that all these distinctive churches are still one church, then there must be some common principles of origin, purpose and communion which ground, generate and embody that unity. These are what Congar called the divine generative principles of every one of the churches outside of which there is no church.

On the other hand, there is one inconvenience in the application of the metaphysical categories to the genesis of the church: In classical metaphysics "matter" is purely passive and receptive; all the initiative and activity is on the side of "form." While there is no doubt that the active initiative in the genesis of the church comes from God, it remains clear that no church is generated unless the divine subjectivity is recognized and received in gratitude by the active responsive subjectivity of believers. Inert matter seems an inappropriate term for such a constitutive role. There are important senses in which the human principles are also *formally* constitutive of the actually existing church.

The genesis of a Christian occurs at the intersection of a life-project and the gospel of Jesus Christ. If it is possible to write a formal theological anthropology, a practice latent in the classical treatises on creation, sin and grace, such justification is always a unique event in which the peculiarities of an individual's life define the subjectivity transformed by the encounter with Christ. One can see this in the New Testament: Simon is not Saul and Peter is not Paul and neither of them is the Beloved Disciple. One can see it in the variety of metaphors that embody the great encounter, some of which are natural and illuminating to certain individuals and not to others, or to some moments in the same life and not to others. Think of darkness and light, weakness and strength, depth and height, thirst and water, hunger and food, lameness and dancing, muteness and speech, filth and cleansing, etc.

A theology of the local church tries to achieve something similar in an ecclesiology that supplements a general field-theory of the genesis of the church with specific accounts of what it means for the church to be born in various specific situations, in the face of varied challenges and among differing communities of men and women. Here we can think of the differences among Paul's many churches, and between them and the Johannine communities, between the house churches of the first century and the great church in any large metropolis today, between the church today in Mali and in Peru, in Thailand and the United States, or in the United States between the church that meets in a suburban town and the churches that meet in a prison, a nursing home, or in an inner city. Across the generations and across the situations of a single generation, something wonderfully different happens: the church remains *circumamicta varietate,* clothed in a many-colored garment.

Catholicity and Particular Cultures

These postconciliar emphases remain valid and still need to be urged against tendencies in governing bodies of the church toward uniformity and top-down management. Other tendencies also need to be acknowledged and resisted, in particular the tendency for individual churches to consider their own sets of assumptions, expectations and challenges to be so normative that others are regarded as tolerable exceptions at best. Catholicity is not simply variety or diversity. The word refers to a "whole," and a whole interrelates and integrates a multiplicity. For the church, the principles of this integration are the word of Christ and the grace of the Spirit, two principles that have their own integrity and substance, which are not reducible to any one of the principles that differentiate individuals or groups. Particular cultures make a community a *local* church, but it is the word and grace of God, received in faith, hope and love, that make a community a local *church.*

I would like to recount a few things that have led me to wonder whether it is not time to start re-emphasizing the integrative dimension of catholicity. First, I read some months ago the following plea by a theologian:

> To every age the eternal gospel must be proclaimed. But to every age it has to be proclaimed differently, as an answer to the specific questions of that age. . . . At the time of the Reformation the question of salvation was the question of deliverance from guilt, of peace with God. . . . Today we are an utterly political species. And our quest for "salvation" comes alive in the political dimension. People of our day are not concerned about peace with God, but with overcoming political calamity in the broadest sense — the mortal distress of a people, the destruction of the national community, the freedom of the people for its

> own life, the fulfillment of its particular mission. If that is the key question for our age, the gospel must be preached to it in terms of its "political" concept: the kingdom of God, the Lordship of God.

With a few changes, this could have been a paragraph of my composition about twenty years ago when I was arguing for the legitimacy and need of the "political turn" in theology. You may understand my distress, then, when I learned that "people" in the original language was "*Volk*" and that the Kingdom of God was here invoked as part of an apologia in the service of the Third Reich.[3]

Second, last night on the evening news I watched a bishop walk along a very long trench and sprinkle holy water on three hundred bodies, mostly of women and children, victims of the latest slaughter in Burundi. The church accompanied European colonists to Burundi and to its partner in horror, Rwanda, but over a century a church that calls itself Catholic, so far from preventing the colonialists from turning tribal differences into racial differences, reflected this view in the structure and membership of its hierarchy and religious orders, and some of its leaders may even have participated in the recent genocidal spiral of violence.

Third, there is the great paradox that where a communist regime was able by force to preserve peace for forty years among Roman Catholics, Orthodox Catholics and Muslims in Yugoslavia, the two Christian churches, finally set free, were unable to prevent the disinterring of ancient hatreds and even at times seemed to be blessing policies of "ethnic cleansing."

Surely such examples should give us pause. If we want still to promote and defend the possibility of an Asian church, an African church, an American church, etc., do we not have some reservations today about promoting a Hutu church, a Tutsi church, a Croat church, a Serbian church?

How did it happen that genuine catholicity failed so miserably? Perhaps one reason was that ecclesiology often so stressed formal and universal elements that catholicity was commonly seen in exclusively theological and ecclesio-centric terms. In a rapid review of recent work on the theme, I have been struck by how little space is given to the *historic* significance of catholicity. The classic texts are cited, of course: "Teach all nations," ". . . neither Jew nor Greek nor barbarian nor Scythian," ". . . from every race and language and people." But the focus tends to remain on the inner inclusiveness and variety of the church, with little discussion of the implications of catholicity for the redemption of history and society.

A book like Henri de Lubac's *Catholicism: The Social Aspects of Dogma* might have taught the lesson. Its argument was based on the recovery of biblical and patristic christology and ecclesiology. These were presented as redemptively overcoming the fatal disjunction between person and community that modernity has fostered and as integral dimensions of a divine plan which began with the creation of a single human race. That plan was splintered by sin's fratricide and Babel, was renewed by the all-embracing love of Christ, the new integrative Head of humanity[4] and will be fulfilled in the communion of saints that is the Kingdom of God. De Lubac wrote the chapters of that book in the late 1930s at a time when a renascent nationalism was threatening once again to give more importance to particular adjectives ("French" or "German") than to the one great integrative adjective: "Catholic."[5]

A second factor in this failure may be the relation between the divisions within Christendom that followed upon the Reformation and the rise of modern nationalism, particularly when religious and national identity were thought to coincide: *Cujus regio ejus religio* (for each region its own religion). In both Protestant and Catholic countries, nationalism moved in a direction contrary to the inclusiveness of the catholicity both traditions claimed for themselves. The stronger the nationalism the more powerful the tendency to remove from catholicity its this-worldly redemptive finality and either to forget it entirely or to conceive it in solely intra-ecclesial terms.

Finally, as secularization proceeds, the nation-state tends to become the sovereign social unit within which any integration of variety occurs. Religion is sent to the margins to take care of the realm of the private in all its particularity, not to say idiosyncrasy.

Religion is given a sectarian definition that is the opposite of catholicity and, as in the U.S. today, is far more commonly thought to be divisive and disruptive of national unity than integrative or catholic.

In this situation passions that were once summed up in the term *odium theologicum* often are transferred to the realm of the political as *odium politicum*. And it not infrequently happens that these latter passions appear within the Church itself and at times become more powerful principles of association and unity than the distinctive principles of the church. Yves Congar was already describing the problem in 1961:

> It is only natural that we attempt to achieve a synthesis between the realities of culture or nationality, of social or even political engagement . . . and our faith, our service of God and neighbor. Natural, yes, but how dangerous! Historically, many schisms arose from such syntheses. In two unfortunately posthumous articles, Dom Nicolas Oehmen showed that the "place" of schisms, that is, the point of ambiguity and danger, is precisely that too close a link is drawn between Christianity and a culture, a national interest, a human, a personal and above all a social enterprise. For if this link is too tight, it entails the practice — I use examples without passing judgment — of an Egyptian or a progressive or a middle-class Christianity indisposed to communion with an Israeli or a conservative or a working-class Christianity, or even quite simply with a universal Christianity. A Church of the Elect, which in fact is a chapel, is more important than the Church itself. The "Other" is banished from a communion that is reduced to my personal and spontaneous orientations.[6]

It is perhaps not necessary to cite examples in which in the past and present this "*esprit de chapelle*" has been found among us, those instances in which, as Congar put it in the same article, this spirit leads members of the same church for social or political or ideological reasons to become strangers to one another and to "sense more communion with a non-Catholic or a non-Christian of the same tendencies than with their brethren in the faith." It is not rare to find groups who passionately desire as great a pluralism as possible on questions of orthodoxy but who carry out their own forms of excommunication on questions of orthopraxis. I take Cardinal Bernardin's "Catholic Common Ground Project" to be an effort to overcome these and other polarities.[7]

The solution is not to promote a Christianity that remains indifferent to economic, political and social problems nor to argue that one's Christianity ought not to inspire and direct one's attempts to address them. But the whole question concerns the relationship between one's specific engagements, intentions and loyalties and the Christianity that is never merely one's own but something much larger and much more inclusive, something of which "others," with different engagements, intentions and loyalties, are not to be presumed to be more unworthy. Here lies the ambiguity of a phrase like "intentional Christian communities," sometimes proposed as a North American parallel to "basic Christian communities." As in Latin America such pioneers of liberation-theology as Gustavo Gutierrez have had to warn against the instrumentalizing of Christianity for the benefit of specific political theories and practices, so in North America the great question is the relationship between and relative weight of specific "intentions" and the church-constitutive "intending" of God in Christ. Similarly, there is the great ambiguity, to say the least, of a name such as "WomanChurch."[8]

Catholicity as Redemptive Integration

I have used before as a parable the example of a parish in the Bronx in the early 1970s. A white teenager, student at the Catholic high school, was murdered by a black teenager, student at the local public high school. It was the second such tragedy in recent months. Racist calls for revenge were being heard in the neighborhood from students at the Catholic high school. The pastor of the parish had to prepare a homily for the victim's funeral.

What is at stake here? What will be represented at that funeral? Consider what a journalist or historian might have to record a few weeks or decades later. Will it be the story that the funeral became the occasion for an intensification of racial hatreds, the religious legitimation for another turn of the spiral of violence? We have seen enough examples of this on television from Northern Ireland, the Middle East, Yugoslavia, Africa and New York itself for us not to ignore the possibility. Or will the story be that the funeral became the occasion for efforts at reconciliation, for new efforts to overcome racial bitterness and social injustice? And what role might the preacher's words at the funeral play in deciding between the two possible stories?

Might he not remind the grieving and angry congregation, white and black, of the unjust and early death of Jesus of Nazareth? Might he not recall that his last words pleaded for forgiveness for his executioners? Might he not speak of how the cross broke down an earlier and equally bitter wall of separation? Might he not remind them that they all, black and white, are about to receive from the table of his sacrifice a bread that is his body and makes them all his body, in which there is neither Jew nor Greek, nor freeman nor slave, nor male nor female, nor black nor white, so that to promote those differences is to fail to recognize the body that they are?

If some such words are spoken and received, two things happen at once. The church is called to be the church in what is most constitutive and distinctive about it: the assembly of those who believe that God was in Christ reconciling the world to himself; and the world — the little portion of the world that is that section of the Bronx — is different because there is a genuine church within it. This world now includes men and women who do not accept the *lex talionis* as the supreme rule of human conduct, who have experienced a communion with God and with one another that transcends their racial and other differences, who seek to make that reconciled communion the reality of their relationships when they leave the church. What is most distinctive about the church is what is most "relevant" to the world, most redemptive of history. The world is history and history is what human beings do and make with their freedom; and the church is supposed to be one of the agents whose exercise of their freedom makes the world what it will become.

The example illustrates a notion of catholicity as "redemptive integration." Catholicity is not primarily a "mark" of the church invoked in order to ground the latter's transcendence and superiority to the world. It is a characteristic that, as a "sign," displays what the world of God's creation is supposed to be like and that, as an instrument, serves the realization of that purpose. Sign and instrument are the words *Lumen gentium* used to exegete the term "sacrament" (LG 1), and the Council both in that text and elsewhere gives this technical term an application that is the opposite of a sectarian withdrawal from the world into some sort of separate ecclesial "communion."[9]

There are several areas that deserve further consideration in the light of these reflections. The first concerns the concrete reference of local community. An ambiguity resides, first, in the adjective "local." Does the at first sight banal reference to a particular physical place have any theological relevance or should it be disregarded in favor of a more meaning-centered, or cultural, notion of the local? This issue arose just before the Council, when some French theologians argued that the word "mission" should not be applied only to non-evangelized areas of the world, but that there were also cultural "spaces," as they called them, which needed to be (re-)evangelized, as, for example, the milieu of the workers. "Space," locality, was here defined by shared meanings and values.

The two meanings are found also in the two sociological approaches to "community," one of which emphasizes community of meanings and values, the other people in a (relatively small) territory. In these terms, it would appear that the post-conciliar phenomenon of "basic Christian communities" and of "intentional communities" reflects the first more than the second, with the Latin American form, largely confined to the poor, reflecting an engagement for justice as a co-constituent of their communal identity and the North American form, often found among middle-class people, gathering for one or another "intention" that distinguishes them perhaps from other "intentional" communities and from the territorial parish. In these cases, a cultural, meaning-ful, notion of local space seems to be primary.

The question for discussion is the one proposed by Hervé Legrand and Gilles Routhier, whether there is not a *theological* justification of the church's traditional territorial differentiation of its life into dioceses and parishes.[10] In the first place, geographical space *per se* is no respecter of persons; everyone within it is supposed to be welcome.[11] This advantage is even more important when one considers that the number of places on the globe that contain people of only one race or culture grows smaller every day. To choose a principle of ecclesial circumscription that in principle is not defined by meaning is, it turns out, remarkably catholic in implication, in the sense of Joyce's comment: Catholic means, "Here comes everybody!" That is, of course, the point: everyone within that territory has a right to come, and barriers of race and ethnicity, economic class and political interest, are supposed to fall. The territorial basis of ecclesial community opens out upon and makes possible the construction of a local church on the basis of distinctively Christian meanings and values.[12] Consider, for example, the comparative redemptive significance of being able to say that an economically, socially, ethnically, racially and politically diverse parish has become a genuine community and saying that a group of people already like-minded economically, socially, ethnically, racially and politically is a community.

A second area that deserves renewed theological reflection is that of nationalism. There was a time when leaders of the Catholic Church regularly warned against exaggerated nationalism, not least of all because its members so regularly indulged in it.[13] Perhaps it is time to echo the warning. More than one observer has predicted that the revival of nationalism will pose the greatest threat to world peace in the coming century. The threat is even greater when it is thought that ethnic identity requires distinct nationhood and when attempts are made to ground national identity on ethnic or linguistic purity, as in the some of the rhetoric of the movement for independence in Québec, Canada, or in calls for an official national language in the United States, both of these mild by comparison to the bloody ethnic cleansings we have witnessed in

Europe and in Africa. Under such circumstances it should give one pause to link distinct ecclesial identities to national or even to cultural identities. The supra-national and trans-cultural identity of the one church in the many churches here surely has something to offer, and perhaps we ought to think of reviving modern papal and conciliar calls for a genuine international community.

Thirdly, one may ask whether these first two considerations do not imply a third: that the point of local insertion of the mystery of the church should not be located in particular cultures but in particular historical moments and challenges. Too often cultures are described as if they exist in some pure form, which has its own integrity, distinctiveness and rights over and against both other cultures and the Christian message. But is there a single culture today that can claim such purity, that is not the result of historical processes of cultural contact and cross-fertilization? And what about situations in which a variety of cultures are interacting and perhaps even competing?[14] The point was once brought home to me by a priest from Singapore who was taking part in a discussion of what it means to be a local church in Asia. All of the conversation was about the church's respecting the integrity of local cultures. At one point he protested that this model of reflection was of little use to him in a country defined precisely by several cultural identities, one of whose major problems was precisely this diversity. To link particular ecclesial identity with culture, he felt, missed the local challenge his church faced.

He had a point. "Culture," after all, is something of an abstraction. Even if one were to imagine a "pure" culture, where representatives of two or more of these enter into regular contact, the immediate challenge is to create a common culture, in the sense that as a minimum they have to learn how to live together and to ground this common life in sets of meanings and values that will not wholly correspond to any one of the particular cultures. These common meanings and values, if they should respect legitimate particular cultural identities and aspirations, must also inevitably relativize the latter in the search for grounds for an integrated common life. If this is a requirement of civil society, surely it applies even more strongly to the life of the church.

Perhaps we ought to think of ecclesiology in terms of a theology of history. By history I mean what human beings have made, are making and will make by the exercise of their individual and collective freedom. (The word "world" has the same meaning, at least in its most relevant theological sense.) The self-realization or genesis of the church then is seen as a moment in the great project of the collective self-realization of humanity. We enter a world, or worlds, created by those who came before us — a world embodying in its achievements and institutions all the grandeur and misery of the human. Enabled and limited by those products of an earlier age, we now have the task of doing something better with our own freedom in order to leave our children a world less unlike the world God's creation intends, less unlike the communion to be realized in God's kingdom. Within this great world there is the body of believers, the church, which participates in the common and grand historic project in the light of Jesus Christ and by the aid of his Holy Spirit. To become a member of that church is not thereby to leave the world, but rather to make the world different because one's individual freedom and one's share in the collective project are inspired by Christ and animated by the Spirit.

But in the one world, of course, are many worlds, like the world of the Bronx in my real-life parable, like Rwanda and Burundi, like Bosnia and Croatia. The challenge represented by these three situations is not most adequately described in terms of culture; in fact, one might be tempted to say that mistaken stress on cultural identity is a very large part of the problem in each. Those terms evoke historical situations, historical challenges, historic opportunities. Certainly culture defines elements of each of them, and respect for cultural difference is a legitimate demand in each. But what in all three of those situations is required is the ability to relativize those differences and to transcend them in the achievement of a reconciled and integrated communion. A church that is not the sign and instrument of that goal falls short of being genuinely catholic.

My point is that we ought to make local historical challenge — local need and opportunity — the primary factor in defining the local character of a particular church. Respect for "culture" or, better, "cultures" defines only one dimension of that challenge, but a church in which barbarians and even Scythians are as welcome as Greeks and Jews should be very wary of making any one culture its locally defining characteristic. The "material conditions," the "matter" awaiting formation from Christ and animation from the Spirit, are the local needs and opportunities that form part of the single grand historical human project.

And the challenge of catholicity is intrinsic to *every* ecclesial community, which is supposed to be internally and intrinsically catholic. It is not a challenge that arises only as a second moment and in terms of a community's relations or communion with other particular communities. The reversal of Babel at Pentecost — a favorite patristic symbol of catholicity — must take place in each community that wishes to be called a church. Everyone should be welcome everywhere.

Finally, redemptive integration or catholicity cannot remain at the level of vague theological affirmation but must be made concrete in conversations, collaborations, communications, etc. These need to be promoted in culturally diverse parishes, dioceses and within the worldwide church. Catholicity is less a given than a task to be accomplished, and where communion is not translated into communication and collaboration one may question whether it really exists in anything but name.

In this respect we might usefully meditate on the apostle Paul's discussion of the dispute over the legitimacy of eating meat sacrificed to idols that endangered the unity of his local churches (1 Corinthians 8; Romans 14). The apostle made it clear on which side he himself stood, but he was also unwilling to allow it to become church-defining to the exclusion or harm of others:

> I know and am persuaded in the Lord Jesus that nothing is unclean in itself; but it is unclean for anyone who thinks it unclean. If your brother is being injured by what you eat, you are no longer walking in love. Do not let what you eat cause the ruin of one for whom Christ died. . . . Let us then pursue what makes for peace and mutual upbuilding. Do not, for the sake of food, destroy the work of God" (Romans 14:14–15, 19–20).

This admirable discrimination and pastoral tact was unfortunately lacking in more than one case of ecclesial dispute in the past; perhaps we have something to learn from it today when multiple variants on food sacrificed to idols once again threaten to destroy the work of God and to banish people for whom Christ died.

Endnotes

1 See *Towards a Theology of the Local Church*. Hong Kong: FABC Papers, 1986; "The Church: God's Gift and Our Task," *Origins* 16 (1987) 735–41; "The Local Church and the Church Catholic: The Contemporary Theological Problematic," *The Jurist* 52 (1992) 416–47; *Foundations in Ecclesiology*. Boston: Lonergan Workshop, 1995.

2 Yves Congar, *Lay People in the Church*, rev. ed. (Westminster: Newman Press, 1965) 30; *Vraie et fausse réforme dans l'Église*, 2d ed. (Paris: du Cerf, 1968) 92–93.

3 Paul Althaus, in a 1933 article entitled "The Third Reich and the Kingdom of God," quoted in Scholder, *The Churches and the Third Reich* I, 104, as cited by M. Hollerich, *Pro Ecclesia* 2 (1993) 316n.

4 "Recapitulation" means being brought under a new Head, Christ, the "second Adam."

5 See Henri de Lubac, *Catholicism: The Social Aspects of Dogma* (New York: Sheed and Ward, 1958; "Patriotisme et nationalisme," *Vie intellectuelle* 19 (1933) 283–300; see Joseph A. Komonchak, "Theology and Culture at Mid-Century: The Example of Henri de Lubac," *Theological Studies* 51 (1990) 579–602.

6 Congar, "Unité, diversités et divisions," *Sainte Eglise: Etudes et approches ecclésiologiques (Unam Sanctam,* 41; Paris: du Cerf, 1963) 123–24; see also "Unité de l'humanité et vocation des peuples," *ibid.*, 175–78.

7 See the statement issued August 12, 1996, "Called to Be Catholic: Church in a Time of Peril," *America* 175 (August 31, 1996) 5–8.

8 For pertinent remarks on the general question, see K. Dobbelaere and J. Billet, "Community-formation and the Church: A Sociological Study of an Ideology and the Empirical Reality," in *Foi et société* (Gembloux: Duculot, 1978) 211–59.

9 See Joseph A. Komonchak, "Concepts of Communion, Past and Present," *Cristianesimo nella Storia* 16 (1993) 321–40.

10 See H. Legrand, "La délimitation des diocèses," in *La charge pastorale des évêques: Décret "Christus Dominus," Unam Sanctam* 71 (Paris: du Cerf, 1969) 177–219; "La rèalisation de l'Eglise en un lieu," in *Initiation à la pratique de la théologie* III (Paris: du Cerf, 1983) 171–76; G. Routhier, "'Église locale' ou 'Église particulière': querelle sémantique ou option théologique," *Studia Canonica* 25 (1991) 277–334, esp. 324–32; "Territorialité et différentiations culturelles: défi ecclésial et problème théologique," in *Espace et culture*, ed. Serge Courville and Normand Ségun (Sainte Foy: Presses de l'Université Laval, 1995) 155–64.

11 Routhier quotes Emile Pin: "What basically distinguishes geographical differentiation from every other kind of differentiation is that it does not effect an arbitrary or voluntary selection among the possible members of the common life. . . . The universality of the Church thus appears on the local level where it is symbolized by this non-discriminating welcome. Thus the parish is not only a link with the universal Church; it reproduces it locally and makes it present. . . ." "'Eglise locale' ou 'Eglise particulière,'" 325n.

12 An obvious exception to this has been the "national parish" which U.S. bishops were allowed to establish in the last century as a way of trying to preserve the faith of immigrants whose Christianity was often expressed in distinct ethnic and cultural patterns. Even then, however, the church did not authorize the establishment of national *dioceses*; this larger unit presided over by the bishop was to integrate all Catholics as a single church.

13 Thus Pope Benedict XV's description in *Maximum illud* of excessive patriotism as a "*pestis teterrima*" ("most frightful plague") was directed at Catholic missionaries; see Claude Soetens, "The Holy See and the Promotion of an Indigenous Clergy from Leo XIII to Pius XII," *The Jurist* 52 (1992) 172.

14 For very perceptive comments on the question, see Peter C. Phan, "Contemporary Theology and Inculturation in the United States," in *The Multicultural Church: A New Landscape in U.S. Theologies*, ed. William Cenkner (New York: Paulist Press, 1996) 109–30.

Chapter 3

Congregational Reorientation

C. Ellis Nelson

Ellis Nelson's work on the local church as the prime locus for the growth of faith has long influenced my own thinking. For carrying through the project that led to this book, his advice and encouragement were the most important elements. In his now-classic work, Where Faith Begins *(1967), he asks what the natural agency is for communicating faith, and answers that it is the community of believers. (p. 30) The family, affirmed as one of the most important units for communicating faith and the meaning of faith, must itself be backed by the community of believers; in philosophical terms, the family is "necessary but insufficient."*

Here he examines the possibilities of moving a congregation in the direction of greater fidelity to the gospel. What are some of the conditions of that possibility, even in the face of its difficulties? He answers these questions by attending to the question of culture and how it works in the formation of a "self" in children. In his first sections, the word "family" is not actually used though the context is family and familial influences. Nelson summarizes research on how children are influenced and then sketches three studies of actual congregational life that disclose a believing community's power to "maintain a religious interpretation in the midst of a changing secular culture." Other studies he cites show how a congregation can become like a social club for the middle class, without transcendent self-critical principles. The account is chilling.

Especially useful here is Nelson's noting how specific sets of procedures produce outcomes: one set a positive outcome, another a negative one. Outcomes are thus demystified. They don't just happen, but are linked to certain observable and specific attitudes, decisions and behaviors.

In the final section, Nelson examines the process of reorienting and refocusing a congregation's belief system towards greater fidelity and, where necessary, towards contesting cultural norms. He pays particular attention to "ever widening circles" of vision and influence in congregations. For congregations wishing to apply Nelson's ideas to its own life, he offers two sets of critical questions.

Some readers will want to know of Nelson's related essay, "Socialization Revisited," Union Seminary Quarterly Review *47:3–4 (1993), 161–76, reprinted in M. Warren, ed.,* The Sourcebook for Modern Catechetics, *vol. 2 (Winona MN: St. Mary's Press, 1997), and* How Faith Matures *(1989), which in many ways is a second volume of* Where Faith Begins.

In Western societies the material conditions of life — including cultural values expressed in laws, form of government and customs — are blended with religious traditions (Warren 1995a). Trying to separate a religion from its cultural setting under these conditions is almost impossible. We can, however, identify extreme cases. Cults, such as those led by Jim Jones or David Koresh, illustrate religious beliefs that reject the dominant culture. At the other extreme are religious movements or congregations which make little, if any, distinction between the material conditions of life and religion so that worship is a validation of their lifestyle. The problem for religious people not in either of these extreme groups is the tension between the lifestyle urged by their religious tradition and the style in which they live.

This tension is not new. The biblical record, from the story of Adam and Eve in Genesis to the description of the seven churches of Asia in Revelation, is an account of what God/Christ wanted and how people actually lived. H. Richard Niebuhr identified this tension as "the enduring problem" and described five ways that the Christian religion has related to culture. Niebuhr concluded there could be no definitive solution to this problem because in each historical situation sin expressed in human values and goals compromised God's will. He did not mean by such a judgment that Christians should therefore accept the lifestyle of their social environment. Rather, Christians should gain an understanding of how they had been influenced by their culture as well as by their faith in God; and in the light of that understanding they should use their reason to decide how to become more sensitive to God's desire for humankind (Niebuhr 1951, 230–56).

Niebuhr's suggestion that we should focus attention on individuals and their ability to bring about change is the subject of this essay. The thesis is: The world view, values and lifestyle of individuals is deeply influenced by the culture of the groups to which they belong, and that significant change will ordinarily take place only as individuals commit themselves to changing their groups. It is necessary first to describe how culture forms the self during early childhood; second, to understand churches in a changing culture; and finally, to suggest how churches can reorient themselves.

Self-Formation

Throughout this century there has been a growing realization that selfhood is formed by one's interaction with society (Mead 1940). This view accepts the notion of an innate motive for a baby to respond to caregivers, to walk, to talk and to think about the environment in which she comes into consciousness. But the self that is formed is indelibly dyed by the social group that brought it into being. This means that the substance of the self — that is, what the person wants and how much she works to get those wants — is socially determined in early childhood. When the child is old enough to reason more abstractly and to take more responsibility for her life, typically at about age 15 to 16, she may begin to change the values and lifestyle she absorbed as a child. However, given the dynamic quality of early social conditioning, such changes do not often happen.

How much of culture a child will absorb and make a part of self depends largely on the social, racial, economic or ethic situation of the parents. In practical terms, the culture that is transmitted to children is that of the groups to which the parents belong. This "belonging" means the groups with which the parents find their well-being in church, school, neighborhood, labor, or kinship associations. These groups may have contrary beliefs about how people should order their lives; but parents work through these issues, prioritize them and communicate to children what they think is right. Children, at least in their preschool years, do not try different lifestyles. Rather, parents demonstrate a lifestyle, provide stories and reasons why that style is right and enforce it with rewards and punishments. If the parents are religious, their children will learn about God and the kind of religious and moral behavior God expects (*Catechism of the Catholic Church* 1994, 537).

The basis on which a person's moral and religious life is built starts at birth. The way a baby is handled, fed, diapered and talked to from the moment of birth creates feelings that become personality traits. According to Erik Erikson, a baby forms a basic trust or distrust in life during its first year (Erikson 1968, 96–107). Other emotional states develop during the first few years according to the baby's relation to caregivers. Although these feelings become unconscious, they produce personality traits that will continue unless the person has enduring relations with people who modify the feelings that were created during infancy. We all know people who are kind, generous and forgiving and have an image of God that fits those characteristics. Contrariwise, we also know people who are legalistic and think of God as primarily concerned about people obeying rules.

A person's moral outlook is rooted in the general feelings that form in infancy, but his moral code is developed during early childhood according to the conduct for which he is rewarded or punished. The process starts as early as self-consciousness begins to form between two and six months of age. The moral training process intensifies as the infant's self-consciousness develops. Between seven and fifteen months infants (1) discover they have a mind, (2) express preferences, (3) are alert to communication by words or gestures and (4) begin to understand motives and intentions which lie behind the behavior of caregivers. When the ability to talk emerges at about 18 to 20 months, the infant's self-consciousness is apparent to everyone. By three years of age, children can imitate what others do, understand themselves as people who respond to others and have personal opinions on food and clothing (Stern 1985, 37–182).

During these early years caregivers are unceasing in their coaching or commands on how to behave. During the course of one day a child will be given hundreds of instructions such as "Do this," "Don't do that, it's not nice," or a slap with "Stop that." Out of the hundreds of daily instructions during the first three or four years, a child formulates and accepts an image of what a good person is, even though he often fails to live up to that ideal. By age four one can often see a child instruct a doll or playmate in what is right or wrong, and by age six his conscience is well formed (Emde, Johnson and Easterbrook 1987).

It is of critical importance that we do not read the above description of conscience formation in an idealistic way. The content of conscience is social. That is, a boy could grow up in a home where the father was a dealer in illegal drugs. The boy at a very early age might learn that preparing and selling drugs was a normal and acceptable form of work. It is reasonable to assume he might help package the drugs and at age five or six enjoy helping his father by delivering drugs to clients in the neighborhood. Indeed, this boy might feel guilty if he didn't help his father (Nelson 1978, 31–53).

A person's religious sentiment is also rooted in the general feelings formed in infancy. A manifestation of religion, however, is less precise than that of conscience. A child growing up in a religious home may develop an interest in God that may or may not be expressed in a church affiliation. A child may grow up in a non-religious home yet develop many virtues of the Christian religion. In any case, a child in America will develop a mental image of God (Rizzuto 1979, 208). This is so because religion, very influential in our history, is carried along in our culture. As a result, about 90 percent of Americans say that they believe in the existence of God (Gallup and Castelli 1989, 4).

Although the image of God that is available to a child is that which is presented by caregivers, the child will respond according to the relationship she has with caregivers. This formulation of an image of God typically takes place between two and a half and three years of age. During this time a child becomes concerned about where she came from and where she will go after death, what created the world, why things happen the way they do and many other questions about nature and human life. The answers provided by caregivers often involve language about God (Nelson 1996).

The questions indicate that the child has discovered a reality between her inner self and outer reality. This "transitional" reality is not transitory; it is the beginning of the child's consciousness of an intermediate reality that bridges herself to the world of people and things. This reality is the place of play, of creative self-expression, of imagination and of God. What happens to a child's religion after she begins to form an image of God depends on circumstances. By age four it is possible to interview children and have them dictate a letter to God or draw a picture of God. By age five a child can process ideas about God. Linda, for example, said to an interviewer that God can see everything that she does. When asked "How do you know God can see everything?" she replied, "My brain tells me." "What about when you are sleeping?" the interviewer asked. The reply, "My brain is working all the time, even when I sleep." At the age of five Russell Baker's father died. His image of a loving, caring God who was in charge of life was so shattered he decided to have nothing more to do with God (Baker 1982, 61). By age six or seven children have a rather clear image of God which they can draw and explain. Researchers who have gathered children's pictures of God show a variety of images ranging from orthodox Christian beliefs to images of an idealized parent or sibling (Heller 1986; Lang 1983).

Moral and religious transformation continues after the age of six or seven along lines that were set earlier. By the age of ten, children have a "moral compass" by which they make moral judgments according to the first long-term efforts to study children's beliefs and moral values. Directed by Robert Coles, this survey concluded that 25 percent of American children were "civic humanists," for they made judgments on the basis of what they thought was the common good. About 20 percent were "conventionalists" who made moral judgments on the basis of what parents and teachers told them was acceptable. Some 18 percent were labeled "expressive," for they made decisions on the basis of what made them happy. The children who referred to God or the Bible when making decisions represented 16 percent of the total. About ten percent of the children used personal interest or concerns as a guide for deciding moral issues. How these "moral compasses" compared with the adult population is unknown; but one can assume that the children reflect the decisions they had seen in their families and the groups to which the families belonged. For example, 94 percent of the children said their parents really cared about them. And when asked "Who you do turn to for advice?" almost all responded by saying their parents, peers, or extended family members (Coles 1989, xiv).

A child not only develops a conscience and an image of God, he also learns patterns of conduct, how to spend time and money, attitudes toward people in authority, how to respond to strangers, notions of what causes lighting and thunder, how he should deal with emergencies and numerous other matters that make up a typical child's life. These learnings tend to persist within a person, rather unchanged by schooling *(Catechism of the Catholic Church* 1994, 440–42).

Howard Gardner has assembled research data from the past few decades that indicate that children prior to entering the first grade have stereotypical ways of thinking and "scripts" that are not easily changed by schooling. Stereotypical thinking is a way to reduce a complex matter to a simply response. Examples are "Girls are not good at math," "African Americans are good at dancing and music," "Presbyterians are rather cold-blooded," "Government workers are lazy," "Politicians are unreliable," or "People on welfare won't work."

A script is about a recurring situation made up of events done in a certain way. Gardner uses a birthday party as an illustration. There is planning for the occasion, a guest list, games, cake and presents. Once a child has experienced a few birthdays, she has a script that will continue with variations throughout life. Children learn scripts for going to church or school, eating with the family, going for a swim and so on.

Stereotypes and scripts vary according to the racial, ethnic, or class of the groups to which parents belong. They are transmitted to children by parents and peers. For example, in some African American communities in New York City, children stereotype policemen as persons you avoid. In white middle class towns of New Jersey children stereotype policemen as persons you trust to get help in almost any situation. Likewise scripts for birthdays, family meals or games are different in various socio-economic strata of society (Gardner 1991, 64–69; 99–101; 110–12).

Churches in a Changing Culture

Culture is a word that encompasses the total life of a people. It includes material conditions such as land, physical resources, food and climate. Culture describes how people respond to their location, govern themselves, interpret history, live together and understand the world. Because American culture is within us, we need not review these aspects of our corporate life. It is important to note, however, that a major characteristic of our culture is change. Moreover, several movements with contrary values may go on simultaneously. For example, we read that Americans are becoming more self-centered, more moralistic than in earlier times. Yet a recent study by Robert Wuthnow shows an enormous amount of compassion in American life (Wuthnow 1991; Sorokin 1950).

In addition to having to sort out conflicting values within American society, we must attend to long term movements that are changing the values most people accept. The term "values" is a neutral, descriptive word that means what most people in a society believe desirable or what they think most people ought to desire. It does not mean that a value is ethically good. For example, in a cannibalistic society most people approve of the custom of eating the flesh of their enemies. A judgment about the ethical desirability of a value must be made on criteria other than the fact that people think a certain type of behavior is expected and accepted.

Trying to identify long term trends that are changing American values is risky because the ebb and flow in society might slow down or stop the changes taking place. The following trends, however, have been underway for fifty or more years, creating changes in values that are now reflected in new customs and laws.

- The civil rights movement is helping African and Latin Americans, Asians and other racial or ethnic people become a part of the mainstream of American society.

- The equal rights movement for women has not yet achieved its goal of a constitutional amendment; but it has changed the role of women in the workplace, politics, community leadership and military service.

- The sexual revolution, which was identified in the 1950s and came into prominence in the 1960s with the introduction of the birth control pill, has changed sexual relations for many people from a committed relationship to a form of recreation (Sorokin 1956).

In addition to trends that change values, modifications in how we live and think are brought about by the technology, economic conditions and political events.

Technological advances in communication through the widespread use of television, for example, have impacted public opinion about persons, politicians and social affairs. The sexual revolution was encouraged by talk show hosts and situation comedies. Our political response to the war in Vietnam was greatly affected by battlefield pictures on the evening news hours. Historians of the civil rights movement write that the TV pictures of police dogs turned loose on peaceful protesters in Birmingham, Alabama during April and May 1963 solidified public opinion for the rights of African Americans.

Economic conditions since the early 1970s have speeded up trends affecting how middle class people live. Wages have not kept up with inflation, more women are working outside the home and automation of plants has eliminated many jobs. As a result the middle class is shrinking in size; with both parents working, children are often without adult supervision for extended periods of time.

The collapse of Russian communism has signaled the end of that economic/governmental system based on an ideology of shared wealth. This leaves capitalism, with its ideology of acquired wealth, as the dominant economic system in the industrialized world. Governments regulate capitalism, but the underlying ideology leads to materialism, a belief that one's worth is related to accumulation and display of property.

How Children Learn Culture

Children growing up in American society are not conscious of either the characteristics of the culture nor of the changes that are taking place. Children in their first six or seven years know only what is presented to them by parents, peers, neighbors and perhaps extended family members. Only that part of American culture that is presented and interpreted to them is absorbed. That is why we have continuity in sub-cultures along racial, ethnic, class or sectarian lines.

To a young child, reality is in her relation to caregivers, her home and neighborhood. Influences from external sources such as television are governed by caregivers. As a practical matter it is the caregivers who present and interpret the meaning of life to a child. Unless the child is in an unusual situation, she has no experience with an alternative to the culture she is absorbing. What is absorbed, especially in the first six or seven years, is considered right, not open to challenge.

Caregivers are the carriers of culture. The questions, therefore, are: (1) What interpretation of culture do they communicate? and (2) How do they deal with changes that are taking place in the culture?

The answer to the first question is that caregivers communicate the culture they received as children along with whatever changes they themselves made in values, lifestyle and world view as they came of age. This could be a Native American tribe, a laboring class neighborhood in the city, a Spanish-speaking enclave, a small farming community or a white middle class suburban environment. Not everyone in a sub-culture has exactly the same set of values, but most people in a social location have a common interpretation of culture. This phenomenon is demonstrated in the polling of public opinion. Many of the Gallup polls interview fewer than 2,000 people, yet the results will indicate how millions of people will vote with a margin of error of only 3%. This is possible because the pollsters ask a few people in each sub-group how they would vote; knowing how many people are in that social location, they are able to project how the whole group will vote.

The answer to the second question is that caregivers deal with changes in culture by discussing the changes with the group to which they belong and then forming opinions based on their group's interest. Many of these groups are informal groups in the neighborhood, at the work place or social club. Often the most influential groups for church members are those clusters of friends one has in a congregation. Through worship (prayer, hymns, sermons, scripture readings), service groups and study classes, churches are constantly describing what human life should be and urging members to make decisions in harmony with the church's beliefs. Adults who are caregivers of children and active church members have the church as a place where changes in culture can be examined, and from these examinations they can work out responses they pass on to their children.

What Children Learn at Home

What children learn at home is how to live in the situation in which they find themselves. This means that they learn what is right and wrong (conscience), an image of God, patterns of conduct based on "scripts," stereotypes and beliefs. These matters are all interrelated within a person and in the first few years of life are inseparable. Later the child will learn to split these things into categories which may become increasingly independent.

What is important for the purpose of this essay is the way culture becomes a part of church life and is then communicated to children through caregivers. Analysis of this situation is difficult because we have so few studies of congregations. An examination of the library of a theological seminary will show an abundance of books on "the church." These studies are on what the New Testament church was, the church in historical periods, or what the church ought to be. Another large collection of books will be available on various institutional matters such as laws regarding the church, ministers or the church and state, how to do evangelism, how to raise money or how to conduct educational enterprises. Studies of congregations are lacking: what life is like in a congregation and how that life is lived by individual members and families. There are probably fewer than ten fairly recent ethnographic studies of congregational life. This situation does not mean we know little about congregations; rather, it means we must depend on our informal observations of congregational life as much as we depend on formal study. The few ethnographic studies we have, however, show a congregational ethos maintained by members which will continue because it is communicated by parents to children in their early years.

Synagogue Life, written by Samuel C. Heilman (1976), is the study of an Orthodox Jewish synagogue with approximately 130 members. This book is a careful description of life within a particular synagogue. The reader learns how the members worship, what members consider important, how they solve practical problems such as assembling a *minyan* for daily prayer, how money is raised and spent, the value and content of gossip, how woman prepare their homes for Passover and all the other aspects of life for an Orthodox Jew.

The title of Melvin D. Williams's book (1974), *Community in a Black Pentecostal Church,* is a clue to its content. This study of a Holiness church with 91 adult members helps us see how a group of people united by beliefs and fellowship can have a profound influence on the life of adults and help them work out acceptable attitudes and patterns of conduct in a society dominated by white people.

Nancy T. Ammerman (1987) reported fundamentalists' beliefs and lifestyle in *Bible Believers*. Her description of Southside Gospel Church with 167 household units includes their theological beliefs, political views, expectations of members in relation to dancing, drinking, divorce, relations between husband and wife, education of children, viewing television and other areas of life about which a religiously-oriented person would want guidance.

These three cases are excellent examples of the power of the congregation to create and maintain a religious interpretation of life in the midst of a changing secular culture. The worship and work of these congregations and the lives of members are governed by distinctive beliefs. Being counter to the prevailing culture, these congregations enroll new members only on the basis of the new members' allegiance to the congregation's beliefs.

In contrast to the three cases above are the congregations of mainstream denominations in which values of secular culture are more dominant. We do not have many studies of these congregations because they consist of members with loyalty to several sets of beliefs and are, therefore, difficult to study. Gary Dorsey devoted all his time for several years to understanding the First Church in Windsor, Connecticut. Toward the end of his study he classified the members into categories according to their real reason for belonging to or attending the church. His categories are as follows.

> At First Church, I had met many kinds of people — people who took religion seriously — like Priscilla — and those who thought of religion as an intellectual game, like Bill. There were those who did not consider religion seriously, like Paul Price, and those who thought of it seriously, but never came to a church service. That was Owen Rockwell. Then there were those who took the church seriously but not religion (many of the older members), and those who took themselves seriously but thought little of either the church or religion (that was me). At last, those who took seriously "spirituality" but not "religion," which was where I finally decided to index Joan Rockwell (Dorsey 1995, 345).

Such diversity of interests and concerns made First Church more of an association of people with overlapping interests than a congregation subordinated to a shared belief in God.

Mary N. Hawkes interviewed a cross-section of the 1,400 members of "Apostles" Church. She selected this 300-year-old congregation of the United Church of Christ because it was large, was growing in numbers and was considered to be "alive and filled with vitality." She indicated why it was considered successful. It had a well-designed worship service, good leadership of music and a trained professional staff for Christian education; and it supported a variety of good community programs. But her interview of adults raised a question.

> A common faith must be inherent in the life in Apostles Church, or else what brings persons together? Yet it is hard to trace the running threads of that faith experience. Persons in interviews seemed reticent to discuss their faith, and some even mentioned that they find it difficult to discuss faith issues and that such conversations make them nervous (Hawkes 1983, 130).

This question "What brings people together?" when a common faith is not evident is the critical issue in mainstream churches, whether they are slowly dying or "alive and filled with vitality." Stephen

Warner's sociological answer is that churches have become more like social clubs for the middle class and therefore "responsive and vulnerable to local cultures" (Warner 1994).

Langdon Gilkey's theological answer is that members in mainstream churches have lost the self-critical principle which leads to repentance and to a concern for building a community such as God desires. Protestants have thus become open to culture and have taken as the substance of their faith nationalism, capitalism and middle class moral standards. Gilkey summarizes his judgment in these words.

> At this point one might note that the denominational church is too secular, too much like its surrounding middle-class culture, not religious or redemptive enough — if religion is to provide, as it traditionally has, the arena in which our finitude, our fatedness, our sin and our death are brought to the surface, honestly looked at and confessed and dealt with. Perhaps the moral silence on national ethical issues overlaps and unites with a religious silence on the pressures of the human condition, and in this combination the lack of a spiritual center becomes lethal (Gilkey 1994, 107–08).

Examples of how middle class values and lifestyle have become dominant in Protestant churches are easy to document, so only a few illustrations will be cited.

Prestige based on design of building and elegance of furnishings abounds. When members want to show off their church, they take friends to the building. Often there is one feature (a tall steeple, organ, gymnasium or stained glass window) which is more revealing of Thorstein Veblen's principle of conspicuous consumption than of any teaching of Jesus (Veblen 1912, 68–102). A building, the result of a congregation's values, becomes the silent but effective communicator of what the congregation considers important.

A congregation's budget is a precise reflection of what it believes. One would expect a large portion of such a budget to be allocated to the care and maintenance of the church as an institution; but many churches' budgets have little or no allocation of funds for human needs in the community, for relief of human suffering elsewhere or to help the self-enhancement of people in third world countries. The congregational budget sets a norm for Christian giving; thus, it is no wonder that members follow suit and use their money for self-development and pleasure.

A congregation's use of leaders is often as self-centered as its use of money. Good, unpaid leaders are hard to locate and churches tend to use and honor them for their service to the congregation. This is proper, but is it in harmony with the beliefs of the church? Church members who are leaders in worthwhile enterprises in the community may get no recognition from the congregation. Why? Because congregations, having accepted the secular "success" goal of institutional life, do not see their mission as helping members to witness in the workplace or as having a responsibility for supporting work of institutions dedicated to community service.

This success motif applies to aspects of congregational life other than the use of leaders. It puts the goal of increasing membership, prominence of individual members, building an endowment fund or other aspects of institutional life before the goal of creating a community which focuses its attention on finding and doing the will of God. If the success motif dominates the life of a congregation, then that church-centered interpretation of religion will be communicated to children through their parents.

This description of the socialization process raises two questions: (1) To what extent do childhood experiences continue throughout life? and (2) Can mainstream congregations become less "responsive and vulnerable to local culture"?

(1) As children grow, they become more conscious of other cultures and lifestyles which they see on TV or observe in school. Their increasing ability to think about and to test how other people live challenges their childhood training. Children raised in cults or sect-type churches tend to maintain their lifestyle/religion, but there are many exceptions.

Children raised in the "First Church" in Windsor, in the "Apostles" Church or in mainstream Protestant churches as described by Gilkey will probably be Christian according to the beliefs and practices of the congregations they and their caregivers attend. This can mean anything from casual membership to a serious effort to be a disciple of Jesus Christ. An adult's religious situation, including a rejection of religious training in childhood, will depend on how the person — after leaving the direct influence of the home — responds to peer pressure in the work place or college.

(2) Although there are many events and conditions that may cause people to become more concerned about their relation to God, the most likely cause for most people is becoming part of a group of people who have this same concern. Sect-like groups, such as the Jewish synagogue and the Pentecostal or fundamentalist churches cited previously, are examples of religious groups which are able to resist secular society as they focus on the kind of life their beliefs require. To these people theology does not consist of ideas that can be tossed about in one's mind; ideas about God do not change or mature people very much. Rather, theology consists of beliefs about God that are to be translated into a lifestyle pleasing to God. The question now becomes: Can mainstream congregations be theological in the sense of trying to develop a lifestyle in harmony with their beliefs?

Congregational Reorientation

Gilkey is right: the basic issue is theological. His observation is supported by a recent survey of Presbyterians. This denomination, like other mainstream Protestant traditions, has experienced a decline in membership for more than 20 years. The causes usually cited for the decline have proven to be incorrect. The real reason, according to researchers, is "lay-liberalism." They use the word "lay" because it does not reflect any liberal theological system. "[I]t is largely a homemade product, a kind of modern-age folk religion . . . . Most 'lay liberals' prefer Christianity to other faiths, but they are unable to ground their preference in strong truth claims" (Johnson, Hoge and Luidens 1993). As a result the typical Presbyterian does not discuss his faith with anyone, not even members of his family.

Given the perseverance and strength of secular values within congregational life, is there any hope for a reorientation toward goals more consistent with the kingdom of God as described by Jesus? The answer is yes, *if* congregations focus on Christian beliefs that apply to contemporary issues.

There are illustrations of congregations which stake out a position contrary to cultural values. The civil rights movement of the 1960s would not have happened without the leadership of Martin Luther King, Jr. and the hundreds of African-American churches which supported the "sit-ins" of the Student Non-violent Coordinating Committee (Mooney and Grossbach 1992). The Mormon Church is an example of a white middle-class denomination which has been able to maintain distinctive beliefs and practices. For example, teenagers are expected to devote two years in missionary work at their own expense. Mormon families explain this mission responsibility to their children at an early age so that at the proper time teenagers have the money and the training to do what is required. Mormon parents would probably not be able to sustain such a radical deviation from secular teenage culture except that such beliefs are supported by their congregations.

The matter of reorienting and focusing the beliefs of a mainstream congregation is difficult. We have very few written cases that can be cited. Church officers, however, in dioceses, conferences or presbyteries can document many cases where a minister over time has been able to lead members to think of themselves as continuing the ministry of Christ.

The process of reorienting a congregation is well-illustrated in the study of a church in Mendocino, California, by R. Stephen Warner (1988). In 1962 this mainstream congregation of about 150 members called a well-qualified minister who represented a "progressive" religion. In 1973 the church called a pastor with an evangelical religion; by 1976 membership had increased to 223.

This reorientation took place because Larry Redford, a member of the church with theological education in an evangelical seminary, developed a cadre of members who were able to orient the congregation to an evangelical interpretation of the Bible.

The case of Covenant Church, a congregation of a mainstream denomination, illustrates the process by which a congregation changes. This church, with a membership of about 1,000, is located in a town of 30,000 and identifies itself as politically conservative. For example, when its minister went to Washington in 1963 to march with Martin Luther King, Jr., he was asked to resign and he did so. Yet in January 1984 the congregation voted to become one of only 150 churches in the United States which would provide sanctuary for South Americans fleeing persecution in Central America.

What caused this action, which was contrary to United States immigration policy? The story as recorded by Nelle G. Slater (1989, 1–27) began with an officer retreat in January 1983. Paul Williams, the owner of a contract business, who was an "economic conservative" and a Republican, spoke to the officers about the need to help disadvantaged people such as Central American refugees. The matter was referred to the mission committee, chaired by Nan Carr. Nan Carr and Hilda Mann, a committee member, with the associate pastor, Carl Gordon, led the mission committee in a three-month study of the Salvadoran situation. This small group expanded their concern and knowledge to the whole congregation through an adult class and statements addressed to the whole congregation. The ever widening circle of concerned people caused conflict in the congregation, yet enough members were convinced of the rightness of the cause to produce the majority vote in favor of the sanctuary status in January 1984; and three Salvadoran refugees were received on February 12.

These cases are cited to illustrate the political maxim that a human institution can be changed if a few people have a vision of what ought to be and then influence others to embrace that vision until a sizable group is committed to the new orientation (Dahl 1956, 132). This process of reorientation is true of a large movement such as a political party, a small local P.T.A. or a congregation.

A more satisfactory and enduring way to reorient a congregation is for the minister and a group of officers to develop a vision because they are in a position to claim theological support for the vision they proclaim; they are also in a position to influence the selection of designated leaders. A central study group can enlarge the number of members who understand and share what the congregation can be and should be doing.

Once members of a congregation begin to ask "What would God want us to be and do because we are Christian?" they are on their way to a goal that will make them more aware of their culturally-formed values and less loyal to such values. Moreover, parents will be given guidance and support as they train their children according to the values of the vision and thus insure some permanence for their beliefs and lifestyle (Nelson 1989, 203–30; Warren 1995b; Wuthnow 1994).

Issues

1. How can Christians live in a secular society and at the same time develop a lifestyle based on the life and teachings of Jesus?

2. How should parents relate to their children so that the children will develop a sense of trust, forgiveness and concern for others on which a faith in God may develop?

3. How can parents teach their young children a moral code without creating a legalistic conscience?

4. Should congregational leaders help adult members sort out the desirable from the undesirable changes taking place in our culture?

5. Is it possible for professional and managerial people who are leaders in the community and the church to administer the affairs of the congregation on the basis of doing the will of God rather than on the splendor and size of their buildings, breadth of programs or acclaim of the community?

Discussion Questions

1. What is the most effective way to influence adults to give a high priority to the Christian lifestyle? Is it through worship attendance, small classes on how Christians should live, support groups for adults who are struggling with personal problems or some other way?

2. How can a church's educational program help parents understand that they are the first teachers of religion? What literature is available for this purpose? How should it be used with parents?

3. Can parents be made aware of how approval or disapproval of their children's behavior creates conscience? If so, what coaching can church leaders give to parents so that the conscience which is formed in children is oriented to Christian values?

4. Is it possible to form groups of adults in a congregation who will commit themselves to a serious and systematic consideration of what their congregation's mission should be in the community? What are the problems and possibilities of such groups? If formed, how should the members be selected, led and related to the leaders who make decisions for the congregation?

5. How does your congregation help members relate the Christian faith to changes that are taking place in American society such as civil rights, women's liberation, or permissive attitudes toward sexual relationships? Do church leaders establish a response or do members participate in the decision-making process?

6. By what means can church members become conscious of how material values — such as size of congregation, beauty of building, public approval of ministers or priests — may conflict with the New Testament example of church life?

References

Ammerman, N.T.
1987 *Bible Believers.* New Brunswick: Rutgers University Press.

Baker, R.
1982 *Growing Up.* New York: Congdon and Weed.

Catechism
1994 *Catechism of the Catholic Church.* Washington, DC: United States Catholic Conference.

Coles, R.
1989 *Girl Scouts Survey on the Beliefs and Moral Values of American Children.* New York: Girl Scouts of the U.S.A.

Dahl, R.A.
1956 *A Preface to Democratic Theory.* Chicago: University of Chicago Press.

Dorsey, G.
1995 *Congregation.* New York: Penguin Books.

Emde, R. William Johnson and M. Ann Easterbrook.
1987 The Do's and Don'ts of Early Moral Development. In *The Emergence of Morality in Young Children,* edited by Jerome Kagan and Sharon Lamb. Chicago: University of Chicago Press.

Erikson, E.H.
1968 *Identity: Youth and Crisis.* New York: W.W. Norton.

Gallup, G. and Jim Castelli.
1989 *The People's Religion.* New York: Macmillan Publishing Company.

Gardner, H.
1991 *The Unschooled Mind.* New York: Basic Books.

Gilkey, L.
1994 The Christian Congregation as a Religious Community. In *American Congregations,* Vol. 2, edited by James P. Wind and James W. Lewis. Chicago: The University of Chicago Press.

Hawkes, M.N.
1983 *The Church as Nurturing Faith Community: A Study in One Congregation.* Ed.D. diss., Teachers College, Columbia University.

Heilman, S.C.
1976 *Synagogue Life.* Chicago: The University of Chicago Press.

Heller, D.
1986 *The Children's God.* Chicago: The University of Chicago Press.

Johnson, B., Dean Hoge and Donald Luidens.
1993 Mainline Churches: The Real Reason for Decline. In *First Things* (March 1993) 15–16.

Lang, M.A.
1983 *Acquiring Our Image of God*. New York: Paulist Press.

Mead, G.H.
1940 *Mind, Self and Society*. Chicago: The University of Chicago Press.

Mooney, C.C. and Barry Grossback.
1992 *The Encyclopedia Americana*, s.v. "Civil Rights Movement."

Niebuhr, H.R.
1951 *Christ and Culture*. New York: Harper and Brothers.

Nelson, C.E.
1978 *Don't Let Your Conscience Be Your Guide*. New York: Paulist Press.
1989 *How Faith Matures*. Louisville: Westminster/John Knox Press.
1996 Formation of a God Representation. In *Religious Education* 91:22–40.

Rizzuto, A.M.
1979 *The Birth of the Living God*. Chicago: The University of Chicago Press.

Slater, N.G.
1989 A Case Study of Offering Hospitality: Choosing to be a Sanctuary Church. In *Tensions Between Citizenship and Discipleship*. New York: The Pilgrim Press.

Sorokin, P.A.
1950 *Altruistic Love*. Boston: The Beacon Press.
1956 *The American Sex Revolution*. Boston: Porter Sargent Publisher.

Stern, D.N.
1985 *The Interpersonal World of the Infant*. New York: Basic Books.

Veblen, T.
1912 *The Theory of the Leisure Class*. New York: B.H. Huebsch.

Warner, R.S.
1988 *New Wine in Old Wine Skins*. Berkeley: University of California Press.
1994 The Place of the Congregation in the Contemporary American Religious Configuration. In *American Congregations*, Vol. 2, edited by J.P. Wind and J.W. Lewis. Chicago: The University of Chicago Press.

Warren, M.
1995a Life Structure or the Material Condition of the Living: An Ecclesial Task. In *New Theology Review* 8:4, 26–47.
1995b Speaking and Learning in the Local Church: A Look at Material Conditions. In *Worship* 69:1, 28–51.

Williams, M.D.
1974 *Community in a Black Pentecostal Church*. Prospect Heights, Illinois: Waveland Press.

Wuthnow, R.
1991 *Acts of Compassion*. Princeton: Princeton University Press.
1994 *I Came Away Stronger*. Grand Rapids: William Eerdmans Publishing Company.

Chapter 4

Tracks into a New Civilization

A View of the Irish Roman Catholic Church

Martin Kennedy

Martin Kennedy's essay illustrates some of the issues of reorientation raised by Nelson. Clearly about Roman Catholic Ireland, its method and angle of analysis will be instructive to thinkers in any denomination. Though Ireland is smaller than New York State and might seem more contained and manageable, its encounter with modernity and Western consumer capitalism has been traumatic and sudden. The reorientation going on is not local or congregational but international and ecclesial.

What is particularly instructive in Kennedy's essay is his quiet, observant and hopeful spirit in the face of the upheavals he describes. He finds seeds of "significant pastoral and spiritual renewal" for the future. He proposes letting go of old metaphors of domination in favor of new metaphors of flexibility, access and adaptation. One of his most perceptive arguments is that the industrial and post-industrial consumerist economy and culture is itself in crisis, signaling the falseness of its promises in its inability to satisfy deeper human hungers. Environmentalists, feminists and liberationists, many of whom are young, are all pointing to this falseness.

Also instructive is Kennedy's way of taking a long historical view of the oral and written history of North America and the explorations of the sixteenth century. Still, his analysis implicitly calls us to pay attention to North American history and the history of our particular denomination in North America. Historical analysis is the compass that gives orientation and bearings to pastoral analysis.

Finally Kennedy describes a specific experiment in a specific local church where adults have gradually taken on new roles and a new say in giving directions.

While Roman Catholics, particularly clergy, find heartening the "reorientation" described by Kennedy, Protestants, particularly Presbyterians, warn that lay control is fine but only so long as the laity have a deep gospel commitment. Lacking that, lay direction could point the church down some blind alleys. This caution echoes Nelson's point in the previous essay, that the issues are "theological." In addition, Kennedy's metaphor of flexible, temporary train tracks addresses the issue of taking new paths.

Kennedy is a well-known theoretician of youth ministry and of adult lay empowerment in Ireland.

In this essay I want to explore current changes in the Catholic church in Ireland and offer a sense of where these changes may be leading. These changes may be of interest to a North American audience in view of our close historical connection and certain similarities in our experiences. The present Irish church was fundamentally shaped in the early part of the nineteenth century by developments I will describe below. The stamp of that church was imported into North America in subsequent decades with the huge numbers of Irish immigrants. By 1890 there were 1,872,000 native-born Irish living in the United States, roughly a quarter of all Irish people. By 1900 fully 50 percent of U.S. Catholics and 62 percent of U.S. bishops were of Irish origin.[1] The First Vatican Council (1869–70), which directed the Catholic church for the following century, had a disproportionate Irish presence. Ten percent of the bishops there were Irish-born and a further 20 percent of Irish descent.[2]

Just as there has been a strong Irish influence on the North American Catholic experience, there is presently a strong North American influence on the Irish cultural experience. And it is in the context of a tension between nineteenth-century Irish church formation and twentieth-century North American culture that the twenty-first century Irish church is taking shape. I believe that this tension is also part of the experience of the North American Catholic church.

Energy and analysis

In the early 1970s the Irish Roman Catholic church appeared, on the face of it, to be very healthy. A national survey at the time revealed that 91 percent of Catholics attended weekly Mass and 97 percent prayed daily. At that time I was part of a group that did street evangelization work with young adults. We spoke with hundreds of young people every week about God. We knew then, as others in youth ministry knew, that things were changing. Many young people were very different from their parents in how they experienced life and faith. The figures cited above would not last.

Twenty-five years later, again on the face of it, the church [here and below: the Irish Roman Catholic church] looks far from healthy. Weekly Mass attendance has been dropping at an accelerating pace and is currently measured at 64 percent. Scandals about sexual abuse of children by clergy and the inept handling of these by church leaders, revelations of the physical abuse of children by women religious and revelations about the private lives of some clergy and bishops have traumatized the institution and deeply distressed the people. Behind these revelations is a general sense of religion in decline, of faith in retreat to the margins of people's lives. There is foreboding and pessimism about the future of faith in our culture. As a church we seem to be losing confidence, losing energy, losing our nerve.

My gut sense is that if the presence of God's Spirit in the church means anything it means that a decline in religious sensitivity is not inevitable. This presence is clearly not magical. It needs energetic human agency to express itself, and this energy in turn needs to be rooted in a solid and hopeful cultural, historical and theological analysis of our situation.

So while I do take seriously the view that we in Ireland could be heading for a post-Christian culture I do not think such a direction inevitable. It is possible that the twenty-first century could be a time of significant pastoral and spiritual renewal. The conditions for such renewal are already present. Now is a time of opportunity when we need to grasp the situation with confidence and energy. My concern is that the prophecy of doom will be self-fulfilling, draining the energy and inspiration needed for renewal. My own sense of a positive future for religious spirituality in our culture is based around three ideas:

- ❖ While the dominant consumerist culture is effectively offering an alternative spirituality, that culture is itself in crisis.
- ❖ This crisis represents an opportunity for the church if we can learn to appropriately express a gospel spirituality for the twenty-first century.
- ❖ Learning such a spirituality requires much pastoral experimentation, experimentation that is already going on in pockets of the church.

Here my understanding has been shaped by a number of cultural analysts who offer a negative, but not pessimistic, view of industrial culture.[3] These thinkers offer a range of complementary interpretive frameworks that seek to account for the ills of consumerist capitalism and at the same time offer hope and challenge for a more positive future. This challenge includes moving from an anthropological to an ecological myth (Berry); from a patriarchal to a feminist consciousness (Lerner); from a mechanistic to a systemic way of thinking and acting (Capra); reshaping civilization in an ethical manner around new technologies (Toffler and Handy); and developing an alternative economics (Robertson). All share an inspiration towards an ethical, inclusive consciousness and a commitment to reshaping civilization in the light of that consciousness.

As the crisis of industrialism deepens, this inspiration can only strengthen and extend; thus there is enormous scope for dialogue between this inspiration and the vision and practice of Jesus. But which Jesus? Over the centuries the church has offered different accounts of Jesus expressed in and limited by the understandings and interests of its time. While present accounts will also be culture-bound and shaped by vested interests, we are in a situation very different from previous generations. There is a wealth of historical, scientific research on the life and times of Jesus that can bring us to a more direct encounter with the original experience of Jesus. Also, analyses of the socio-economic history and structures of our civilization, which were not available in the past, can at the least confront us with the question, From whose viewpoint do we construct our image of Jesus today? Environmental, feminist and liberation theologies construct their images of Jesus from the point of view of those wounded by our industrial culture.[4] These theologies, summarized by Echegaray and others, have something to say, I believe, to the twenty-first century.

Learning to speak afresh to the new century requires a fundamental openness to change in the church. Here I have found Kung's work on paradigmatic change and Handy's work on organizational change very helpful.[5] Küng's presentation of church history as a succession of epochal paradigms — constellations of communally shared beliefs, values, techniques that guide thinking in pre-established ways — relativizes the dominant structures of church in any given time. It shows how these structures rise and fall over the centuries in the context of broader civilizational change. Küng argues that the Roman Catholic church is still dominated by a monarchical paradigm that came to the fore in the eleventh century. This paradigm was reaffirmed in the sixteenth-century Council of Trent against the Protestant paradigm and again in the nineteenth-century First Vatican Council, which was against the modern paradigm. He interprets the proposed reforms of the Second Vatican Council as an attempt to take on board Protestant and modern paradigms. Those with vested interest in the monarchical model are now resisting such reforms. Küng's basic point is that the monarchical paradigm is not credible to the modern or post-modern sensibility. He points both to the struggle for democracy in the church and to the emergence of feminist, liberation and environmental theologies as signs of a new paradigm candidate that can speak to the civilization.

Coming from the point of view of organizational development and change, Charles Handy also works with a rhythm of rise and fall, which he holds endemic to all of life. An organization will only remain healthy if it can flow with this rhythm, anticipate change and allocate in time resources to prepare for that change. This preparation needs to happen when the organization is strong, not when it has already fallen into decline. He images this with an S-shaped curve. The high point of the rising curve (a) is precisely the point that a new curve needs to begin in anticipation of the coming decline. The new curve overtakes the old at a point of decline in the old (b), by which time it would have been too late for the new one to begin had it not already started. The new curve seeks to anticipate the new environment, and through trial and error develops appropriate structures and practices for it. In time it becomes the main curve as the old one declines. The period between the two points is a time of duality, where the past co-exists with the future in the present. The logic that accepts this notion of permanent change Handy calls curvilinear. Such logic is necessary for successful leadership but may be short-circuited by too much attachment to the past.

I find Handy and Kung evocative in coming to terms with the present situation of the Irish church. Handy's curve frames my own efforts towards an energizing perspective that looks at the past with an attitude of freedom, the future with confidence and the present with a sense of opportunity.

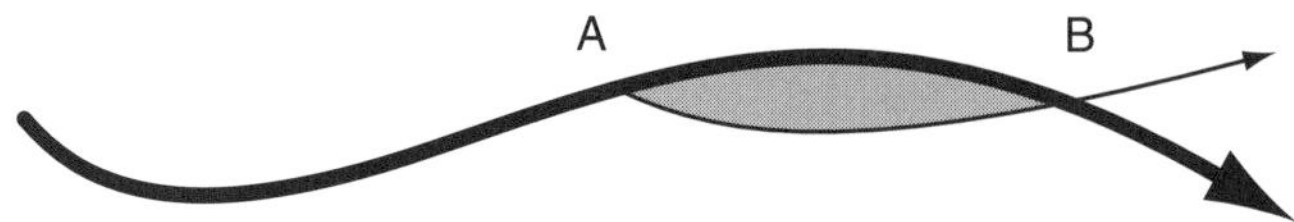

A changing church

The Irish church today is still fundamentally shaped by innovations from the first half of the nineteenth century. These innovations are now in crisis and need to be set in their historical context if the crisis is to be properly addressed. The main point that emerges for me from this history is that religious spirituality has been a resilient feature of Irish culture for millennia, supported in different circumstances by very different pastoral strategies.

When Saint Patrick and other early missionaries arrived in Ireland in the fifth century, they found a Celtic people with a rich culture, well-developed political and legal systems and a body of religious beliefs and practices based around the druids. The basic strategy of the missionaries was to graft the gospel message onto this existing culture, achieving the conversion of the Irish without martyrs or great social disturbance. One of the effects of this approach was the emergence of a monastic rather than diocesan church structure, with many of the most important churches ruled by monks who were not bishops. Such structures better fitted the intimate nature of Irish society, composed as it was of some 150 small kingdoms. It was to be another 700 years before the present diocesan structure was established.

Intimacy with God, love of nature, hospitality, pilgrimage and penance emerge as constant themes in Irish religious literature over the centuries. These themes survived the traumas of the

Viking raids for the eighth to the eleventh centuries and the Norman invasion of 1169. Within a century two thirds of Ireland was in their hands. That invasion from the neighboring Britain initiated conflict between the two islands that has continued in one form or another down to the present day. It fostered severe racial conflict within Ireland and even within religious orders in the country. The invading Normans brought with them English and Continental monks, establishing rival monasteries of the same order and attempting to impose foreign superiors and abbots on communities of Irish monks. This led on a number of occasions to bloody feuding among the monks. "At the 1291 Franciscan chapter in Cork, for example, the sons of the gentle St. Francis decided that action speaks louder than words, so that at the end of one plenary session the chapter-hall was strewn with the dead bodies of sixteen delegates."[6]

Following the Reformation in England in the sixteenth century, Tudor monarchs carried through a sustained campaign of anglicization in Ireland that involved numerous attempts at suppressing Catholicism. These efforts included banning the Mass, execution or exiling of clergy, and confiscation of lands held by Catholics. Many penal laws were enacted severely disadvantaging Catholics. In 1530 Catholics owned 100 percent of the land; by 1778 that figure had fallen to 5 percent. In the early eighteenth century the bounty on a priest was £30, a vicar general £40, a bishop or a Jesuit £50. The impact of all this was that church organization was reduced to a minimum. However, popular faith survived the times by coming to expression in a tremendous devotional blossoming in the form of folk prayers and practices that fed the spiritual life of the people. A collection of 539 of these folk prayers was published in 1974.[7] It shows how prayer was integrated into the daily lives and struggles of the people in a manner not dependent on church buildings or clergy.

By the early nineteenth century the last of the penal laws were removed. Catholic emancipation had been granted and the church set about rebuilding itself. A central figure in this rebuilding was Paul Cullen, Rector of the Irish College in Rome, who was made Archbishop of Dublin in 1850. The centuries of anti-Catholic legislation had left the institutional church organizationally very weak. A strong tradition of emigration had intensified after the mid-century's great famine, resulting in a halving of the Irish population during the nineteenth century. As the bulk of emigration was to English-speaking countries, the Irish language went into severe decline, which greatly weakened the tradition of folk prayers. Further, Cullen disapproved of the tradition of religious practice not centered on the church building or the priest. His efforts were towards replacing that tradition with one more amenable to clerical control.

One of Cullen's first tasks was to call a synod of the Irish bishops in Thurles, the first full and formal synod since the twelfth century. The basic pattern for the future of the church was laid down at Thurles. "This programme for the new age contained little or anything that was really new. It is hard to find anything at Thurles that was not laid down at Trent. Hitherto the full Tridentine pattern had been difficult to implement in Ireland. Now it was to go the way of Catholic Europe."[8]

Mass attendance, estimated at around 30–40 percent in the 1850s, jumped to 90 percent within 50 years and stayed that way up to quite recently. There were only 120 nuns in Ireland in 1800; that figure became 8,000 by 1900 and continued to grow right through to the 1970s. By the 1860s there were 2,339 churches in the country, of which 2,000 had been built since the beginning of the century. From the mid-century the extension of state-sponsored social and education systems was gradually and effectively brought under Catholic control by Cullen. Religious instruction took its form from the Tridentine question-and-answer catechism with emphasis on the Christian life as obedience to concrete rules. The Sunday sermon was the normal supplement to the catechism and was itself supplemented by the parish mission, an intensive week-long program of religious devotions run by specialist teams of priests.

The priests who ran the parish missions (Redemptorists, Passionists) in turn left behind them institutions to nourish a devotional spirituality. The decline of traditional Celtic spirituality left a devotional vacuum in the lives of the people. The mission priests filled that vacuum with a flood of imports from the continent: jubilees, *tridua,* novenas, forty hours devotion, perpetual adoration, blessed altars, benediction, stations of the cross, devotions to the Sacred Heart and the Immaculate Conception, sodalities, societies, scapulars, missals, prayer books, medals, holy pictures and so on. People adopted these with enormous enthusiasm. This shift in religious practice was not without its critics:

> The nineteenth-century apostles of the Church achieved their aims in Ireland, not necessarily because of their personal worth or the message they had to offer, but because of the vast reserves of faith in the hearts of the people. At the same time these nineteenth-century churchmen virtually ignored, and sometimes openly opposed, what were in fact the very sources of that faith, namely, fourteen centuries of unbroken and life-giving Christian tradition passed on in the erstwhile vernacular — Irish — and the tradition it embodied.[9]

Irish Catholicism, thus shaped by Cullen, flourished for the remainder of the nineteenth century and for three quarters of the twentieth century. Now, many of the devotional practices have virtually disappeared; the number of seminarians at Maynooth College is at its lowest for over a century; the numbers in religious orders are declining dramatically; Mass attendance in many urban areas is back to or below mid-nineteenth century levels. Viewed from Handy's or Küng's perspective, this development is not tragic or disastrous. It is simply another example of the pattern of rise and fall. A particular religious strategy flourished in a particular culture. As the culture changed, the strategy became less effective. The challenge is not to recover the past but to develop a new strategy in anticipation of a different future.

A changing culture

The stress of many in ministry today is that we are attempting to straddle at once a slow-moving church and a fast-moving culture.

Irish society changed little from the nineteenth century to the 1960s. Relative to most of Western Europe it was poor, rural and insular. A fundamental change in government economic policy at the end of the 50s led to the creation of an open industrial economy in place of a largely agricultural, protected economy. A huge influx of European and North American multinational companies brought a great increase in wealth for two-thirds of the population. At the same time the first national television station opened in 1962 and within four years 85 percent of Irish homes had television, giving the nation an unprecedented view of Western culture. Within a decade Ireland was fully integrated into that culture.[10]

Western society has 20 percent of the planet's population and consumes 85 percent of its income. Western culture is a function of this statistic, justifying and sustaining it by offering a vivid fantasy of what it means to be human in terms of consumption, a fantasy that has entranced Western civilization. This reduction of the human has, according to Thomas Berry, brought our imaginations to their narrowest since consciousness emerged from its Paleolithic phase: "We are made for consumer goods and our hearts are restless until they rest in these." Put this way the culture emerges as an alternative spirituality, seeking to shape what we believe in, what we hope for, what we love. Jesus opens up much different, much bigger possibilities for us: intimacy with God, love between neighbors, a delightful sense of our innate self worth; but an imagination entranced and reduced by the consumer culture has little space for the vastness of this Christian vision.

In this difficult situation any attempt to communicate that vision through medieval authority structures and a sixteenth-century Tridentine pastoral strategy will simply not work. A survey of the pastoral practices of parishes, dioceses and religious orders will show that much of the Irish church has not faced up to this reality. But it will also show that there are many, often lonely, efforts at pastoral experimentation around the country. Groups of people — islands of creative re-imagination — struggle with the question of how to offer the gift of the gospel in a way that can spark the religious imagination of the people of our time.

These groups have, in the language of Handy, embarked on a second curve. The challenge facing them is to discover a language and a strategy that can effectively communicate the gospel's good news to the people of the twenty-first century and exploit the chink in the culture. The challenge to the church on the main curve is to support these groups in the messiness and frequent failure that will attend their experimentation.

A key inspiration among these groups is the Second Vatican Council, with its inclusive vision of church as the people of God. The Council arrived at the exact moment in Ireland when pre-conciliar church structures were encountering a new culture here. The first generations that were to move away from Paul Cullen's church had already been born.

The Tullamore experiment — creative restructuring

Tullamore town has a population of some 9,000 people and is located in the Irish midlands. It is a single parish and has come to prominence in the church in recent years for what are seen as innovative practices. In its endeavors to facilitate the full and equal involvement of lay people, the parish is among the first in the country to attempt to move beyond the structures and practices initiated a century and a half ago by Paul Cullen. I will examine three features of this endeavor: how authority is practiced, how money is spent and how formation is facilitated.

Authority

In the last six years the authority structures have shifted in stages from a simple monarchical model towards a more complex democratic one. In making that shift in virtually uncharted Irish waters, there were inevitable tensions and confusion that the parish has since been struggling to deal with.

Up to 1990 the parish priest or pastor was the sole authority figure. He consulted with a small group of financial experts on matters requiring major expenditure. These constituted the parish finance committee who understood themselves as advisory to the parish pastor. None of the other priests of the parish had access to the finance committee meetings or minutes. When the church building was destroyed by fire in the mid 1980s, the parish pastor took full charge of the rebuilding project with the finance committee. They managed finances adroitly and on completion of the rebuilding had over one million pounds left over. This was placed in a trust fund for the ongoing development needs of the church. The details of the fund did not become public and only the parish pastor and finance committee members had access to information on how it was performing at any time.

A new parish pastor arrived in 1990 and within a year had changed the authority structures. A team system of working was established among the priests and sisters. Decisions that formerly rested with the parish pastor now came before the weekly meeting of the team for consideration. Shortly after that, a Pastoral Council was established on an area election basis as a decision-making body for the parish. Tensions quickly emerged among the three bodies (pastoral council, finance committee and parish team) regarding areas of authority. The finance committee continued to function as before in its capacity as advisor to the parish pastor and resisted recognizing the new institutions. The pastoral council was slowly coming to grips with its decision making role, and the minutes of a 1993 meeting record its rejection of a proposal from the parish pastor to build a parish center. The Pastoral Council opted instead to commission a parish needs survey. Meanwhile, parish team members struggled for and eventually gained access to finance committee meetings. Later they even succeeded in publishing a full disclosure of parish finances and securing a substantial budget for the pastoral council.

In autumn 1994 the parish team engaged in a planning exercise from which emerged its own vision for the parish: "to make Tullamore Parish a place that puts its total resources at the disposal of the poor and alienated." In a continuation of these creative tensions, the council questioned whether the pastoral team had the right to come to a vision statement on its own, raising thereby the question of where final authority rested in the parish. A full review of the role of the council was the outcome of this questioning. That review resulted in the establishment of a parish coordinating group whose task would be "to facilitate the implementation of Pastoral Council policy." This coordinating group was made up of representatives from the council, the team and the finance committee. The coordinating group meets every two weeks, prepares the monthly agenda of the Pastoral Council meeting by acting as a clearing-house for all parish business and is responsible to the council for the implementation of council decisions. At this juncture, the parish team discontinued its regular business meetings and the finance committee was deemed advisory to the Council.

Money

Patterns of money distribution offer clear indicators of the priorities of any grouping. In church terms every budget is a theological statement. Significant shifts have taken place recently in the parish's financial priorities. The employment on a trial basis of a lay parish pastoral coordinator exemplifies these shifts. His later retention on a reduced job description and an increased salary is a further indicator of long term commitment to the principle of lay involvement and of the need to allocate resources to the work of calling, forming and sustaining lay ministry. At a time in Ireland of deepening hostility to Travellers, who are a minority ethnic nomadic community, the parish is taking an unambiguous stand. It has committed money to the Tullamore Travellers movement for the employment of a community education worker whose role is to help the non-Traveller or "settled" community come to a better understanding of the experience and orientation of Travellers.

The parish has also recently funded the establishment of a local and independent rape crisis center, initiated by local women following a lay woman's homily given at all the Masses about the abuse of women and the challenge of the gospel. A further commitment of substantial parish funds helped establish an unemployment center, the initiative of the employment committee of the pastoral council. These commitments have put substantial strain on parish funds. As a result, a new tithing system was agreed upon, to which the people responded by tripling overall weekly contributions.

Formation

For most of its history the Catholic church has emphasized the pre-eminence of the vocation of priests and religious over the lay vocation. Against this background the current crisis of vocations is viewed by some as *a crisis of a system without people to lead it,* with a "shortage" of priests and religious because not have enough people are willing to enter the priesthood and religious life. Ironically, despite this sharp decline in the numbers entering seminaries and novitiates, huge financial and personnel resources are still put into these institutions of formation. A 1989 study revealed that for every four people being trained in Ireland as priests, brothers and nuns, there are three people working full time on their formation. At the same time there are many dioceses in the country without a single full-time adult Christian education coordinator.

This apartheid approach to the distribution of formation resources is being challenged by a new perspective based on the Vatican Two vision of the church as the people of God. In this perspective, baptism — not ordination — is seen as the decisive sacrament of vocation, and the many lay people in the Irish church with energy and commitment for ministry are finally being recognized. What they need and often lack is a system of roles and formation that will provide them the space to develop and express that commitment. In this view the crisis of vocations is seen as the failure to recognize and adequately cater for the lay vocation. *This crisis can be defined as a problem of a people without a system.*

A key corrective decision taken in Tullamore was the employment of a parish pastoral coordinator to foster the involvement of lay people in the work of the parish. This decision responded to the very practical difficulty that greater involvement of lay people brings. Who is going to call, form and sustain them in their ministry? If it takes years of formation and considerable expense to equip priests and religious for their roles, it is unreasonable to expect lay people to engage in ministry without serious formation. Priests and religious open to lay involvement often feel they cannot provide the formation. They feel ill-equipped, or they find they have to straddle (in Handy's imagery) both the new and the old curves, providing the services traditionally expected of priests and religious while seeking to develop new ministries. They are left with little time or energy for the formation and support of lay people.

The decision to employ the coordinator was taken by the pastoral council. The job was formally advertised and an interview committee put in place. The person appointed was an ex-priest, the first and only such appointment in the country. This was a very practical application of the principle of the primacy of baptism. Though the official church position effectively prohibits ex-priests from taking up formal pastoral roles, the pastoral council took the view that this man's baptism and giftedness for the role outweighed considerations about his ordination — effectively relativizing ordination *vis á vis* baptism.

In his first two years the coordinator had a very broad brief that overlapped with the traditional coordinating role of the parish pastor. Included in this brief was the support and coordination of the council and its working groups. The pastoral council has some 60 members, each of whom also belongs to one of nine working groups covering liturgy, justice and peace, communications, youth, employment, adult education, care, prayer and administration. Each of these groups required support and training in developing and maintaining their programs. The council itself needed the same support and training as it struggled to take up its full role in deciding and implementing parish pastoral policy.

As noted above, at the end of this period the pastoral council signed a new contract with the coordinator, increasing his salary and reducing his duties. For a number of reasons his title was changed from parish pastoral coordinator to coordinator of adult religious education. First, the former role was so broad as to have been unsustainable. Second, the coordinator saw that the new model of church emerging would require a focused and sustained adult education thrust among the community at large. Hitherto this thrust had been largely confined to the pastoral council. The council itself recognized that the formation it still needed was needed also by the whole parish.

In an aptly titled article, "A Journey of Discovery,"[11] the coordinator outlined the main elements of his approach. He explained his role as exploring questions rather than offering ready-made answers, maintaining that "any real progress in adult education will depend on whether the real needs of the intended adult education participants have been surveyed and identified . . . there is no bypassing such real needs." Efforts to determine such needs have included a detailed study of the parish, using questionnaires, interviews and a number of "listening surveys" among youth and parents.

It is too early in the process to offer a detailed account of this phase of his work. Based on this needs assessment, his initial approach has been to organize 1) training for basic Christian communities, 2) a course in Vatican II theology (given by a lay woman) and 3) a series of dialogues with parents involved in the parish sacramental program. His work is basically about popularizing adult religious education. In a society where 73 percent of the adult population have never been involved in adult education of any description, his task is formidable.

New tracks

These and other efforts, and the difficulties that accompany them, need to be viewed in the context of experimentation. They are simply efforts at discovering what works and does not work in the Christian formation of lay persons. Through such efforts a wisdom gradually builds up that can inform the church's pastoral strategy for the future. Without them the church will not have the insight and experience needed to develop an effective strategy, and the negative prognosis of a post-Christian culture in the twenty-first century will surely come to pass.

This idea of experimentation does not come easy for us in the Irish church. It is associated with small, insecure projects that often fail. Coming so soon after the big, certain and (by its own lights) very successful experience of Paul Cullen's church, experimental ministry looks like a big comedown. Some years ago I was planning for a young adult liturgy in an urban parish. The parish pastor asked me how many young people I was expecting. “Two hundred,” I said. He told me he would have expected 2000. While this expectation deflated me, in the following months I began to understand where it came from. The parish pastor told me he had been on the foreign missions. There were so many people coming to him for baptism that once he had to turn the water hose on them to confer the sacrament! That image of the priest hosing the masses with salvation has remained vividly with me. It summarizes very well where we as a church have come from, and why we find it so hard to leave that behind.

A final image I have found encouraging and inspiring in my own pastoral work comes from where I live. There the turf harvesting company, called Bord Na Mona, carries off the turf by rail cars on light rail tracks. When they move into an area to be harvested, they lay the tracks and harvest the turf; when the turf is finished, they lift the tracks and lay them in a new place. Obviously the tracks are meant to be temporary, not permanent. Workers are trained in building and laying new tracks and in removing those same tracks. The pastoral strategy of the church as we have known it here is much more like a mainline track, laid firmly in place in the expectation that it would never have to be moved. Yet in these decades of major cultural change, when there has been a migration of peoples’ hearts and minds, our tracks are becoming more marginal to the people they seek to serve. There is a need for new, flexibly laid tracks to reach into the heartland of a new civilization.

If some of our priests and religious in the past were like the drivers of big trains full of passengers, sure of where they were coming from and going to, some in the future will be quite different. They will leave behind their important jobs driving the big trains and, with some of their erstwhile passengers, struggle with picks and shovels in the muck and the mess learning how to lay new tracks. Indeed, some, like the parish of Tullamore, are at it already.

Endnotes

1 Owen D. Edwards, "The Irish Priest in North America," in *The Churches, Ireland and the Irish* (Basil Blackwell, 1989), pp. 311–52.

2 Patrick Corish, *The Irish Catholic Experience* (Dublin: Gill and McMillan, 1985).

3 The material I have found particularly helpful here includes: Thomas Berry, *The Dream of the Earth* (San Francisco: Sierra Book Club, 1989); Frijof Capra, *The Turning Point* (London: Fontana, 1983); Alvin Toffler, *The Third Wave* (London: Pan, 1981); James Robertson, *Future Wealth* (London: Cassel, 1990); Gerda Lerner, *The Creation of Patriarchy* (Oxford: University Press, 1985).

4 The best I have read on this is Hugo Echegaray, *The Practice of Jesus* (New York: Orbis, 1984).

5 Hans Küng, *Christianity* (London: SCM Press, 1995) and Charles Handy, *The Empty Raincoat* (London: Hutchinson, 1990).

6 John J. O'Riordan, *Irish Catholics: Tradition and Transition.* (Dublin: Veritas, 1980), pp. 33–34.

7 Diarmuid Ó Laoighre, *Ár bpaidreacha Dúchais*. (Dublin: B.A.C., 1975)

8 Corish, p. 201.

9 O'Riordan, p. 74.

10 Marguerite Corish, "Aspects of the Secularization of Irish Society," in *Faith and Culture in the Irish Context* (Dublin: Veritas, 1996), pp. 138–73.

11 Shay Claffey, "A Journey of Discovery," *St. Anthony's Brief* August/September (Dublin: Franciscan Publications, 1996), pp. 20–21.

Chapter 5

Going to Church: Parish Geography

Marianne Sawicki

Martin Kennedy's essay ended with his description of pathways: the new tracks needed for a new time. Marianne Sawicki begins by referring to the principle that "a Christian is where a Christian goes" and locates the key ecclesial organs in the feet — getting at a different sense of tracks and pathways with a different concern for direction and access.

The clarifying distinctions that bubble out of her essay come from her educational background and her current interests: an M.A. in Communications; a Ph.D. in religion; and an additional more recent Ph.D. in contemporary philosophy. Throughout her essay she sketches with philosophically elegant but accessible language and historical savvy the specific conditions of our acting and knowing — in her own words, "the comings and goings that the architecture enforces." Her reader-friendly prose is conceptually challenging in the sense that she asks us to reconsider our usual ways of thinking. She demands attentive reading but offers astonishing clarification.

As the theoretical anchor of her essay, Sawicki proposes the priority of path over place and casts suspicion on the half-baked character of "situated knowledges." She does not dismiss place but chooses to view it in terms of the comings and goings to and from and through a place. With this strategy she uncovers a new way of seeing the materiality of the local church and its pastoral meaning. "If Kentucky were Camelot," she remarks, "I would have no criticism to make against Mary Queen," the parish from which she departs on a galloping visit to the darker, pastorally ignored sinful side of the bluegrass region and then on a fence-jumping tour of the multiple ecclesial sites she proposes to us.

During the 1980s, when I taught ministry in seminary, I would lead students through an exercise that I used to call "the designer Christian." First we brainstormed to compile a list of characteristics that the ideal member of the congregation would have or would develop. We listed these qualities on the blackboard in six columns under the following headings: Beliefs, Knowledges, Abilities, Behaviors, Attitudes, Expectations. Next we would map the items onto a large gingerbread figure, with each category assigned to the appropriate region of its body. Knowledges were written inside the head, beliefs across the heart, abilities and behaviors on the two arms, and attitudes and expectations on the two legs for support. Once constructed, our "designer Christian" poster-child was prominently displayed to serve as a criterion for assessing the rationales and successes of various ministerial

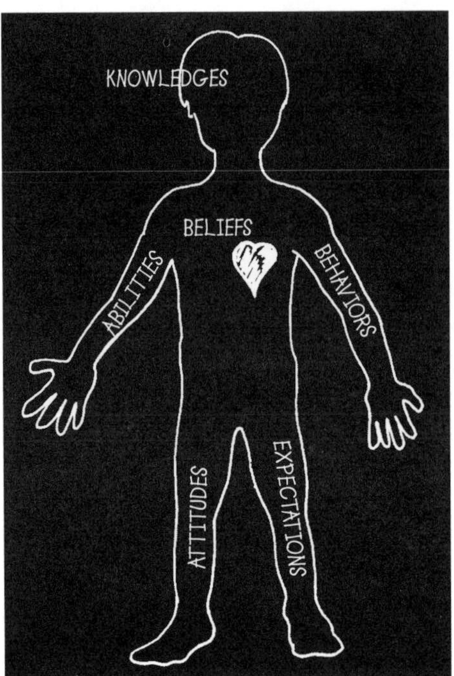

practices. (For example: How do catechists foster age-appropriate historical knowledge? How does the congregation learn to pray aloud and sing and keep silence? What can staff do to model and foster attitudes of toleration and forgiveness? And so forth.)

That was then. Today, I would leave out everything but the feet. Moreover, I would treat those feet literally, not metaphorically. A Christian is not "what a Christian stands for." A Christian is "where a Christian goes."

Figure 1: Designing a Christian — What the blackboard might look like after a brainstorming session

Where do Christians go? This essay makes a three-part answer. First, I criticize the slogan of "situated knowledge" in contemporary social theory. I argue that every location is materially placed and thus traversable by many paths; therefore, location alone cannot determine knowledge. *The priority of path over place provides the theoretical anchor for the rest of this essay.* Second, drawing on observations of my own parish, I describe the comings and goings that the architecture enforces there. While this case may not be typical in all respects, it serves to illustrate the principle that path determines knowledge and geography determines path. This shows why Catholic parishes no longer are what they were in the 1940s and 1950s: landscapes of resistance. Third, I consider some possibilities for generating an action agenda, preferring *diffused agency and access* rather than ideological structuration of ministry delivery systems. I argue that churches of the next century must be built to house variant cohabiting paths for ecclesial agency.

"Where I'm Coming From" and Other Bogus Locations of Knowledge

Knowledge is local and perspectival, as any sophomore will happily inform you. One's "viewpoint" is largely prescribed by factors such as income, gender and age. These determinants of knowledge often are conceptually summarized by the metaphor of "social location." According to that metaphor, demographic similarities are said to "place" people into "sectors" within the population, each affording access to its own distinctive knowledges. Unfortunately this *metaphor* of "location" muddles the inquiry when we try to think about how *real* places affect the understanding and distribution of messages and when we try to design real pathways for delivering information.

The metaphor of "situation" cannot be entirely disentangled from the realities of place, placement and movement. Nevertheless, an adequate analysis will distinguish among three general senses in which knowledge is "situated." 1) The *social* situation of knowledge is a function of the knowers' membership in kinship and other affinity groups. For example, mothers and wives have a particular "take" on reality that is not available to Norwegian bachelor farmers — and vice versa. One's gender, nationality, race and age all lend dimension to one's knowledges. Republicans inhabit a different planet from that where Socialists abide, so to speak. African Americans live in a country where Polish Americans have never set foot.

Related to the social location of knowledge is 2) its *material* location. What you know, and what you *can* know, is radically determined by the work you do and the level of income that it brings you. The plumbing subcontractor has a very different understanding of what goes on in the neighborhood than the sociology professor or the trial lawyer. Manual labor of all kinds puts us in touch with realities that cannot be known as mere theory. (Karl Marx figured this out.) Who makes the bread that you eat? Who eats the bread that you make? The answers to those questions are what constitute the material situation of your knowledge. Facts, histories, arguments and truths are all artifacts engineered to help in the struggle for survival. The ruling classes *rule* precisely by promoting the ideology that serves their own material interests, by passing it off to everyone else as if it were absolute truth. But this hegemonic knowledge is inherently unstable, thank goodness. The submerged or muted knowledges of working people continually find ways to subvert hegemony and to speak other truths.

The social and the material "situations" of knowledge must be distinguished from 3) its *physical* situation. If the first two are "placements," it is only in a metaphorical sense. Access to information requires structures and landscapes in the *literal* sense as well. Yet it has become difficult even to talk about these literal layouts, because the space-words that we need already have been used up for the other two senses. The physical, built environment itself is epistemologically potent. Spatiality imposes relations of proximity and distance, relation and disjunction, access and want.

Let's consider some examples on various scales. There are regional determinants of knowledge. In the United States, the Southern territories are inhabited by people who once fought to preserve a slaveholding economy and experienced invasion, brutal devastation and occupation when they were vanquished in the War between the States. Today these same territories offer conditions for the possibility of understanding American history that differ from those offered by the physical territories that Yankees inhabit. Different realities persist on the opposite banks of the Ohio River. Regional epistemologies also distinguish the U.S. from Canada and the Southern Hemisphere from the Northern. Human and civil rights vary as one crosses borders.

On the local scale, architecture and landscape affect what we can know. The authority of academic theories is supported by the granite blocks of university walls and the tendrils of ivy that climb them. The city is a logic unto itself. A middle-class kid is someone who has his or her own bedroom, bicycle and TV, learning thereby what it means to be an individual. The American housewife of the 1950s found her role laid out for her in the "modern, labor-saving" kitchen of the tract home, which concealed life-support functions in private space. Does it seem "natural" to you that shopping malls include cinemas and banks and restaurants, but not schools or clinics or libraries or tailors or hardware stores? If so, then your knowledge of "nature" has been spatially engineered. What appears "natural" for the human body itself is prescribed by the design of the buildings and streets that we inhabit: we "should" be able to climb steps, sit still in enclosed spaces, breathe cooked air and endure long intervals between opportunities to drink or urinate.

The "location" and determination of knowledge by regions and borders, by architecture and landscape and by differential assignment of people and tasks among them, all point toward a final, crucial characteristic of physical space: *we move through it*. The built environment is *built* precisely so that it can channel the movements of people and their stuff. We go out to work, play, visit, vote, buy and so forth. We bring stuff home. Locally, regionally and globally, one sees that distinctive circulation patterns are enforced for commodities, capital and labor. Each of us is assigned somewhere to stand in the cycle of production and consumption; we *tap in* to the gravy train, and/or we *are tapped* and induced to contribute our labor and our resources into a stream flowing elsewhere. Information also flows. The character of your access to goods and services necessarily affects your access to information, and it may well determine the *kind* of information you receive. Thus in the literal sense, "situated knowledge" is tenuous and fragile — because situation is access, access goes both ways and knowers are mobile.

Therefore, physical space does not *entirely* determine the information that it houses, generates or transmits. Several different knowledges can "occupy" the same space at once. People can move through any given space for different purposes. *You* may go to the mall to shop; *I* may go there to eat, or to steal, or to dispel loneliness, or to do my aerobic walking. A racially segregated neighborhood does not keep blacks and whites apart, but rather juxtaposes them intimately in roles of householder versus domestic laborer, supervisor versus craftsperson. Locations bring us into contact with people and goods that are moving along various trajectories; we share the places where our paths intersect. But we may very well know those places differently. To coincide *spatially* is not necessarily to coincide socially, materially or epistemologically.

Conversely, people who are physically far removed from one another may still share the same social or material "location" and the knowledges that go with them. This brings us to a particularly troublesome corollary of the equivocation between metaphorical and literal senses of "situation" in contemporary social theory. Both of these senses are invested in *the human body itself*. Literally, the body is my only permanent location, just as it is the means for me to travel among locations in the built environment. My body situates me, because it is the one situation that no one else can have. Although people can accompany me on my travels, nobody else can climb inside my skin.

Now, if the social and material senses of "location" are confused with the physical sense, then the individual human body comes to be construed — wrongly — as the ultimate repository of knowledge. Accordingly, knowledge becomes utterly relative, and it's impossible to transfer information. Like my tasting of a green popsicle or my terror in a nightmare, whose intense tang or fear I cannot impart to you, my historical and theological information would have to remain mine alone — "just my opinion." The validity of information would be entirely biographical and idiosyncratic. Only I could understand it. I would be able to claim absolute incontestable authority to assert whatever facts I might entertain in consciousness. However, *my* claims would roll off *you* like water off a duck's back, because your own biographical "location" would necessarily differ from mine and would carry its own set of equally incontestable knowledges. All science would reduce to autobiography. We could not understand one another; we could only trade echoes.

The relativism that results from confusing metaphorical and literal "situation" not only isolates individuals but can ruin exchanges among social groups as well. This confusion is the root of the mistaken belief that nations, races, genders and classes cannot really understand one another. The thesis of a racial foundation for truth and knowledge was vigorously argued earlier in this century by the pet philosophers of National Socialism: Ernst Krieck, Alfred Rosenberg and their colleagues. (Today this particular evil wheel is being reinvented by critical race theorists who, though they mean no harm, would do well to heed history's lesson about where such a wheel is bound to roll.) Undeniably, the various human genders and races are capable of their own distinctive raw experiences that remain unavailable to others *as raw experiences*, yet something true and valuable can be communicated from them. That's the point of being human: one can share something out of one's distinctiveness. We can achieve understanding and consensus. We can establish a factual basis for action to build a common future.

How so? How is it that knowledge is not sealed into the physical organisms and locations where it originates? How is it that information and action, conditioned as they are by built environments, still are not *entirely* determined by them? The mobility of our bodies suggests the answer. One person understands how another moves, because the one has the possibility of following along after the other, *or not*. Knowing needs only following, not displacement.

Any portion of the built environment offers particular pathways to be followed; but the same physical spaces always present additional possibilities for movement that their builders did not intend. People deploy themselves ingeniously and strategically. This gives hope for the future of the churches. On one hand, new places and new landscapes can be designed for ecclesial life. On the other hand, resistive co-inhabitations of existing structures can be fostered, and old borders can be pierced.

The real space that we have got to share — this *here* world, the only one — is crossed by many paths. Our resources drain away in many directions. The next section of this essay describes the circulation of people, cars, ideology, commodities, money and information through a parish in Lexington, Kentucky. But first it shows how the history of the church can be told in terms of strategic subversive spatial deployments and re-routings.

Churchscapes

In this section I invite readers to use social geography to reformat what you already know about church history. I would also invite you to set aside any nostalgic personal attachments you may have to the churches of the New Testament or of your own youth. In other words, as you follow along with my descriptions let them "re-situate" your knowledges.

The texts of the Pauline and deutero-Pauline epistles and of the Gospel of Matthew, reflect ecclesial "structurations" that are decidedly urban. The canonical three-tiered ministry of "bishops, presbyters and deacons" was developed to work in Roman imperial cities. The antecedent pattern of "prophets, apostles and teachers" also presumed the metropolis and inter-urban travel.[1] Therefore, neither "structuration" originated with Jesus or came from his era. The gospels depict a village milieu for Jesus. Although he may have visited cities, he did not design administrative institutions for them.[2]

Now, in the first century, Galilean villages were not insulated from Galilean imperial cities. On the contrary, Herodian urbanization had as its express purpose the cultural and economic penetration of villages. That program was only partly successful. The cities of Sepphoris and Tiberias sucked labor and commodities out of the countryside, and pumped Greek language and imperial ideology back into it. Nevertheless, indigenous cultural practices proved both resilient and ingeniously adaptive in the face of urban imperial incursions. For example, Jewish kinship and cultic systems seized upon the imperial vernacular architecture of water and light, using it to develop architectures of cultural resistance. Thus when the urban tentacles of the aqueducts snaked out across the Judean and Galilean landscape, they were opposed by the "separatism" of domestic ritual baths (*miqva'ot*) with their "pure, undrawn" water supply. The Roman city secularized daylight itself, with dark narrow streets opening into sunlit plazas and shaded colonnades. But synagogue architecture responded by capturing light directly "from heaven" through clerestory windows and tiered benches focused into the central "tank of light" in which scripture was read.

This resistive architecture did not offer a way of keeping oneself physically apart from the city. Rather, it offered the means of inhabiting a secular city "Jewishly." Jesus did something different, but it was something that made sense in this context of Herodian-

Roman occupation of the land together with evolving Jewish cultural resistance to it. He avoided the Galilean cities; he preferred village venues and, in fact, he seems to have rejected the imperial architectural vernacular by staging events *outdoors* whenever possible. Jesus accepted his vocation in a wilderness baptism, not in a *miqveh*. He taught people seated on hillsides, not benches. In the gospels, cities cannot receive and house Jesus. He died outside, on Calvary. His lieutenants ran away — back to Galilee, to their established practices of circulating among villages and receiving hospitality there.

Between 30 and 60, however, there was a major transition in the "structuration" of the nascent church. The "ministries" mentioned in the New Testament, with their urban spatiality, evolved after Calvary and after the urbanization of (some sectors of) the Jesus movement. Saint Paul's churches were deployed and were led quite differently than the bands that followed Jesus before Calvary. Theologically, then, if we accept the authority of the canon, then we must accept its testimony that *spatial adaptation, entailing the evolution of ministerial structuration, is a constitutive element of the church as God intended it to be*.

Let's come forward rapidly in history. The urban church of antiquity gave us the spatial patterns that still constitute the institutional Catholic Church: dioceses, subsidiary parishes and a superordinate or "capital" see in Rome. These structures work like hubbed wheels nested within wheels. Transactions occur along centripetal and centrifugal lines of force, unobstructed by any frontiers, like this:

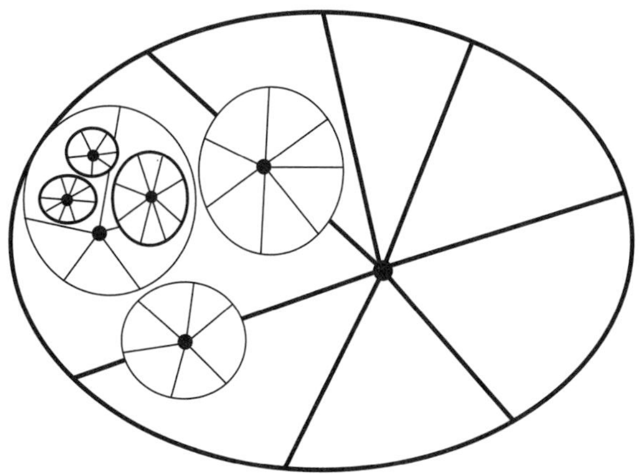

Figure 2: Hub-spoke structuration of urban parishes, dioceses, Rome

Ignatius of Antioch (died about 107) and Augustine of Hippo (died 430) both ran churches that worked like this. The ancient church confined itself largely to the cities and ex-urbanite villas, leaving the countryside to "paganism." But the urban clockwork gummed up and wound down by about the fifth century. With the disintegration of the western empire, we see the emergence of a contrasting spatial pattern, the monastery. In post-imperial Europe, monasteries were rural enclaves of civilization, ecclesially self-sufficient but linked to other outposts in the pagan barbarian wilderness. Abbots and abbesses now had the "oversight" roles, and they came into conflict with bishops when their spheres of influence overlapped. This feudal rural mission system, after "Christianizing" Europe, was transplanted to the Americas with the dawning of a new imperial age. On this side of the Atlantic it became the *encomienda* system. Although this ecclesial spatial practice is rightly criticized for its collusion with European conquest, it effectively counteracted some of the worst exploitations that the conquerors inflicted upon the indigenous population. Within the mission walls, Christian native peoples were somewhat shielded from slavery, prostitution and other brutalities. The price they paid was acceptance of a European ideology and loss of many indigenous cultural and economic practices. Instead of wheels within wheels, the monastery-mission church consisted of islands of security amid a sea of exploitation. Like this:

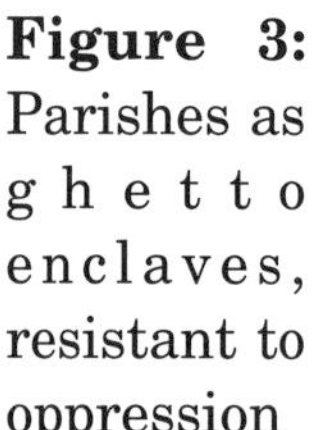

Figure 3: Parishes as ghetto enclaves, resistant to oppression

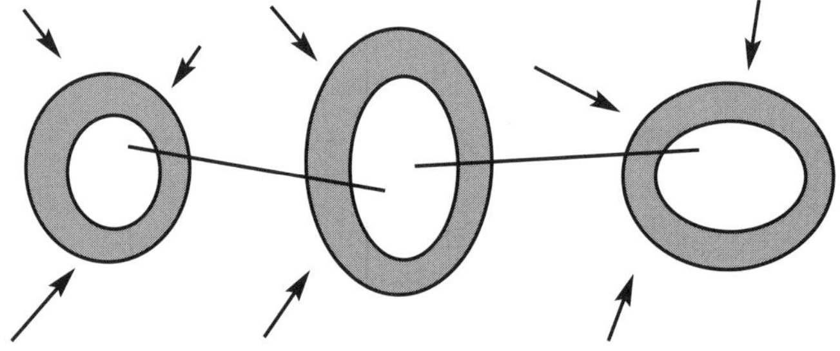

The urban Catholic parishes of Anglo-America were not direct descendants of the Spanish mission/*encomienda* system. They were its cousins, thanks to their common ancestry in the medieval monastic institutions of Europe. From about 1830 through 1950, Catholicism was built in America largely through the leadership of vowed religious women (and some men) whose communities were transplanted from Europe and adapted to social conditions here. Bishops had the good sense to invite and promote these evangelizing efforts. The American Catholic Church thus grew as a hybrid of the two ecclesial spatial expressions: the ancient urban diocese of parishes and the feudal rural monastic enclave. The American diocese was urban, but in many ways it was still an insulated self-sufficient plantation. It differed from the *encomienda*, however, in that the people built it for themselves, hence the separatism of the ghetto-church of my own 1950s childhood.[3] My little feet never walked into a school, a youth club, a gymnasium, a hospital or a home that was not Catholic.[4]

We were not prepared at all for what happened next. The suburbs happened. Population shifted onto a terrain too expansive for Catholics to establish their accustomed seamless web of cradle-to-grave institutions.[5] The suburban parish had to be built, oxymoronically, as a pierced ghetto. Without the means to build for physical isolation and self-sufficiency, Catholics now designed campuses that produced *symbolic* isolation even as they facilitated physical mutual inter-accessibility to the other structures of suburban life. At the same time, Catholics built to strengthen the "centripetal" attraction of the parish as hub. For example, parish schools now became magnets for parents who found the public schools deficient. In older cities like Detroit and Baltimore, the cream of diocesan resources now is funneled into these newer, more populous suburban "pierced-ghetto hub" parishes, while inner-city parishes are left to wither. This episcopal policy is difficult to justify, for inner-city parishes often evolve their own ingenious breaches of boundaries in regard to ministries and the utilization of space. No longer ghettos in their own right, the endangered older parishes have become a distinct way of inhabiting the inner city.

The suburban parish campus retains motifs of insularity but cannot maintain the defensive social perimeters or the self-sufficiency of its predecessor. The traditional ghetto parish was an urban landscape of resistance. With a working-class and immigrant population, it propagated a counter-hegemonic symbolization of the unique value of each individual. It cultivated indigenous leadership by lifting out some of the daughters and sons of workers, educating them as nuns, brothers and priests, and returning them to the community. It demonstrated another way of assigning meaning and value to the hours and years of one's life. Although it could fall in step with secular cultural trends, it could also muster significant political power for righteous causes.[6]

How well did these capabilities translate to the suburbs? I'll discuss the case that I know best. My parish is called "Mary Queen of the Most Holy Rosary Church" — for short, "Mary Queen."[7] Since I am not a native of Lexington, Kentucky, the nickname still strikes me funny because it sounds like "Dairy Queen." The resemblances go deeper than the sound of the name. Like a Dairy Queen, Mary Queen is surrounded by an extensive parking lot as one of its most distinctive surface features. Nobody walks to Mary Queen. We drive and park, which means that "going to church" has to compete with other transportation needs in our scheduling of the family cars and their drivers. The parish is sub-urban in ethos, although no longer in reality, the city having engulfed the surrounding subdivisions as its population climbed toward a quarter-million residents. While we still have blue laws here, Sunday-morning Lexington offers many enticements besides going to church. In fact, it is increasingly common to go to church *on the way to or from somewhere else*. Mary Queen is one stop among many.

Monday through Friday, the parking lot becomes a rodeo for cars and minivans twice a day, as students are delivered to or retrieved from the parish school. Car-pooling alliances, along with cooperative arrangements among working and non-working parents for after-school supervision of the children, form the major social bonds that structure the community of Mary Queen. There are two categories of kids in our parish: those who are shepherded through this daily convergence and dispersal, and those who are not since they ride the bus to the public school next door. Public-school families and people without children have no comparable opportunity to be stitched into the fabric of parish life. Sunday "CCD" classes don't require the complex kid-sharing arrangements of the car pools and after-school play groups, yet the practice of shepherding children to and from classes has taken over as the rationale for adult Christian education in the parish. Adult classes are conceived and designed merely as something to keep the CCD parents occupied while they wait for their kids to finish Sunday catechetical sessions. Accordingly, parents whose children attend the parish day school do not participate in the Sunday adult education programming; if they did, where would their children "wait for" them? These anomalies arise because of the suburban siting and design of the parish plant as a place that we must drive to.

What, then, is near Mary Queen? The parish campus is on the way to a neighborhood public swimming pool and a ball park. MQ's campus is between my home and a very good bakery. A little further along the same route lies Fayette Mall, the largest in central Kentucky. Our city's Catholic high school is across the street from the parish plant, and attracts graduates from MQ's grade school and from the surrounding city and county parishes. Lexington, unlike many cities, has excellent public schools with a relatively high standard of deportment for all kids. Thus when parents here choose the Catholic schools, it is primarily because of the schools' intentionally religious atmosphere and instruction. Why is that? Catholic grade school education seems to be a virtual vestige of the physical isolation that parents remember (or fantasize) from ghetto Catholicism. They think of their faith as something projecting *boundaries* and something inhering in an *information base*. That sort of faith-information cannot be homegrown; it is thought of as something imported from elsewhere and delivered in a cloistered environment by experts, as when formerly their daughters and sons returned home transformed by veils and collars and mystically endowed with vowed expertise.

A peculiar sociology of knowledge persists in the suburban pierced-ghetto parish. I see it as arising from a perverted nostalgia for the urban ghetto parish. Pathologically, my parish is built to house circulation patterns mimicking those that once resisted cultural pressures; yet now, in the suburban situation and under changed conditions, these channelings render Mary Queen indistinguishable from many other features on the suburban map.

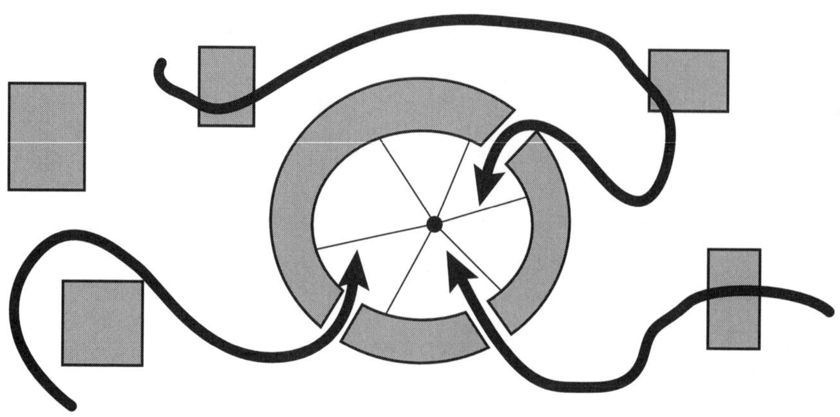

Figure 4: Suburban parish as pierced-ghetto hub

Let's consider the flow of personnel through the parish. Basically, there are three unconnected streams: the indigenous population, split into school-affiliated families versus others, and the professional leadership. Ordinary parish members (like me) move into the territory of the parish for reasons that have nothing to do with the church. We show up at the rectory door one day to register; thereafter, we show up in the parking lot on Sundays, or bring our children when it's time for a sacrament or for school. Children cycle through the day-school or Sunday-school programs. We all are there as receivers for installments of info-grace; the analogy to medical procedures of transfusion or dialysis is difficult to avoid. There are physical slots to hold us: parking spaces, pews, schoolroom desks, places at folding tables in the gym for potluck dinners, hangers in the cloakrooms to hold our jackets. I have no place of my own at MQ; when I go there, I just temporarily occupy one of the berths. By contrast, the professional staff have personal places. Three priests reside at the rectory: one retired, one our pastor, and one recently ordained and presumably gaining experience for a pastorate of his own. There are still some sisters teaching in the school, but I'm not sure where they live. We know the names of these professionals. They do not — cannot — know most of ours. They are not "from here." They *bring* the gospel *to* us.[8]

We, in turn, are spatially trained to regard the gospel — and Catholicism itself — as commodities delivered to us parentally by experts from afar. The parish campus is laid out like piglets on a sow. This place is built to let one suckle many. The herringbone motif of the parking lot repeats in the sanctuary seating. Partly because the sanctuary is built like a theater, people routinely applaud the conclusion of the liturgy. They have not participated in worship; they have merely been entertained. The churchscape of Mary Queen, then, is architectural rhetoric. The very bricks insist that "church" means thousands of berths and one dispenser. In a city of a quarter-million people, we Catholics have only seven places like this.[9] In the diocese, churches are being shut down and parishes are being consolidated because they outnumber the diocesan priests by 67 to 39.[10] The built environment makes it nearly impossible to imagine a Catholic Christian community without a priest at its hub. We have some 42,000 non-ordained Catholics with various talents, but they figure into diocesan planning chiefly in terms of the additional miles they will have to drive on Sunday to reach the new consolidated parish center. The architecture, including those parking lots, argues for the inevitability of precisely that structuration of ordained ministry that we have inherited *through a series of historical accidents*.

Paradoxically, thanks to this architecture, the parish becomes the termination point for the gospel: its last stop, its dead end. The word stops here, it does not circulate further. It is consumed. No one tells you this, however. They tell you that we "carry the word home in our hearts" and "pass it on to our children." But that is exactly my point. These alleged further passages *do not materialize*. The parish literally is not built for them. What goes home from the sanctuary and the schoolhouse are people — people whose paths are utterly indistinguishable from the paths of people who happened to pass through the mall or the public school instead of Mary Queen. As far as I know, MQ sends no missionaries to Africa, Appalachia or South Central Los Angeles.[11] We do not send young people into convents or seminaries any more. A number of mature couples have completed training for the diaconate, and the men have been ordained, but they typically do not leave their parishes and remain largely invisible even there.

How does the built environment of Mary Queen divert and redirect the other resources that circulate through it? Money from the weekly collections is spent to support parish operations, for the most part. The practice of the "offertory collection" could hardly be more alienating. The only one of "my gifts" that the parish wants is my money. When I registered at the parish, I listed my skills on a machine-readable form that was entered into a computer. I also spelled out my own name for the computer. This data is used to issue pre-printed envelopes in which I am supposed to make my weekly offering. They appear in my mailbox quarterly. Since I am a married woman, the computer refuses to address me by my own name. So every week, "my gifts" go into an envelope stamped "Mr. and Mrs. Robert Miller." Every week, women and girls, men and boys take turns carrying "our gifts" up the aisle to the foot of the altar. This is another terminal journey. The women stop there, turn around and retreat. Only the money continues in circulation.

Happily, I can report some significant diversions of resources that occur occasionally in and around the MQ campus. Sometimes canned goods are collected for distribution to the poor. There is a barrel for spare baby clothes and furnishings, to be distributed to mothers with problem pregnancies.[12] The parish maintains a club called "Queen's Service," whose members do odd jobs for older people and shut-ins. MQ also supports the traditional charities of the Saint Vincent DePaul Society and the Knights of Columbus. There is a "prayer network," and some parishioners occasionally have gone picketing at a local outpatient surgery center where abortions were being performed.

If Kentucky were Camelot, I would have no criticism to make against Mary Queen. But the Bluegrass has some distinctive social sins that a parish could address. Let me just make a partial itemized list.

Sins of the Bluegrass

- Tobacco farming and marketing
- Racial segregation in housing in Lexington
- Race hatred and anti-Semitism
- Intolerance of the multi-racial Muslim community,

expressed in a "NIMBY" movement to block construction of the new mosque

- Horse industry excesses: multi-million-dollar maternity hospitals for mares, while mountain mothers die in childbirth for want of education and medical care
- Exploitation of migrant labor on horse farms and other farms
- Family violence, especially among families economically displaced from the mountain counties
- Women political prisoners held underground in federal prison, now designated a "medical facility"
- Political corruption, nepotism, bribery
- Sports idolatry. Exploitation and corruption of athletes at the University of Kentucky
- Legal liquor production
- Illegal liquor production: the "moonshining" tradition as infrastructure for drug trafficking with offshore sources
- Union busting: collusion of local governments in establishing non-union manufacturers like Toyota
- Collusion of state government with big coal companies; removal of mineral resources from the land without compensating the local people; loss of homes and lands through the "broad form deed"
- Collusion of the urban county government with business to promote real-estate "development" and circumvent democratic discussion of it
- Corruption in waste management oversight: dumping of household and industrial waste, and disposal of nerve gas stockpiles on federal property
- Special-interest collusion to repeal the Kentucky Educational Reform Act (KERA) and neutralize Kentucky's health insurance reforms.

There are Bluegrass Catholics working to resist and repair these evils, but they do so outside of parish and diocesan structures. That means that activists do not receive the emotional and financial support that parish backing could provide. More importantly, resistance to these evils is not identified as an expression of Catholic Christian faith, and is not modeled for other Catholics, especially young ones.[13] In our region, one of the most popular and effective organizations for grass-roots social action is Habitat for Humanity, which builds houses for people who could not qualify for a mortgage on their own. Catholics participate in Habitat, but this occurs largely "off the map" of parish and diocese. It is disconnected from the "going" of "going to church."

This sketch of the landscape of Mary Queen parish is not meant to be definitive, but merely to suggest what a spatial reading can disclose. By investing itself in the suburban "pierced-ghetto hub" spatialization of its parish campuses, Catholic America has mortared itself in to a "time out" model of Christian life. "Going to church" is a tune-up, a scheduled download, a dialysis of the soul. We "come back from church" feeling better, knowing better, but not *doing* better. Little Cities-of-God with names like Mary Queen do not alter the landscape of the Suburb-of-Man within which they nestle. We don't violate the zoning. We don't interrupt the traffic patterns of this world.

Agenda

How can we become an obstructive and redirective church? How can our inhabitation of the suburbs make a difference to those whose paths we cross here? It seems to me that we need smaller, more specialized sites and more of them. Two of the evolved elements of the "pierced-ghetto hub parish" should be retained: its magnetism and its porosity. That is, ecclesial sites should attract by actualizing values that people desire, and they should be nexuses of crossing paths rather than insular citadels. On the other hand, most of the administrative functions of today's discrete parish should be further centralized. (Let the bishop bean-count me as "Mrs. Robert Miller" on a downtown computer if he wants to; better yet, let the archbishop do it from over in Louisville. I would find remote depersonalization less alienating and abusive.)

The so-called geographical or neighborhood parish is an anachronism. Multiplication of ecclesial sites will mean multiple memberships and allegiances for individual Catholics and for families. A suburban network of sites or cells could be schematized like this

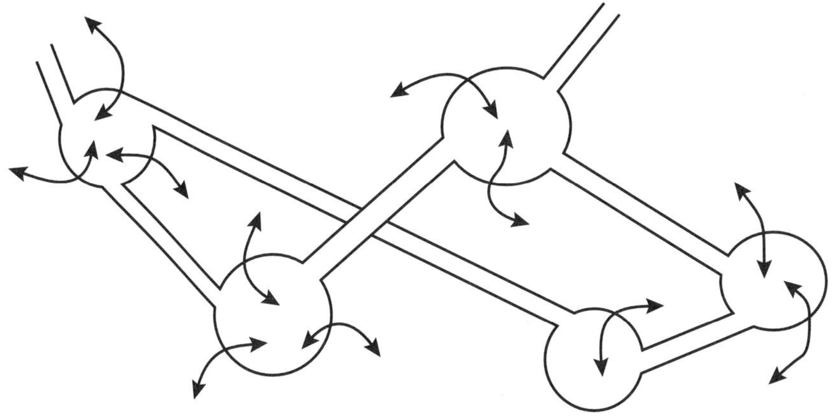

Figure 5: Multiple ecclesial sites

Its salient features are satellites and circulation. It is best thought of as a disruptive ecclesial habitation of places and pathways that already house the projects of everyday American life. Some potential sites already are in place in Lexington. Under Christian auspices we have two major hospitals, a food pantry, a center for the homeless that offers shelter and various other resources, and women's refuge houses. For the most part, these very fine sites unfortunately confine their efforts to "providing services" for the needy. They don't know what the Catholic Worker movement knows: that God is found in prayer and celebration and companionship *with* the poor; otherwise *we ourselves are bereft of God's presence.*[14] The new ecclesial sites that I propose would be friendly and nonhierarchical. Thus the arrows are bi-directional, indicating mutual benefit.

We can imagine three kinds of ecclesial sites: bases, mobile units and electronic sites. Here are illustrations that occur to me for Lexington.

Ecclesial bases. There is a small enclosed shopping mall called Turfland about a mile from Mary Queen. The stores there open at 10 A.M.; but at 8 the mall fills up with middle-aged and older people in athletic shoes who have come to do their aerobic walking in a safe environment sheltered from the weather. They meet their friends, have lively conversations, check out the window displays and wind up with coffee and muffins in the Food Court. About noon, a different population claims the space: teens on the loose from Lafayette High School or from the nearby alternative high school. White girls with dreadlocks, black guys with shaved heads, individuals of indeterminate gender in bandannas and capacious plaid shirts — they gravitate to the pizza place, psychedelic Spencer's Gifts and the dollar cinema. Turfland Mall lost its JCPenney and its Thom McAn some years ago; their spaces are still empty.[15]

What if Mary Queen opened a storefront inside Turfland? What if the walkers were invited to gather for ten minutes of morning prayer at 8, 9, or 10? What if there were some cozy tables in the MQ annex where they could spread out their coffee and muffins? What if there were a bulletin board, maybe even a newsletter? And after 10 A.M., what if the storefront had an alternative bookstore, a juice bar, an Internet parlor? Could there be office space for Christian counseling and psychotherapy,[16] both by appointment and for drop-in emergencies? A parents' resource center? An after-school tutoring service? A *supervised* video arcade?[17] These activities could be commercially viable. They would not compete with the merchants presently doing business in the mall and might even enhance its ambience and commercial attractiveness.

For Catholics, what is missing in this picture, what would make it recognizably ecclesial, is a tabernacle and the eucharistic presence. *We could not find a priest to say Mass in the mall.* We can barely staff the regular Sunday Masses scheduled on the Mary Queen campus. This is because the Vatican has forbidden the ordination of wo[*oops, can't talk about that.*]

Mobile units. The church must learn again how to make house calls. For a long time at Mary Queen, parishioners have organized themselves into crews that do chores for the elderly. My suggestion is that traditional Christian activities such as "Queen's Service" receive more visibility and become recognized as a vital materialization of the church. In the 1970s I knew a Catholic couple who ran a "home grocery-shopping service" with their own car. Their clients were shut-ins, mostly elderly. Each client received a weekly phone call and dictated a grocery list. Then a volunteer college student would take the car and the cash kitty, buy the groceries, deliver them, visit briefly with the shut-in, collect reimbursement for the kitty, then return the funds and the car back to the sponsoring couple. A great system; everybody benefited. But there was no explicit moment of reflection and celebration of God's hand in this. There was no connection to a parish.[18] I say, buy a van and paint the sides to tell the world what is going on. But I also say, provide time and space for the "volunteers" to pray and reflect together before and afterwards. Getting the van on the road and the kids on the van is not enough to engineer a disruption in suburban pathways. It must happen mindfully, mutually and prayerfully.[19] We must learn to believe in *a "real presence" through diffusion* by mobile units and satellite bases. Bust Jesus out of the tabernacle and the church campus. He wants to escape the black hole of the parish parking lot. He's sick of the rodeo.

Electronic sites. The most potent diffusion of the gospel will be through electronic means. My two examples are the cable channel and the homepage. In Lexington we can watch extremely boring city business conducted over a government channel, which also provides traffic and weather information. On another channel, we see live or taped services at local Protestant churches, also pretty boring. The communicative potential of local cable origination for religion has never developed. It has now been overtaken by the more exciting and user-involving medium of the Internet. There are thousands of active religious sites on the Net. Importantly, the texts of the Bible — by book and chapter, or broken down into the daily readings of the common lectionary — as well as texts such as *Catechism of the Catholic Church* are instantly available. Anyone can compile a site that links to those resources selectively, with helpful commentary.

Internet access is available to any parish in North America with the will to write and maintain a home page. What would a church post on its home page? The weekly lectionary readings (i.e., links to established sites where the Bible is available online). Educational materials. Notices of coming events. Homilies. *Responses* to those homilies. Photographs of parish events. We won't know what works on a parish home page until we start using them. There are already virtual dioceses. Partenia was a place in northern Africa until the Sahara Desert swallowed it many centuries ago. Bishop Jacques Gaillot, a trouble-making advocate of the homeless in France, was appointed in 1995 to shepherd this non-place, in an apparent attempt to banish and silence him. That move backfired gloriously. His diocese has been an online witness for about three years at www.partenia.fr, and its structure has evolved along with the medium. The multilingual site now hosts a forum, a topical e-catechism, a log of the bishop's ministry and his homiletical letters. It has the capability for projecting timely critical witness into fast-moving political situations.

From the standpoint of evangelization, Partenia compares favorably with the home page of the archdiocese where I grew up, Baltimore. At www.archbalt.org you'll see a crisp and efficient portal to the many offices and services comprising this vast bureaucracy. It takes five or six clicks to burrow down through the links to anything recognizable as a gospel message. I could find no mention of Kosovo when I visited archbalt.org in June 1999.[20] This reflects the Archdiocese of Baltimore's choice to turn an institutional face to the web world. The archdiocesan web portal perfectly mirrors the centripetal hub-and-spokes structure inherited from two centuries of urban experience in that city, where national plenary councils used to meet. Unfortunately, when such a pattern is projected onto the Web, it puts the Cardinal Archbishop in the place of the spider.

What is *webby* about the Web is the subversion of hierarchy by the medium itself. Sites are just nodes; there is no top or center. The Web is more like a communion of saints or a mystical body, with all parts equidistant from and responsive to one another. Alliances and coalitions form between "service providers" and "clients" that override institutional allegiances; this is increasingly the experience of businesses that incorporate web presence into their existing organizations.[21] Sites such as "archbalt.org" and the site of my own diocese, "cdlex.org," are hierarchically designed, like traditional organization charts. But the *use patterns* of these sites are not hierarchical. They are opportunistic: "pulled," not "pushed." What kind of a church will the online church be? Can a church of immediate access to scripture, to catechesis and to prophetic critique of social sins perhaps be a more *sacramental* church, a more *catholic* church, than one in which a professional must drive somewhere in his or her car in order to "deliver" the gospel in the mountains or the suburbs?

This is not a choice between personal contact and a computer screen. Models for integrated media use are already available in initiatives such as the distance-learning operations of Kentucky Educational Television. At www.ket.org, in-person contact with learners in isolated homes is supplemented by one-on-one tutoring through e-mail, coordinated with traditional broadcast or cablecast instruction. The Internet does not solve every problem, but it has profoundly changed the architecture that contains and disperses information.

What does this do to the *local* church? In Lexington, when I want to hear a bishop's teaching about social justice, it's easier for me to get it from Bishop Gaillot of "partenia.fr" than from "my own" Bishop Kendrick Williams of "cdlex.org." Online I live in "Partenia," not "Lexington." Or when I want to urge a lawmaker to support a progressive social program, I make email contacts and alert people in my neighborhood to sites with relevant information: the career of the bill in the legislature, the representative's voting record, email address, fax number and so forth. Dioceses and parishes can find new and very appropriate ministries along these lines, including the catechetical ministry of helping adult parishioners perceive the possibilities — while they are waiting for CCD to be over, if need be.

Two objections may arise, and I wish to address them briefly. First, you may say that gospel on the Internet would be something restricted to people wealthy enough to own computers. In Kentucky that is not the case. The publicly supported University of Kentucky (with a far-flung community college system) has an open-use policy for its extensive computer labs, which are staffed with consultants twenty-four hours a day. Anybody at all — street people, the homeless, eight-year-olds, bag ladies in tennis shoes — can enter and be trained to peruse the Web. (In fact, they're now crowding out the grad students.) Public libraries and other municipal facilities also offer free public online time, so access to ecclesial sites would not be hindered by lack of money. On the contrary, what hinders some middle-class, middle-aged academics from exploring the Internet is lack of *time* to learn the skills, coupled with a certain perverse pride that prevents them from asking teenaged techs for help.

The second possible objection is that I have ignored the electronic media of videotape and audiotape. But this was not an oversight on my part. These media, although electronic, are not live and interactive; thus they belong to the model of ecclesial organization that I termed the suburban pierced-enclave-hub. They are one-way delivery systems for messages *from* authoritative experts *to* receptive mute lay people. The audiotape, perhaps played for meditation or just for company when the suburban Catholic is in the car commuting, effectively isolates and soothes the person. It incorporates a religious message into the cocoon of the automobile — along for the ride, on the way to somewhere else. By contrast, the videotape may be viewed together by a group as a prelude to discussion; but we still have a clerical professor or some other talking head as personification of a *message that comes in but does not go out.* The video discussion is conveniently scheduled, like an entertainment. It does not arise out of the people's material practices, their comings and goings across the suburban landscape. It is just one more thing that they "go to."

Conclusions

In this essay I have criticized both the practices that domesticate the church in a suburban Catholic parish, and the theories that would identify Christianity with its metaphorical inscriptions and situations. I have proposed instead that the material siting of Christianity be reconsidered. Churchscapes today function to prop up the elite and dwindling institution of the celibate professional male cleric. They are spatially ill-suited to every other ecclesial purpose. They materially impede the redirection of suburban pathways.

The physical placements of ecclesial sites will determine people's access to the gospel and the gospel's access to the world in the coming century. My proposal is that we develop diffuse ecclesial satellite bases, mobile units and electronic sites. As these new placements emerge, the educational ministry of the churches must of course be overhauled. New interpersonal, organizational, creative and interpretive skills must be developed and taught. The *places* where this happens will not be islands of privilege or ivory towers, like traditional seminaries were. Tomorrow's seminaries themselves will be increasingly depending on remote sites, mobile resources and home page contact. Moreover, these concrete placements won't be designed for the "inscription" of individual bodies. They will rather be training feet to go where Jesus went. That is what the real scripture says. Christianity is a way to follow. Displacement is more than a metaphor.

Endnotes

1 Theologians routinely contrast these two structural patterns as "institutional" and "charismatic." Such a contrast obscures what they have in common: their adaptation to ancient *urban space*.

2 More information about the social world of Jesus is presented in my book *Crossing Galilee: Architectures of Contact in the Occupied Land of Jesus* (Valley Forge PA: Trinity Press International, 2000).

3 A great deal has been left out of this story, of course. What American Catholics insulated themselves *against* was the cultural and economic hegemony of Protestantism, particularly as expressed in the public schools of the nineteenth and early twentieth century. Moreover, Catholic enclaves were safer for some than for others. From within the Catholic Church itself, the English-speaking Irish-Americans were able to engulf and suppress the German-speaking and Slavic cultural institutions, for the most part. Thus the ghetto-ization of American Catholicism also produced its ethnic homogenization.

4 I attended the parish grade school at Saint Francis of Assisi in Baltimore from 1955 to 1963. During that time, on rare occasions when I visited a secular institution such as the public library, a museum or an amusement park, I went with a group of Catholic children on a special day and under strict supervision.

5 There were non-spatial factors at work in the demise of Catholic schools and other separatist institutions, of course. Nevertheless, the sheer scale of suburban life and the consequent impossibility of "neighborhoods" were of decisive importance.

6 I am thinking of the unholy alliance between Irish-American Catholics and the Democratic Party. But I am also thinking of the boycott of the racially segregated Gwynn Oak Amusement Park by the Catholic parishes of Baltimore in the 1950s.

7 Although the more prudent and charitable course might have been to disguise the identity of this parish, a description of "material conditions of the local church" requires concrete particulars. I participated in this parish from 1995 until 1998, when I moved to another parish. During that time, MQ erected a new and larger sanctuary building across the parking lot from the old one. The old church building, which had gradually been surrounded by the school, now serves as a meeting hall.

8 With the very best of intentions, one of the priests habitually remarks to the congregation that "you moms and dads preach a better sermon than I ever could, just by bringing your kids to Mass." He does not perceive the boundaries enforced by his words: that parenthood is the normal condition of the laity, and that its *mute* witness is the *only* kind of communication that lay people are capable of.

9 Another one is about to go up on a magnificent lot in the newest, whitest, costliest Southside subdivision. Inevitably another older ecclesial terminal will be terminated when this parish, now meeting in a shopping mall, builds its centralized and centralizing campus. Our diocese regards the decreasing priest-to-campus ratio as a personnel crisis. Recently a diocesan-wide consultation process called "New Faces in Ministry" was undertaken in an effort to acquaint people with the notion of priest-sharing parishes, on the pretense of brainstorming for fresh approaches to future staffing needs.

10 Many of the 39 are nearing retirement age. We also have 24 priests serving here from religious orders or other dioceses.

11 In fact the diocese of Lexington consists of one urban area, plus forty-nine rural counties in the mountains of southeastern Kentucky. Thus our diocesan staff spend a good deal of their time and effort on the road in Appalachia. My impression is that most Catholics who live in the Bluegrass prefer to have nothing to do with mountain people.

12 Unhappily, the barrel looks a lot like a trash barrel. The symbolism of this is very different from that expressed in a student parish I used to visit. Young parents there had taken over a large corner of the hall and set up a kids' clothes exchange. Everyone — not just "the poor" — deposited clothes and toys, as their children outgrew them, and picked out what they needed. Miraculously (maybe), there always seemed to be more than enough stuff for everybody. Periodically the collection was weeded out and shared with other clothing banks. The same parish maintained an emergency food supply as well, under similar terms.

13 The diocese supports a lobby in the state capital, Frankfort, to communicate the Catholic ethical position on various issues to lawmakers. One applauds those efforts, but they are almost invisible to ordinary parishioners at Mary Queen.

As this book goes to press in the spring of 2000, the Catholic Conference of Kentucky is lobbying the legistlature to kill a bill that would require insurance companies to pay for birth control pills, diaphragms and intrauterine devicesif they cover the cost of other medical prescriptions. The executive director of the Conference characterized the bill as "anti-Catholic" in an interview with the local newspaper. This, of course, gave us a front-page story in the local section. Citizens, non-Catholic and Catholic alike, now "know" that Catholics are those who oppose an initiative in favor of women's health. We are failing to communicate the depth and range of the Catholic ethical tradition. In the case of reproductive rights, we are ignoring the complex rationale behind Catholic teaching, and we are retreating once again into a ghetto: "us against them" has again become the whole story.

14 For Protestant readers, perhaps I need to identify *The Catholic Worker* as a newspaper started in New York by Peter Maurin and Dorothy Day during the Depression. The movement — with its soup kitchen, hospitality house, farm, philosophy and the lifestyle that grew up around it — all go by the same name and have been cloned in various cities across the country. Diverse and decentralized, the Catholic Worker movement might be characterized as radical practical personalist Christian communist pacifist anarchism.

15 Turfland Mall underwent renovation in 1999 and still has many vacant spaces.

16 I don't know about the rest of the country, but "Christian psychotherapy" certainly seems to be a growth industry in Lexington.

17 Formerly, Turfland had a very popular video arcade; it was a victim of its own success because it lacked both the personnel and the rationale for supervising its young customers.

18 One can easily name other services that religious and secular groups provide via "mobile units." For example, I know of a dentist with a mobile practice among shut-in clients. She had to make a large investment in the dental equipment that she transports to their homes. The expense of a mobile dental or well-baby clinic could be underwritten by an ecclesial community. There are also low-tech needs, such as providing hot meals for AIDS patients.

19 In Lexington on Saturdays in springtime, I often see a contrasting spectacle. Kids from church youth groups hold car washes to raise funds to send themselves on recreational trips to Kings Island or some other regional amusement park. Everyone smiles on them for being such good Christian young people and taking care of themselves. In other words, they are not making trouble. This teaches the kids that Christianity is the opposite of troublemaking — which is heresy, in my view.

20 However, bishops' statements on Kosovo were available at the site of the United States Catholic Conference, www.nccbuscc.org

21 This phenomenon is explored in the *Journal of the Hyperlinked Organization*, www.hyperorg.com, with related links.

Chapter 6

Local Learning: A Congregational Inquiry

Edward Farley

Edward Farley's lifelong work in practical theology is behind much of the current thinking and reflection on the dilemmas facing the churches today — even when writers do not refer to Farley. Starting with Ecclesial Man: A Social Phenomenology of Faith and Reality *(1981) and* Ecclesial Reflection: An Anatomy of Theological Method *(1982) and continuing through* Theologia: The Fragmentation and Unity of Theological Education *(1983) and* The Fragility of Knowledge: Theological Education in the Church and the University *(1988), Farley's writings have disclosed both the problems lodged in our way of reflecting on the church and in our way of preparing leaders and everybody else for life in the church.*

Farley's essay explores the transformative power of education as effortful and rigorous learning in the life of congregations. Only through such education can disciples become steeped in the Christian tradition and skilled in interpreting the situations that arise in individual and social life. A childish faith will not hold up against the winds of modernity or postmodernity.

Farley is clear that education-toward-gospel-interpretation is an indirect sign of the work of the gospel in congregations but one that makes possible the direct signs of various kinds of loving action. Interpreting the world according the Spirit of Jesus is a foundation for the features that make up the congregation's institutional distinctiveness. A key section of his essay explores the resistance to learning and inability to reconsider found in so many congregations — a preference for "a perpetual, religious childhood." Here are echoes of issues found in his Deep Symbols *(1996). His "curriculum" suggestions foster the interpretive skills needed for Christian living in today's culture.*

Two splendid essays of Farley's for those serious about practical theology are: "Theology and Practice outside the Clerical Paradigm," in Don S. Browning, ed., Practical Theology: The Emerging Field in Theology, Church and World *(San Francisco: Harper and Row, 1983, 21–41) and "Interpreting Situations: An Inquiry into the Nature of Practical Theology," in Lewis S. Mudge and James N. Poling, eds.,* Formation and Reflection: The Promise of Practical Theology *(Philadelphia: Augusburg Fortress Press, 1998).*

This essay joins with others to explore how "concrete patterns of living in the local church (congregation)" can become "credible signs of the gospel," not simply in another preachment that confronts congregations with their ideal responsibilities but, rather, as a close scrutiny of the way the specific distinctive social features and processes of congregations are open or closed to what David Kelsey calls "the Christian thing." I take up here a very specific strand of this theme: the possible role of educational activities in the mobilization of congregations toward being what they are called to be.[1] Easy as it is to make proposals about what congregations should be and do, about their transformation and responsibilities, my own past proposals along these lines have about them a certain sociological innocence, a tone of ideality that comes from ignoring the congregation's distinctive social reality. While I do not expect this innocence to totally disappear, I hope it can be partially corrected. For example, I have strongly criticized Protestant congregations for their inability, if not refusal, to engage their members in serious, effortful, ordered learning.[2] I traced this inability to inherited paradigms that make preaching a privileged if not exclusive means of salvation and that remove educational elements from the tasks of ordained clergy. Such paradigms do play an important role in accounting for the virtual absence of ordered learning in the lives of congregations, but it is also clear that this absence is also promoted by their cultural situations and by their distinctive institutional features. Accordingly, in the light of a general description of the congregation as a distinctive institution, I shall explore the way certain institutional features create a deep resistance to ordered learning; yet paradoxically some features of congregations open them to fairly rigorous activities of ordered learning. These too must be identified. Finally, I shall offer a few guidelines for what a curriculum of ordered learning might look like in a contemporary congregation. Such learning does have some characteristic requirements. Casual, sporadic, spectator events that require no effort and totally lack sequence will not produce disciplined skills of interpretation. Minimally, genuine education requires effort (textual work, reading, thinking) and creates sequences in which some things are the basis of other things.

A program of studies whose aim is disciplined interpretation may be an indirect indication of the work of the gospel in a congregation. Many are the direct signs of the work of the gospel. Any account of them inevitably reflects an interpretation of what "gospel" is all about. Typically, signs of "gospel" are a face-to-face community of mutual *agape*; recollection and attestation of the agent of "gospel" (Jesus); agendas of ministry beyond the congregation to larger circles of need; action on behalf of groups marginalized by gender, color, age, ethnicity, class, or poverty; and activities of regular worship that embody these orientations. Interpretation (as the skill of bringing normative tradition to bear on situations) can be an element at work in all of these "signs." If activities of learning do discipline skills of interpretation, ministry and even Christian life, it would seem that learning too is an indirect sign of the gospel in the life of the congregation. And it would seem that a program of ordered learning eventually would affect every aspect of the congregation's life, influencing what it expects from its ordained leader, how it envisages its trans-congregational responsibilities, how it treats its own marginalized people and even its expectations for preaching and liturgy. In other words, Loren Mead is right in pointing out the transformative power of education for congregations.[3]

Institution

Awareness of the congregation as a distinctive social entity is not new.[4] This awareness is a stepchild of earlier applications of historical and social sciences to religious communities: thus, for instance, the work of Ernst Troeltsch, Dietrich Bonhoeffer, H. Richard Niebuhr or James Gustafson. New to the scene are the recent studies of the congregation as a distinctive type of social entity. This literature is already too vast and complex to be easily summarized.[5] Recurring themes are the programmatic call for serious congregational study (Wind), proposals for how to proceed, histories of *types* of congregations (Holifield), typologies of theories that guide basic approaches (Wheeler), versions of the distinctive problems American congregations face, critiques of the older notion of the congregation as confined to the private sector, critiques of facile accusations that American congregations simply internalize the larger culture (Wind and Lewis), in-depth studies of particular congregations (Wind and Lewis) and specific descriptions of the congregation's social structure and dynamics (Hopewell, Carroll).

Social structure and dynamics is our theme. I sense two complementary approaches at work in congregational studies. One works from a definition of the congregation. The congregation's social or institutional characteristics are thus elaborated from the definition: for instance, a group of people that regularly gathers in a place for purposes of worship.[6] The other approach presses beyond (though probably presupposes) the formal features of a succinct definition to the social dynamics that constitute the congregation's organizational structure and identity over time. Its characteristic concepts are identity (plot), world-view (perspective), ethos, processes, etc.[7] In the following brief account, I shall draw on both approaches and add to them certain features that may help us to understand both the congregation's actual resistance and possible openness to ordered learning.

The Douglas and de S. Brunner definition states the most general and probably essential social features of the congregation: a human group that gathers on regular occasions in a particular place for purposes of worship. I shall call these features the social facade of the congregation, the first and most external characteristics apparent to an observer.

The weekly event of worship is not merely one among many instances of the gathering of the congregation, but is the one event in which the whole congregation is regularly together in a way that is open to the public and therefore to potentially new members. The centrality of the weekly event is closely connected to the way congregations interpret the function of regular worship (as sacrament, preaching) in salvation as both conversion and edification. So central is this event that the congregation's viability, vitality and attractiveness to potential new members are measured first of all by the quality of this event. This is why a major, if not *the* major, criterion of Protestant congregations for their ordained leader is her or his capacity to manage this event, to be a "good preacher," etc.

Closely related to the centrality of the weekly event is the physical building congregations deem necessary to their repeated meeting. Building defines their place; hence the building's history, cost, spaces, furnishings, functions and aesthetics are a crucial part of the congregation's self-understanding, ethos and even story. Most congregational events take place in and from the building. The "sanctuary" as the initial and primary space of the building is required by the weekly gathering for worship. Other activities (education, fellowship meals, staff offices, etc.) prompt the creation of other spaces. Also apparent to both the social scientist and casual observer is the congregation's leadership structure that distinguishes the paid or "professional" leadership, the lay leadership and the non-leader members.

When we move behind these public and visible social features, we quickly discover a number of social dimensions less apparent to external observation.

Individuals. The first social dimension originates in and is carried by the individual human actors. Attending to this dimension of human sociality has been the concern of a line of German social thinkers from Wilhelm Dilthey, Max Weber, Max Scheler and Alfred Schutz.[8] Congregational social analysis so far seems to have passed over this Weber/Schutz tradition of attending to human action, life-worlds, sociology of knowledge and intersubjectivity. One problem that arises when we turn to individual members is *how* they experience, belong to, "mean," the congregation. In some sense the most general relation of a member to a congregation may be the distinctive loyalty which the group evokes.[9] The problem congregational analysis faces is just what form (or forms) loyalty takes as members commit themselves to the larger religious tradition, to a sub-institution of the congregation, to the pastor, to an ideology, etc.[10]

The Interhuman. A second dimension behind the visible organization has to do with the way individuals are distinctively together in a congregation. Douglas and de S. Brunner note that a congregation is constituted by face-to-face relations. Such relations inevitably attend any local gathering for worship, but the being-together of people in a congregation is clearly much more complex and convoluted than what is expressed in this statement. A distinctive and quite determinate kind of intersubjectivity arises with congregations and with each congregation. Congregations are made up of both face-to-face and anonymous relations. The face-to-face element ranges from the relations that form in brief and fairly superficial meetings (e.g., in the weekly gathering) to deep interhuman structures of expectation, affection or competition, all tied up with corporate memory and anticipation.

Semi-autonomous sub-institutions. While some local congregations and even denominational types are organized by way of strict hierarchical structures and authoritarian styles, most congregations retain semi-autonomous groups that more or less live a life of their own. Officially, these groups may be part of the church's organizational map and subject to the church's leadership. Actually, their agendas, constituency, ethos and dynamics are more internally generated and maintained then externally determined. They are not like a department in a college, a division of a sales organization, or a bureau of a state government. They have little formal accountability and their survival depends primarily on the vitality of their membership. The original entity of this sort was the virtually autonomous Sunday school that became a kind of co-institution within the congregation.[11] In spite of the weakening of its original autonomy, the Sunday school remains a semi-autonomous sub-institution of the congregation along with large (or even small) long-standing Bible classes, women's circles, missionary societies, the music program, etc. Loyalty to the congregation can, accordingly, be primarily to the tradition, activity and membership of one of these sub-institutions. These groups are and are not subject to the congregation's central leadership. Why congregations have developed this cluster of loosely interdependent groups deserves inquiry. It may have something to do with their voluntary membership, American individualism, the hidden or not-so-hidden lay *ressentiment* of the elite leadership, and the rather strange non-authoritarian relation between the leadership and the members.

Economics. The way economics is a structural feature of congregations appears to be relatively hidden both from social analysts and the congregations themselves. Because a congregation occupies a building that typically includes a sanctuary, "educational" and staff spaces, and because it depends on a paid leadership, it requires for its survival not just face-to-face relations or the retention of its religious tradition but money. Insofar as growth and not just maintenance is a goal of the congregation, the need for money intensifies. However intense is the ideal discourse about missions, morality, justice and worship, however much the congregation would minister beyond itself to the community through benevolences and various programs, it must attend first of all to the material conditions of its own existence. With the rare exceptions of endowed congregations, the main source of money is the periodic, voluntary contributions of the members. Accordingly, to exist at all, a congregation must generate an ethos of loyalty, enthusiasm, contentment and mutual harmony among its members. For these reasons, the issue of money is paramount among the concerns of the leadership.

Generations. For reasons of location, history, context and ethos, some congregations are constituted by a single, near-retirement aged membership. Unless they attract new members, such congregations will disappear. Accordingly, a *sine qua non* of a congregation's survival is its intergenerational constitution. To survive, the congregation must pass on its "story," ethos and vitality to oncoming generations. Thus, congregations are not simply accidentally made up of children, adolescents, young adults, middle aged and aged members; they are, rather, structured not only by semi-autonomous sub-institutions but by age groups. The needs and interests of these groups evoke a variety of programs and set criteria for selecting the "professional" leaders. Two of these age constituencies are of paramount importance for the congregation: children and adolescents. Something about the ethos of American religion prompts even religiously alienated young adults to join congregations "for the sake of the children." Thus, congregations who are not "child friendly" put themselves at risk. Generations, therefore, contribute to the distinctiveness of the congregation as an institution. We do not find this generational structure in a corporation, a denominational bureaucracy or a department store; most American institutions and social entities lack it.

Social fragility. All social institutions are vulnerable to demise. Combined in this vulnerability are external conditions (large societal movements and events) and internal dynamics and effectiveness. Congregations can be diminished or even eliminated by changes in the larger ethos of society (e.g., the popularity of fundamentalist religion) or by demographic changes in their own neighborhood. The delicate balance of semi-autonomous sub-groups, the vicissitudes of age groups, the possibility of a catastrophic professional leadership, and the variety and degree of membership loyalty can all endanger the internal conditions of a congregation. Available to leadership-seeking congregations is a pool of "professionally" educated clergy whose members vary enormously in basic ability, perspectives and agendas for ministry. Thus, the transition of "professional" leadership is a highly charged event in the life of a congregation, one whose outcome can seriously advance its health or bring about its demise. Congregations are not unaware of their fragility. With the exception of the rare "political-cultural" type of congregation, congregations create an environment in which preaching, education and ministry are expected to maintain a balance of contentment among its various groups. The congregation's activities should comfort, console, maintain and address the problems of its individual members.

These features together constitute the congregation's institutional distinctiveness: place (building), weekly public worship, face-to-face relations, ordained and lay differences, membership loyalties, semi-autonomous sub-groups, generational structure, paramount financial concerns and social fragility.

Resistance

Effortful and cumulative learning is only rarely a significant part of the life of American Protestant congregations. Something other than ordered learning is going on in the weekly hour of Sunday school classes, communicant or new-member classes, church retreats and occasional lecture series. American congregations display a certain resistance to programs of adolescent and adult learning.[12] This resistance, this inability to make learning an intrinsic part of the life of the congregation, has many roots. The deepest roots are the paradigms both Protestant and Catholic congregations inherit from their past that dispose how they interpret salvation, the Christian life, the character and function of the congregation and the responsibilities of the ordained leadership. In these paradigms the salvific transformation of human beings requires preaching, sacraments and, possibly, individual "spiritual" disciplines — but not ordered learning, that is, the deliberate and effortful attempt to understand the tradition (stories, texts, doctrines) of the church and to obtain skills of world interpretation. Perhaps this paradigm that marginalizes ordered learning comes from an early period of churchly life in which widespread literacy would not be taken for granted. In this period of Christendom, monks, priests, ministers and nobility had access to learning; the rest of society did not. In the church, clergy were expected to read, know and interpret the sacred texts to the laity. Now, in spite of the democratization of literacy and education, the presumption persists that Christian learning is for the clergy only.

In some early periods, the Protestant minister was thought to have an important teaching function. This function now has been entirely removed: first, by the Sunday school as the lay-led educating institution in the congregation and, second, by the institutional resistances to learning. Absent in present imageries of the "good" minister is the minister-as-teacher. The minister is not expected to actively teach the skills of textual interpretation, the narrative and doctrinal tradition, or the hermeneutics of situations to adolescents, adults or the congregation's teachers.[13]

In addition to persisting paradigms that dominate how congregations think about the ministry and education, there are powerful social factors at work in their cultural context and in their very institutionality that make resistance to learning almost inevitable. The first of these factors originates in religion itself. Religion or religiousness makes its primary appeal not to the intellect but to what Jonathan Edwards called the affections. In individuals, the vitality of religious faith is carried in passions, desires and powerful convictions; thus, for the "religious" individual, knowledge, interpretive skills and precise forms of understanding are secondary (if needed at all) to the passionate and active life of faith. In short, religiousness is ever suspicious of, if not at war with, the distancing orientations of learning and the cool objectifications of thinking. Whole denominations and theological movements have arisen to embody just this suspicion.

A second factor of individual resistance to connecting faith and learning also has its roots in religiousness. Religiousness (or to use the older term, piety) tends to entertain its content and whatever mediates that content (e.g., scripture) in modes of certainty and cognitive security. Through proclamation, doctrinal motifs, moral maxims and rites, the religious person is consoled, secured, rooted in ultimate meaning. Learning, with its inquiries and efforts to understand, not only objectifies what is existential but opens up the complexity and ambiguity of what to the religious person needs to be simple and settled.[14]

A third social factor at work in the resistance to learning comes from the way a postmodern society impacts the congregation. Two results of this impact are especially prominent. First, attitudes about learning in the larger society re-appear in the congregation. Second, the exhaustive and all-consuming busy-ness of modern life constrains the way individuals are able to exist in congregations. As to the first, learning in an advanced industrial society appears more and more a matter of information rather than understanding. Vocationally relevant skills rather than interpretations of life situations in the world orient us more to useful technical methods than to retrieval or understanding of past tradition; yet the learning required by a faith's self-understanding inevitably involves tradition, symbols and metaphors, written texts and a variety of modes of understanding. Given this larger ethos that devalues learning in its traditional senses and alters it toward the technical, it would not be easy for people socialized by such a society to have strong convictions about the importance or possibility of learning as part of their religious life. More serious yet, even if this anti-learning social ethos had never developed, the character of modern (mostly urban and suburban) life works powerfully against programs of genuine learning in the congregation. From early adolescence through the end of high school or college-level schooling, the young experience education as all-consuming; hence to add an educational element to their religious or congregational life seems unthinkable. For adults, modern patterns of family (two working parents) and work are also all-consuming. With the exception of the very rich and the poor underclass, working Americans divide into well-trained and well-paid masters of some expertise and low-paid workers with little or no special training. Pressed hard by these patterns of work, both groups divide life between the effortful and stressful world of work and the privacy, rest, leisure and entertainment of the weekend and home world where one recovers from the strains of work. Accordingly, the congregation is a kind of haven and alternative to the stressful world of work. To introduce effortful learning in the congregation is to make an already burdened everyday life complicated and stressful. For these reasons the societal situation of the congregation's members conspires with the inherited paradigms to resist ordered learning.

According to the analysis so far, resistance to learning is prompted by powerful paradigms, features of religiousness and the patterns of postmodern society. Is there anything about the congregation as a distinctive *institution* that contributes to this resistance? In my view, there is nothing about the social reality of the congregation that is absolutely incompatible with ordered learning. At the same time the distinctive institutionality of a congregation works against local learning in the sense of lay theological education. Let us first recall that congregations are highly fragile institutions. A typical modern congregation (which in mainline Protestantism tends to be relatively small) senses two things needed for its very existence: a sound enough financial situation to maintain its building and pay salaries and a weekly service of public worship that is "comfortable" to its members and helps maintain their loyalty. Accordingly, most congregations (whatever their preachments) must focus first on ministries and events that assure these two conditions necessary for survival.

It is just this self-oriented social fragility with its *sine qua non*s of survival that marginalize learning in the life of the congregation. Because the bills must be paid and the institution maintained (and ideally enlarged), the paid leadership is first of all expected to attend to whatever administrative tasks the institution requires. Securing the institutional health of the congregation is the paramount, even if unstated, requirement of the paid leadership. What this means, of course, will vary from church to church, but two tasks stand out. The first is to maintain the quality of the weekly event of public worship. If that is a failed event — that is, dull, meaningless or angry in the experience of the members (and visitors) — the congregation's survival is in peril. The pastor, therefore, must give close attention to the sermon, liturgy, music and general tone of that event. The second task is to foster an environment in which the semi-autonomous sub-institutions can flourish and in which the age groups the congregation deems important are served. In this way administrative, managerial, personal relational, pastoral, homiletic and liturgical duties determine the primary tasks for the minister and subtly form an imagery of the "good" minister. To the degree that these concerns are paramount, necessary and definitional, they exclude, or render secondary, programs of adolescent and adult learning. Education in this sense is external to the image of the "good" minister and not definitional of the "good" congregation. Contemporary congregations have been accused of what has been called their "suburban capture." Their programs and ethos show only minimal concern for societal transformation, global crises and disenfranchised minorities. I think it could be shown that the same institutionality that forces congregations to make their own survival central also presses them toward an ethos of neutrality about most real, and therefore "controversial," societal issues.

The distinctive institutionality of congregations is not without its advantages. Survival, balance of sub-institutions, satisfied attenders of the weekly worship event and a solvent bank account are not trivial matters. At the same time, a congregation pays a price for what it must do to survive. Familiar are the criticisms of at least mainline Protestant churches offered up in recent decades: secularity (Berger), religious illiteracy or "the strange silence of the Bible" (Smart), the triumphant therapeutic ethos (Rieff), prevailing civil religion and individualism (Bellah). These criticisms are only slightly qualified when we consider the many types of congregations, the national shift to religious conservatism and recent studies of their "public" connections.[15]

Two features of contemporary Protestant congregations seem especially related to their refusal of programs of ordered learning. The first is the failure to deliver in a meaningful way the content of Christian tradition (its narratives, major symbols, history, doctrines and scriptures) to the congregation's adolescents (middle school through college). The loss of the majority of this group from the church seems to be the major reason for the statistical decline of the mainline churches. Driven already by familial and cultural youth-adult alienations, adolescents rarely see ways to merge their "Sunday school faith" and religious world-view into the youth subcultures of punk and rap, science courses, computer games, male cultures of violence, media-orchestrated leisure activities and multiple value worlds. The second is the religiously illiterate adult who has not moved very far from the modes of belief and interpretation that were in place prior to adolescence. Apparently, Protestant adults know very little about the Bible, the history of Christianity, their own denomination or the content of major Christian beliefs. According to John M. Hull, Christian adults are socialized by their congregations into a perpetual religious childhood whose typical state is a kind of religious bafflement.[16] The failure to pass on the traditions of faith to the young and the superficial acquaintance of tradition among adults make both groups open to the appeals of both fundamentalism and of thoroughgoing secularism or religious skepticism. They also help maintain what Hull calls an "unlearning culture" in the congregation that constrains congregational commitments and activities in serious ways.

Possibility

Resistance to local learning originates in part in certain institutional features of congregations. This need not mean that congregations are fated by their very nature to exclude lay theological education. We speak rather of their inertia or resistance to learning. Some congregations do in fact create in their midst programs of genuine learning. Furthermore, certain things are at work in the situation of congregations that open them to the possibility of theological education.

One of these is the total legacy and character of Christianity itself. Because of this legacy, churches and individual Christians are related paradoxically to learning. Christian religiousness (spirituality?) is suspicious of learning's objectivity and relativity, yet oriented to the truth and reality of the things of faith. Prior to the democratization of literacy and learning, this orientation was restricted to that part of the church responsible for teaching and preaching: the priests, ministers, "doctors," of the church. Learned clergy and unlearned laity was an assumed distinction of pre-democratic societies. With the democratization of education, this distinction collapsed. Most American Protestant congregations can assume a literate or educated laity. In the Christian past, the world of learning and the world of faith were connected: theological education with its tools and pursuits was present in the clergy. At least for them the church valued knowledge of biblical languages, conceptual clarification of basic beliefs, the apologetic struggle to relate the faith to science, cosmology and history, and the appropriation of various sciences in service of practical theologies. This commitment to learning has roots in the very nature of faith as faith in the creator God. When the world has the status of creation, willed and ever reshaped by God, faith has a certain seriousness about what is real and true. Thus, the Christian life is life in terms of the real: real nature, real, embodied human beings, real societies and their problems. Sin and salvation thus have to do with the corruptions and redemptions of actual human beings and their communities.

In addition to the legacy of learning in the Christian movement, certain institutional features open congregations to the possibility of local learning. Flexibility is one of those features. This means in part the possibility of paradigm and world-view change. Paradigms that interpret the character of redemption, the duties of the ordained leadership and the nature and importance of education do not change easily, but they are changeable. Further, the social environment that permits semi-autonomous sub-institutions makes possible new sub-institutions, for instance, those given to learning. For example, nothing about a congregation's institutionality would prevent it from developing a program that gave adults the opportunity to move from introductory to more advanced levels of interpretation, that offered both self-study and teaching programs, that created very brief units of commitment (three to six weeks), and used evenings and week-ends for such courses. New institutional possibilities also reside in the fact that a congregation has voluntary members whose roles in the congregation are not absolutely determined.

Further, almost all congregations tend to have resources for local learning already built into their situation. Some of these resources are present in the congregation because of the Sunday school. As a sub-institution, the Sunday school functions in congregations as an alternative to learning. Nevertheless, the Sunday school has brought with it physical spaces of potential teaching, the idea (if not the reality) of teachers, the idea of a written curriculum and regular gatherings of classes. Some congregations have small libraries, though rarely do these function in educational processes. Because the Sunday school does not require genuinely trained teachers, effortful study or phases of movement through a curriculum, it is not an institution of ordered learning; yet it has created in the congregation expectations potentially useful for a program of learning. Another important built-in resource is the congregation's "professionally" educated leaders who can, if given the opportunity, teach a variety of biblical, ethical and theological subjects.

In addition, Protestant congregations have strong traditions of lay leaders who give significant time to the church. In many congregations there are people who are seriously interested in learning, who would enjoy studying the Bible, the church's history and theology and contemporary religious topics both by way of directed individual study and in ongoing groups.[17] Masters of Theological Studies degrees attract numbers of church laity in cities that house seminaries or degree-level programs in theology. Specially designed lecture series by visiting clergy or professors tend to be popular when they are offered. It seems apparent that most congregations have in their midst some people who would respond positively to opportunities for genuine theological study. And it would be just these individuals who, after a period of serious study, would become, along with the pastor, teachers of programs of genuine learning in the congregation. A final congregational feature that opens it to the possibility of lay theological education is one of the necessities of its existence, its determination to transmit religious tradition to children and adolescents. Most congregations that include these age groups are seriously committed to this transmission. What they do not have in place are programs of ordered learning, especially stretching from early to late adolescence, in which the young would learn to read and interpret scripture, learn something of the church's history and beliefs and grapple with the way these things impact their own experience.

Because of the importance of the real and the true in Christian faith, paradigms that include at least the idea of education and available institutional resources already in place, the prospect of learning in the congregation should not be a lost cause. It will, however, take place in congregations only as they seriously overcome old paradigms of "education" and replace their "unlearning culture" with a new institutionality. This institutionality would include serious teaching responsibilities of the paid leadership, a sub-institution of learning outside the Sunday school, a theologically educated group of lay teachers, pedagogies that call for some minimum preparation by the students, a genuine curriculum with texts, field education events, courses that actually progress toward some aim (e.g., an exegetical skill, knowledge of Arian controversy), a possible symbol system for moving through the curriculum, a solution to the difficult problem of attracting adolescents to Christian learning, and inter-congregational shared programs and possibly staff. While this institutionality resembles formal degree-oriented education, it would necessarily depart from such at many points. While units of study would be inevitable, they would typically be short-term. Adolescents or adults may be able to commit themselves to a three to six session sequence that would introduce the synoptic problem or liberation theology. Long courses may be unsuited to theological education in congregations.

Curriculum

I began this exploration with the contention that the Christian life involves an *interpretive* way of existing in the world. It is not simply action but interpretive action. If situations (political, personal, institutional and global) are *what* we interpret, something about the gospel orients our interpretation. Minimally, the gospel calls forth interpretations of situations that combines critical suspicion and hopeful expectation. But interpretation is not inevitably reality-driven, morally pure or cognitively insightful. Human beings inevitably interpret the situations in which they live, but their interpretation can be misinformed, idolatrous, irrelevant, racist, superficial, superstitious and truth-indifferent; when it is these things, it loses the dialectic of suspicion and hope that originates in the gospel. Accordingly, learning does not so much create interpretation as make it self-aware, deliberate and subject to proper criteria.[18] Christian learning then is a disciplining of the interpretation ever going on in Christian existence. Such learning can provide the interpretive life of the believer with profound images, conscious criteria, powerful narratives, typical pitfalls, influential ideas and skills of thinking.

I also contended that, in spite of a legacy of anti-learning paradigms and institutional elements that promote anti-learning, congregations possess paradigmatic and institutional resources for programs of learning. By "programs of learning" I mean a curriculum of studies.[19] Two features reside in the idea of a curriculum: discipline and teleology. Discipline names the effortful aspect of genuine study. Learning to paint, hit a golf ball, organize a constituency and make sense of a text all involve effort; in genuine learning, the student is never utterly passive. Teleology names the expectation that continuing effort can move the student toward the sought knowledge or skill. Since the subject of this essay is the plausibility of congregational theological education, it must explore the possibility of a curriculum whose aim is disciplined interpretation. In this brief review I shall omit almost all the important things needed to frame an actual course of study: field education and contexts of praxis; the need for historical-critical, literary and contextual approaches to biblical and other texts; the special problems presented by programs of study for adolescents.

I shall make no proposal concerning pre-adolescent church education. I have a single criterion for the adequacy of such education, although I acknowledge many other criteria may be appropriate. The one thing that adolescent and adult theological education need to presuppose is a good knowledge of the church's narrative tradition: that is, the basic stories of the Bible and, ideally, stories having to do with the origin and development of the Christian movement. This implies that the teachers of the church's children, whatever else they are, should be gifted storytellers.

For adolescent and adult theological education, I propose three criteria for curricula whose aim is to develop skills of situational interpretation under the gospel: knowledge of the biblical and theological past of the Christian movement; acquaintance with dimensions of contemporary religious and cultural life; and the interpretive exploration of contemporary situation. The one aim of this exposition is to argue that programs of adolescent and adult theological education are inadequate if any of these three themes are absent.

Tradition. To most congregations, knowing the tradition of the Christian movement may be the most self-evidently valuable aim for lay theological education. Tradition, here, refers to the texts, doctrines, imageries and events that in some way define the Christian movement and the strand of that movement from which the congregation draws its identity. In Protestant communities, scripture is the primary vehicle of the normative past, although a secondary normativity is given to events, literatures and histories of the Reformation. To interpret situations in and from a Christian community is inevitably to think from and in relation to tradition in this sense. In some way the narratives, imageries, event (of Christ) and scripture dispose how a Christian community thinks about evil and salvation, suffering and hope, the world and God and, beyond those things, a multiplicity of moral and personal issues. Accordingly, lay theological education must employ serious historical tools to study the texts, periods, literary structures, motifs and theologies to be found in the Bible. Yet the Christian movement is not simply a blank tablet on which the ancient texts of scripture rewrite themselves. It has inherited and been structured by decisive doctrinal disputes and resolutions of the post-biblical past: early Christian-Gnostic controversies, Roman Catholic and Protestant mutual polemics, historical-critical and anti-critical theologies. The outcome is present in the languages of liturgy and piety.

Religion and culture. When human beings interpretively respond to a situation, something much more complex is at work than simply the application of a biblical passage or a fourth- or sixteenth-century doctrinal motif. All interpreters interpret by way of their own contemporary world, that is, they interpret in a milieu of interpretation set by past habits and preferences, past interpretations which have often found textual expression and which have a kind of authority for the interpreters. For example, African-American, feminist and liberation theologies are instances of contemporary Christian interpretation. In addition, untold numbers of advances are taking place in the contemporary world, knowledge of which assists interpretation to open up a situation under the gospel: analyses of the phenomenon of post-modernity, insights into the way language and metaphor work, knowledge of the texts and traditions of other religious traditions and faiths, inquiries into the way religious faith relates to modern science, politics or music and arts. To study these sorts of things is not so much to study specific situations as contexts, aspects of contexts or literatures of contexts. Thus, in addition to tradition studies, one part of a curriculum of lay theological education should include various contemporary texts and movements: contemporary theologies, ethics, faith in relation to various cultural phenomena, the history of one's own congregation. I presume that studies in tradition would be somewhat central to adolescent theological education although studies of religious and cultural issues would not be absent.

Situational explorations. The third guideline, or strand, of an adolescent and adult curriculum would be deliberate, self-conscious explorations of specific situations. Human life is only generally and abstractly a matter of larger cultural phenomena such as "ethics," types of theology, or types of world faiths. Specifically and concretely, it is comprised of situations in which we exist. The young must survive not just "post-modernity" but the specific youth subculture of which they are part. Contemporary human existence contains situations of gender conflict and ways of being gendered, of sexual preference, the distribution of wealth, situations of leisure, the consumer ethos of the larger society and even the situation of the congregation itself as it relates itself to these things. Here we have theological education in the sense of "practical theology," the interpretive responses that take place on the moving edge of actual existence. Christian individuals do interpretively respond to these situations, of course . I am arguing that they need to do so together in the context of learning, that is, the context in which in a disciplined way they self-consciously attempt to bring these situations into relation to the world of the gospel.

Omitted in these three guidelines, or strands, of curriculum are pedagogies devoted to interpretive skills themselves. I omitted them on the assumption that interpretive skills can and should be taught in connection with each of the three groups: skills of interpreting a biblical text or theological passage. Failure to make such skills a separate part of the curriculum should not mean that there should never be specific educational units devoted to skills; hence, each of the three strands should contain specific, even if very brief, units that focus on exegesis, analytic reading, ethical argument and symbol interpretation.

I conclude with a repetition. Curricula are easy to frame. Many impressive curricula have been prepared for congregations in the past. Virtually all of them fail because they are offered to an "unlearning culture." I argue that one sign of a congregation's commitment to the gospel is an institutionality that takes up Christian learning — lay theological education — to the end that its individual and communal praxis can be informed and disciplined by the interpretation of situations under the gospel.

References

Becker, Ernst
1968 *The Structure of Evil: An Essay on the Unification of the Science of Man.* Chapter 4. New York: The Free Press.

Bonhoeffer, Dietrich
1960 *The Communion of Saints: A Dogmatic Inquiry into the Sociology of the Church.* Translated by R.G. Smith. New York: Harper and Row.

Carroll, Jackson, et al.
1986 *Handbook for Congregational Studies.* Nashville: Abingdon.

Douglas, H. Paul and Edward de S. Brunner
1935 *The Protestant Church as a Social Institution,* p. 82. New York: Harper.

Fallow, Wesner
1960 *Church Education for Tomorrow.* Philadelphia: Westminster.

Farley, Edward
1987 "Interpreting Situations: an Essay on Practical Theology," in *Formation and Reflection: the Promise of Practical Theology.* Philadelphia: Fortress Press. Edited by Lewis Mudge and Daniel Poling.
1988 "Can Church Education be Theological Education?" in *The Fragility of Knowledge: Theological Education in the Church and the University.* Philadelphia: Fortress Press.

1990 "The Tragic Dilemma of Church Education," in *Caring for the Commonweal: Education for Religious and Public Life.* Macon GA: Mercer University Press. Edited by Parker Palmer, et al.

Fishburn, Janet E.
1988 "Leading: *Paideia* in a New Key," *Congregations: Their Power to Form and Transform.* Edited by C. Ellis Nelson. Atlanta: John Knox.

Foster, Charles
1985 "Abundance of Managers: Scarcity of Teachers," *Religious Education,* vol. 80, Summer.

Glenn, J. Stanley
1960 *The Recovery of the Teaching Ministry,* p. 9. Philadelphia: Westminster.

Hopewell, James
1987 *Congregation: Stories and Structures.* Edited by Barbara Wheeler. Philadelphia: Fortress.

Hull, John M.
1984 "Agreed Syllabuses, Past, Present, and Future," in *Studies in Religion and Education.* Philadelphia: The Falmer Press.
1985 *What Prevents Christian Adults from Learning,* Chapter 3. London: SCM.

Lynn, Robert W. and Elliott Wright
1971 *The Big Little School,* p. 96. New York: Harper and Row.

Mead, Loren
1994 *Transforming Congregations for the Future,* pp. 59–61. Bethesda MD: Alban Institute.

Nelson, C. Ellis
1988 *Congregations: Their Power to Form and Transform.* Atlanta: John Knox.
1989 *How Faith Matures.* Louisville KY: Westminster John Knox.

Royce, Josiah
1916 *The Philosophy of Loyalty.* New York: Macmillian.

Scheler, Max
1954 *The Nature of Sympathy.* London: Routledge and Kegan Paul. Translated by P. Heath.
1972 *Ressentiment.* New York: Schocken. Translated by W.W.Holdheim.

Schutz, Alfred
1967 *Collected Papers.* The Hague: Nijhoff. Edited by M. Natanson.
1967 *The Phenomenology of the Social World.* Evanston IL.: Northwestern University Press. Translated by G. Walsh and F. Lehnert.

Weber, Max
1947 *The Theory of Social and Economic Organization.* New York: Oxford University Press. Translated by Henderson and Parsons.

Wheeler, Barbara
1970 "Uncharted Territory: Congregational Identity and Mainline Protestantism," in *Presbyterian Predicament: Six Perspectives.* Louisville: Westminster John Knox. Edited by Milton Coulter, John M. Mulder, and Louis Weeks.

Williamson, Clark M. and Ronald J. Allen
1991 *Teaching Minister.* Louisville KY: Westminster John Knox.

Wind, James P. and James W. Lewis
1994 *American Congregations,* Introduction, vol. 1. Chicago: University of Chicago Press.

Endnotes

1 This essay builds on and goes beyond three other essays on church education (ordered learning) by the author. See Farley (1988, 1987 and 1990).

2 The subject of this essay is not such general notions as religious socialization, maturation, spirituality, nurture or "education" defined by these terms, but "ordered learning" or "schooling," to use C. Ellis Nelson's expression, or "Christian learning," to cite Jack Seymour. "Learning" is also the subject of John M. Hull (1985).

3 Loren Mead (1994). He states that "each congregation must be a center of teaching" and that this is especially critical in a situation of a displaced Christendom and a culture where the stories of faith are absent.

4 See H. Paul Douglas and Edward de S. Brunner (1935).

5 See Barbara Wheeler (1990).

6 Douglas and de S. Brunner define the congregation as a "group which comes together frequently in direct face-to-face relationships" and at a "habitual place of meeting." (1935) They supplement this minimal definition with features of the congregation's organized life such as voluntary membership, paid leadership and distinctions between lay and clergy. James P. Wind and James W. Lewis virtually repeat this definition but replace the face-to-face element with worship. A congregation is a "body of people who regularly gather to worship at a particular place."(1994) The social elements of a congregation are: 1) a group of people, 2) a regular gathering, 3) a particular place, and 4) the occasion of worship.

7 The second approach does not try to replace the elements of the definition of Douglas and de S. Brunner but apparently thinks that such things are only the skeleton of a congregation's sociality. To correct this, it thus focuses on distinctive "dimensions" of the congregation's life, and what these dimensions express is the distinctive way the congregation is a social identity. Thus Hopewell's comprehensive metaphor of narrative enables him to inquire into a congregation's world-view, plot (history), and character (ethos). See Hopewell (1987). Jackson Carroll and his co-authors follow a similar route. See Carrol (1986).

8 Early German sociology debated the status and viability of "scientific sociology," the issue being the obligation and ability of social science to acknowledge the human actor. For an account of this issue in the German literature, see Alfred Schutz (1967).

For a similar debate in American sociology, see Ernst Becker (1968). The main work of Max Weber that poses this problem is *The Theory of Social and Economic Organization.* See Weber (1947). For Scheler's way of attending to the contribution of individuals to social entities, see Scheler (1954 and 1972). Alfred Schutz devoted most of his writings to this problem. See Schutz (1967 and 1967). Dietrich Bonhoeffer (1960) applies this sociological tradition to ecclesiology.

9 See Josiah Royce (1916). This work had major influence on the American theologian, H. Richard Niebuhr.

10 An exception is John M. Hull (1985) who makes some use of Weber, Schutz and others in his analysis of the "education of the ideological community."

11 Janet E. Fishburn (1988) argues that originally the Sunday school was so autonomous it was virtually a second church within the congregation. On the same point see Nelson's Introduction (1988). See also Robert W. Lynn and Elliott Wright (1971). Lynn and Wright describe the tension that arose between the "old-timer" adherents of the Sunday school and the new professional church educators especially after World War II. They conclude, "Despite better materials the classroom scene in most Sunday schools is approximately what it was fifty years ago." Now, twenty five years later, the statement still holds true.

12 According to J. Stanley Glenn, "a strange subordination of the teaching function pervades its (the church's) life, work, worship, and proclamation." And, "a strange resistance even from the most unexpected quarters makes the teaching ministry harder to develop than any other." Glenn (1960). One of the fullest accounts of the resistance to education (ordered learning) comes from an English author. See Hull (1985).

13 According to Janet E. Fishburn, "the pastoral role as the teacher of the congregation was gradually replaced by the laity-led Sunday school." Fishburn (1988). This paradigm of the non-teaching minister has not gone unchallenged. Many authors not only note the phenomenon but call for the restoration of the "teaching office" to the minister. *The Quarterly Review: A Scholarly Journal for Reflection on Ministry* devoted a whole issue to the pastor as teacher (Fall 1983). A generation ago several monographs on the teaching minister appeared. See Glenn (1960) and Fallaw (1960). More recently, see Williamson and Allen (1991) and Foster (1985).

14 John M. Hull expresses this point in the phrase, "the need to be right and the pain of learning." See Hull (19985). Inquiry, open learning, ever poses the possibility that one's judgments are wrong. Cognitive dissonance is thus introduced into one's belief system and that is painful. Hull thinks there is a parallel between being disabused of the belief in Santa Claus and experiencing the mythical character of childhood ways of believing religious matters. Thus, insistently determined to believe things, one dissociates the whole of religious discourse from the world one knows and from the rest of knowledge. For Hull this empties faith of growth, excitement, novelty. One knows "only Jesus" but the knowing self is simply empty.

15 Some studies now qualify the Berger description of the congregation as a phenomenon of the private sphere and the argument that American congregations largely mirror the secular values of the culture. See Wind (1994). In my view this qualification is somewhat ambiguous. One issue is how accurately ordinary social scientific methods, e.g., the questionnaire, capture the deep values and ethos of a congregation. A very "religious" and "biblical" discourse can characterize a congregation's preaching and beliefs, yet at the same time have a primarily therapeutic content. Have the new studies actually overturned or strongly qualified Phillip Rieff's thesis about the therapeutic uses of faith? Further, to argue that congregations embody in a certain way the public world may not contradict the way their paramount concerns have to do with the stresses and strains of individual and familial life. Are the "culture wars" issues really being taken up and given expression in mainline congregations so that they have altered their programs, ethos, and expectations of their leaders?

16 Hull (1985), p. 9. For a similar point, see C. Ellis Nelson (1989), Introduction.

17 C. Ellis Nelson has urged churches to form a central group that will commit itself to weekly study for the purpose of building up the congregation. See Nelson (1989).

18 "Learning" in the sense of the academic establishment, its disciplines, methods, movements and the like, can of course itself be racist, idolatrous, absolutistic, etc. I am using the term "learning" here not to describe the academic, but as the process of deliberate inquiry and self-criticism.

19 Many curriculums are written for lay church education. An example of curriculums written for public schools are the English "Agreed Syllabuses." The Education Act of 1944 required religion to be taught in the schools, resulting in a number of Agreed Syllabuses — Surrey, Birmingham, etc. In the Surrey Syllabus, two themes are present as the curriculum develops over the years: the Bible, and, the Christian life. Seniors take up Christendom (history) and "Christian work in the modern world." See Hull (1984).

Chapter 7

Raising Lay Consciousness

The Liberation of the Church

Paul Lakeland

Paul Lakeland's work on the concrete conditions of church practice is well expressed in his 1990 book, Theology and Critical Theory: The Discourse in the Church *(Nashville TN: Abingdon, 1990). This book is perhaps the most luminous and readable treatment in English of Jurgen Habermas's writings on communications and critical theory and their theological implications. Where Habermas seems obscure, Lakeland is able to concretize and apply his thought to institutions and situations common in English-speaking countries. Lakeland's "translations of the translations" of Habermas are valuable, but his applications of his ideas to the circumstances of the local churches and to current theology are priceless. Behind his book is the question: Under what circumstances can the word of the gospel come to be on the lips of the people in original ways? This is the great question for discipleship in our time.*

In the following essay, Lakeland does not move beyond Theology and Critical Theory *and its seminal, even timeless, issues. Instead he goes deeper, using a liberationist perspective to get at the marginalization of the "lay voice" and its consequences for the local church, particularly the Roman Catholic one. In his lay voice, he describes a situation of concern to lay persons but also to the most thoughtful among the clergy: the systemic divorcing of authority from expertise, of teaching authority from living faith and of local gathering from community of inquiry. [See, "Tradition, Theology and Discourse," in* Theology and Critical Theory.] *While not claiming the oppression he describes is the most serious one in our world, he does claim it to be an authentic oppression and diminishment of the humanum and on a continuum with other oppressions.*

Here Lakeland sketches the story of his own coming-to-be as a lay theologian, moving from the pulpit to the pew. Ecclesial re-location has opened up critical questions for him about discourse in the local church. These questions, here given a Roman Catholic focus, seem to be pressing ones in all denominations, even in denominations where, as some at our conference claimed, there can be too much of a lay voice directing congregations only from the angle of efficiency.

1.

This essay has proved to be the occasion for me to bring several previously unrelated factors into focus in my own mind. First, there is my very long-standing concern with the question of liberation theology, and the perennial issue for white males about whether there is anything in it for them (Lakeland 1986a, b).

Second, there is my equally long-standing attention to ecclesiology, a gaze which — for a Catholic — is not always benign and is always complex (Lakeland 1990). Third, there is the increasing pressure, stemming partly from a deeper acquaintance with the family of liberation theologies, partly from domestic pressures, to get something of my own life into the words I write — in other words, to make *my* experience a source for theology, rather than simply to write at length, and at arm's length, of the importance of experience as a starting-point in theology.

Let me then begin by sketching the context out of which I work. I am writing this paper a few weeks before my fiftieth birthday. It is not unusual, they tell me, for this milestone to be a moment of taking stock. I left my parents' house in 1964 at the age of eighteen, never again to take up residence there. The thirty-two years that have elapsed since then have been equally divided between two very different worlds. From 1964 until 1980 I was a Jesuit; since 1980 I have been a layman ("reduced to the lay state" is the telling juridical designation), have been married for twelve years and have been busy now for five and a half years raising a child. I have already chosen the title of my memoirs: *All Seven Sacraments . . . and then some*. The common factor of these three decades has been allegiance to the Catholic tradition, an identification that has never been without question, unease and doubt, but which has always remained more or less intact. I suppose that what has kept me with it all has been the perception of the persistence of truth, even within an apparently increasingly dysfunctional religious family. Of course, the ways in which I have reconciled these two elements have not always been the same. Indeed, the answers I once thought I possessed have grown more rather than less tentative over the passing years.

In the midst of my middle-aged tolerance for ambiguity, and despite my growing lack of confidence in any conclusions to which my earlier self may have come, one judgment stands out more and more clearly. I am sure that my own Catholic tradition squanders lay experience, and convinced that this is directly connected to the degree of its dysfunctionality (Lakeland 1990: 180–83). This is most tragically apparent in the effective absence of lay experience from the formation of teaching on personal, and particularly on sexual, morality. In the Catholic tradition, of course, laypeople have neither active nor passive voice. They are silent in and out of church, occupy no positions of leadership and, at least formally, exercise no teaching responsibility within the church.[1] There are clear and understandable historic reasons for this split between a clergy who teach, preach and exercise jurisdiction, and a laity who do not. For most of the last two thousand years, to be clergy was to be educated, and to be lay was to be uneducated. While that has been a long time changing, it has certainly changed now, and it is no disrespect to the ranks of the Catholic clergy to say that most educated Catholics will now be found outside the clerical ranks. Indeed, in the United States one could probably make the more remarkable claim that most theologically educated Catholics are not clergy.

I want then in this paper to expand on my ideas of how the discourse of the ordinary people is essential to the practice of the church and to what extent their everyday lives are an important theological source for the community. And I want to do so against the background of a more general concern to explore the conditions under which the local church may become a credible sign of the gospel.[2] I shall begin with some brief comments on the theological value of "the discourse of ordinary people," and then turn to a summary pathology of why that discourse is not available to the church. In a final and lengthier section I shall reflect on what it will take to reverse this clearly dysfunctional aspect of the life of the church.

One of the most striking characteristics of much contemporary theology is the attention paid to the context of the theologian or the community engaged in theological reflection. Indeed, this is one reason why I begin this paper with a few brief biographical notes of my own. Attention to context is a direct result of the turn to experience as normative for theology. From the stress placed on context in the 1960s in the work of Juan Luis Segundo, through the entire development of Latin American theology of liberation and those other theologies sharing a family resemblance — especially in feminist, womanist and *mujerista* thought — the concrete circumstances of the doer of theology come into prominence (Freire,

Gutierrez, Isazi-Diaz, Schreiter). In the past, they were not merely in the background; they were invisible.

Few, if any, authors in the Catholic tradition have reflected upon the particularity of *lay* experience as a starting-point for theology, or have recognized the context of lay Catholics as being just as distinctive as that of *mujeristas* or gay and lesbian Christians.[3] One obvious reason for this oversight is the fact that lay Catholics include many people who are already self-identified as members of more obviously distinct groups. There are many Hispanic women lay Catholics, lots of gay and lesbian Catholics and not a few African-American Catholics. In the liberation theologies that emanate from these groups, their being members of the laity never seems to emerge as worth comment. A second and perhaps less obvious reason for the lack of a sense of the laity as a distinct group is that the very notion of being "lay" includes within it connotations of passive acceptance of one's place as recipient of grace, of the Spirit, of the sacraments. Rarely, if ever, does being "lay" seem to imply a particular activity or ministry within the community.

The laity as laity have never been valued as a distinct group within the church, despite recent conciliar and papal nods in their direction.[4] In consequence, they have only with difficulty seen themselves as gifted in particular ways *as* laity. Where and if such lay consciousness emerges, the following concerns are commonly articulated: the psychological distance of much worship from the life lived by the majority of worshippers; preaching of uncertain quality that consistently represents a disembodied spirituality; inadequate teaching on personal, and especially sexual, ethics; the absence of young people from the life of the church; the lack of clear prophetic witness on any issue other than abortion; and, above all, the absence of the voice of the laity in the day-to-day management and organization of the church, most particularly in the formation of teaching, particularly in those areas, like sexual ethics, where lay experience might be thought to be more fully developed than among the ranks of a mostly unmarried clergy.

While it is possible to argue that what is included or not in lists such as the above is more a reflection of the author's "discontents" than it is a description of any particular imaginable lay group and that therefore one should not insist on any particular item on the list, one issue is — I believe — beyond dispute. No one questions the fact of the exclusion of lay voice from formal participation in ecclesial leadership. Differences between passive and involved laity, or between liberal and conservative lay Catholics, on the question of lay voice in the church do certainly occur; but these largely have to do with whether lay people *ought* to be accorded leadership roles, not with whether they as a matter of fact possess them at the present time. While conservatives would be content with lay levels of participation and leadership, and liberals would not, all would agree that laity are juridically excluded from leadership positions in the church.

2.

The greatest problem with the kind of hypothetical discussion just conducted is that it has to be conducted at all. Given the fact of lay exclusion from voice in the church, why is it that there is little or no organized attempt to change this? There certainly exist groups such as "Call to Action" which stress the democratization of church structures, but they involve a tiny minority of lay people and — much more importantly — only a small fraction of those who are dissatisfied with the current role of the laity. Why, if the problem of lack of lay voice exists, is resistance so spotty? Is it that most people do not see a problem, and those who do are just constitutionally indignant, or is there some other explanation?

The case I wish to make is that the low level of lay protest at the role of laypeople in the church is a product of the systemic or structural oppression of the laity in the Catholic church. The concept of structural oppression was developed in religious reflection first of all in the Latin American theology of liberation, but is now a commonplace in all liberation theologies (Segundo). It is particularly important to understand the precise character of this notion of oppression. The concept draws attention to actual structures within a particular society, in this case the Catholic church, that result in oppression, while they may or may not have been set up with the intention of oppression. It also leaves open the question whether or not those who benefit from the oppressive structures do so consciously, accidentally, or by default. Certain oppressive social structures, such as chattel slavery or apartheid, are consciously intended systemic oppressions. Others, such as societies that are de facto rather than de jure racist, or that demonstrate elements of patriarchy, reveal systemic oppression that may not be so consciously intended, at least in its origins, but that is not necessarily any less oppressive. Thus systemic oppression by no means requires that we understand the individuals occupying positions of power within the system to be consciously engaged in the physical or emotional abuse of those victimized by the structures.

The accusation of systemic or structural oppression of the laity in the Catholic church does not, then, require the claim that clergy consciously oppress or abuse non-clergy. Indeed, as we shall see, there are good reasons to see the oppressors in this particular structure as themselves, to a degree, oppressed by the very same divisions. The claim is only that the division between clergy and laity, as understood in the Catholic tradition, systematically subordinates and undervalues the lay lifestyle, lay talent, lay leadership, lay experience and lay spirituality. While the patterns cannot be equated to those of slavery, they certainly reproduce in striking ways the structures both of racism and sexism. Racism, sexism and clericalism all at root are moved by a belief, however inchoate, in the lesser humanity or lesser intelligence of the oppressed group, thus justifying the subordinate position in which the underclass is then to be maintained.

It may seem to be a serious exaggeration to argue that the Catholic clergy believe the Catholic laity to be less human or less intelligent than priests and bishops. Of course, none of them would ever say that, and perhaps none of them would ever think that. But the patterns of behavior and the structures of the lay/clerical divide within the Catholic church suggest that in fact the laity are systematically treated *as if* they have lesser talents and are of lesser account. Lay people are of course not ordained to celebrate the Eucharist, and there is no good reason to take seriously any lay demand that they be permitted under normal circumstances to do so (though of course it is a far different claim to want patterns of ministry and ordination to be transformed so that the lay/clerical distinction no longer is operative). What is not in dispute here is that at least at the present time some are ordained to celebrate the Eucharist and lead the community at worship, and some are not. The problem lies much more in the historical accretion to this segment of the clergy of *all* formal manifestations of leadership, power and authority in the church.

The problem I am attempting to address here is more fundamental than a mere call for a better attitude on the part of the clergy to the laity, or for the laity to be allowed to exercise more non-sacramental functions in the daily life of the church.[5] On the one hand, the "clergy" in the clergy/lay distinction simply indicates those members of the church who happen as a matter of fact to have been singled out to lead the community in its sacramental worship, while the "laity" are those who do not feel called to this particular ministry. This in itself is not oppressive. The problem lies much more in the fact that "clergy" in the clergy/lay distinction is also a designation for a group of people who hold all authority and exercise all leadership in the church by virtue of possessing a calling to preside at worship, which is by no means the same thing. The problem is greatly exacerbated by the fact that for purely historical reasons a series of entirely extrinsic factors (maleness, willingness to commit to a celibate lifestyle) delimits not only those whom the church considers to be truly called to ordained ministry, but also those who can lead the church, preach the homily, teach with authority, or even be formally incorporated in the communal discernment of the gospel.

The problem endemic to the lay/clergy distinction is then not solely an administrative or attitudinal one, though there are elements of both of these at work. It is at root a theological problem inherent in the notion of the relationship between ordained ministry and various forms of leadership, although one that becomes as apparent as it does only because of the purely accidental exclusion of women and married men from the ranks of (ordained) leaders. In other words, any questionable or even negative elements in the historical association in the Catholic tradition between ordained ministry and authority are masked just so long as the restriction of ordination to celibates and men goes unquestioned. When such restrictions are scrutinized, particularly when their connection to leadership is examined, and the essentially ideological argument for their continuance is uncovered, a theological argument against them is the more likely to be mounted. While a theological argument for the ordination of women is by now unremarkable in the Catholic tradition (Lakeland 1977, Swidler, Tavard, van der Meer) the less common but arguably more necessary theological challenge is the one to be mounted against the traditional connection between ordained ministry on the one hand and positions of leadership and authority on the other.[6]

While it would undoubtedly be beneficial to the church to have many more laypeople in visible leadership positions and while their exclusion is symptomatic of their subordination, it is not there that we should locate the principal battleground of systemic oppression. Much more troubling is the crippling effect on lay consciousness of lack of voice and its concomitant marginalization, a phenomenon that, as a matter of fact, has as one of its consequences the decreased probability that many laypeople would be qualified to put themselves forward for just the sorts of positions of leadership in the church that are listed above. In her great book on the origins of liberation theology, *Cry of the People,* the late Penny Lernoux made an important sociological distinction between "poor cultures" and "cultures of poverty." The former are not problematic. Though distinguished by lack of material means, they are communities with a rich cultural life in which the dignity of their members is not in question. However, a culture of poverty is one in which the poverty has become so overwhelming that its psychological effects are such as to deprive the community of hope and to substitute a climate of demoralization and decay. Clearly, for Lernoux, structural oppression is what turns a poor culture into a culture of poverty. A similar distinction may be instructive in plumbing the depths of lay oppression; while the notion of "the laity" is not in itself degrading or inappropriate, the impoverishment of lay culture and lay expectation resulting from systemic oppression is deeply problematic. Like the denizens of a culture of poverty, the laity are depressed. And because they are depressed, they are less likely to be aware that they are oppressed. Indeed, as studies of clinical depression tend to show, they may even be unaware that they suffer from depression.

The first step in emergence from structural oppression is for the laity to move from depression to a recognition of their oppression, and the prerequisite for this is to be able to name their own oppression. In liberation theology, such a step is called "conscientization" and it is the primary awakening of a community, through which it begins the struggle to pass from being object or victim of history, as defined by someone else, to subject of its own history. Through "conscientization," people begin to take charge. In whatever context, it represents achieving or reclaiming adulthood from those who have reinforced the infantilization of the victims. In whatever context, it is the moment at which the patriarchs, patronizers or "parents" are challenged to abandon their stranglehold on power and, all too frequently, the moment at which they often redouble the strength of their hold.

3.

Infantilization. "Conscientization." Self-definition. These are the Egypt, Sinai and Promised Land of lay liberation. While Latin American liberation theology has been able to make more direct links to the Exodus narrative of how a non-people is chosen by God to become a people, indeed to become God's people, the Catholic laity *as* laity must do a lot of tacking to get to the same point on the other shore. But the fundamental predicament is structurally identical between the two groups. Historically, their reality has always been defined by their particular structural oppressor, and their objectification and alienation have been reinforced by all kinds of social sanctions and cultural codes. The parallels are striking.

The poor of Latin American liberation theology are submerged in their culture of poverty until awakened through encounter with the scriptures in a context in which they are encouraged to vocalize their sense of the relationship between their own oppressed condition and the voice of God in the Bible, singling out the marginalized as God's special object of concern. Strengthened by their new awareness of the preferential option for the poor in the God of the Hebrew Bible and the Jesus of the gospels, they can take simple, humble, but nonetheless courageous, steps to change the structural oppression under which they live. For the most part, this is less a matter of a direct challenge to political authority than it is the attempt to take charge of their own lives in their own communities, and to insist on the right to a dignified human life in which their basic needs are met. Such "agitation" was most frequently identified as subversive, and struck down in often-violent ways. Often the local church sided with the poor, but sometimes not; sometimes the national and international church sided with the poor, more often not.

These basic historical moments in the story of liberation theology may well be paralleled directly in the story we shall one day be able to tell about lay Catholic experience and the emergence of a lay theology of liberation. In the local parish situation at the present day, most of the laity are relatively passive and uncomplaining, at least in public. Some parishes allow for considerable lay involvement in the conduct of worship and the organization of the parish community, but the majority do relatively little of this, sometimes because the laity willing to involve themselves do not exist, in itself a further sign of the reality of the culture of oppression/depression. But even where lay involvement is encouraged, perhaps beyond what is strictly permitted by higher authority (in preaching, for example), while there is some erosion of the lay/clerical distinction, there is no possibility of real change in that formal relationship.

A major element in intensifying divisions between laity and clergy is the issue of clerical lifestyle (celibate, male), which creates a class division as pronounced as that between rich and poor in Latin America. The division is, of course, not largely on economic lines, except in the poorer parishes where the pastor may sometimes be living at a level of material comfort unknown to his parishioners. More important than economics, the characteristics of the lay and clerical lifestyles represent two different worlds. This is not only or even principally a matter of celibacy; it is much more the different forms of security, responsibility and accountability that mark the two ways of life.

Catholic clergy have the most secure lifestyle in the community, except perhaps for the fabulously wealthy. While not highly paid, their material circumstances are never in doubt; downsizing, outsourcing and the other manifestations of the new social barbarism that render even the upper middle-classes anxious today are unknown to the clergy. While frequently managing parishes with doubtful financial solvency, they have few if any such worries for themselves. As celibate individuals, many of the more demanding forms of personal responsibility are unknown to them. And as essentially private, bachelor individuals, their ethical accountability in small matters and large is entirely located in their own consciences. The laity, on the other hand, typically live with those who hold them accountable, and to whom and for whom they are responsible.

The lifestyle divide between clergy and laity is not the source of the problem of lay oppression, though it is undoubtedly symptomatic. The real problem is that all forms of authority, influence, leadership and power in the church are reserved to a small minority of Catholic Christians distinguished from the others only by their possession of a radically different lifestyle. What we see is a true caste system, by vocation if not by birth. The laity are defined by the clergy. Their respective rights and responsibilities are defined by the clergy. Laypeople, however well-qualified or with whatever virtues and talents, are children in the house of the Lord. Attempts at real resistance to this situation, sporadic as they are, are interpreted as troublemaking, grumbling or "dissent" that is not to be tolerated and that, at least in Nebraska in 1996, could earn swift excommunication if your dissent took a form that the bishop disliked.[7]

If real change in the church is to occur, then there must be a mechanism and an agenda. There is a clear need for mass "conscientization" that, while it may only ever affect a minority, will at least be sufficiently widespread for it to be taken seriously. If the laity are ever to be given voice in the church, they must speak out. They must take voice. But we must also have something to say; we need an agenda. If we can find a way to raise consciousness but then have nothing serious to say, the charge of needlessly polarizing people might stick. If, on the other hand, we have an agenda but no mechanism — the condition of church now, at least in my estimation — there is a danger of the church falling further and further into ineptitude, if not irrelevance. To be irrelevant is to have nothing important to say, and the Catholic church cannot be accused of this, even in its present wounded condition. But to be inept is to be dysfunctional in discharging its responsibilities to history, and it is here that the problem of lay voice becomes crucial.

The agenda of a lay theology of liberation must then be to achieve voice in the church, that is, to be taken seriously on a par with clerical voices, priestly or episcopal, according to the degree of expertise one can claim and according to the measure of good sense and gospel insight that seems to inhabit what we have to say. Of their nature, the majority of lay people are not likely to be specialists in academic theology or in philosophical or theological ethics; while some will (and do) contribute to the scholarly dialogue on such matters, most do not, cannot and do not want to. But there is an enormous reservoir of lay experience of the challenges of living life according to the gospel, both theologically and ethically, that remains untapped because the clerical teachers in the church draw upon it little, if at all, and because those whose experience it is are hobbled.

Most of what is wrong with the church today is to be found in precisely those arenas where lay experience would be crucial if it were attended to at all. Aware once again of the danger that any list will reveal more about the writer than about lay consciousness as a whole, I would yet venture the following brief list of pathologies: the attempt to stifle debate by invoking authority; the exclusion of most married men and all women from ordination to the priesthood; the continued insistence on "banning" so-called artificial means of birth control; the voice of the Vatican in international debate on population policies and the rights of women; patterns and practices for the appointment of bishops; church teaching on homosexuality; clerical sexual abuse of minors. Lay experience has an impact on each of these pathologies, either by shedding light on the problem, by rejecting the notion that there is a problem at all or, perhaps, by cutting down to size some of the issues that seem blown out of proportion by the seemingly unhealthy level of interest the teaching church seems to display in sexual sin. Nevertheless, items on a lay agenda are less important than determining the means of lay "conscientization."

If "conscientization" is demanded and the "culture of poverty" makes such an event unlikely to be spontaneously generated, the need for a historical catalyst becomes apparent. In this context one more parallel to liberation theology is helpful. While liberation theology certainly emerges in the encounter between the faithful people and the word of God in scripture, the turn to scripture itself needs to be explained. The truth, in Latin America, is that it was in some sense occasioned by a growing desperation. As Jon Sobrino has said, "true theology begins in indignation."[8] The indignation of the Latin American people and the institutional church itself was aroused by the experience of the assault on human rights conducted by the many governments of national security that flourished in Latin America in the sixties and seventies, and that are by no means absent today (Lernoux 1981:155–202).

The catalyst for the emergence of lay "conscientization" may well lie in the experience of living within what we may perhaps call, with some poetic license, "a church of national security." In other words, there are definite and important resemblances between the prevailing ideology of the Catholic church at the present time and the ideologies of the governments of national security experienced in Latin America over the past three decades. Governments of national security invoke higher ideals of the constitution in order to justify (temporary) suspensions of constitutional rights. The Church condemns dissent and — where it can — outlaws dissenters in the name of fidelity to the gospel. It invokes the example of Christ and the representative status of the priest to exclude women from any leadership role in the worshipping community. It rests its exclusion of (almost all) married people from priestly ministry on the traditional connection between such ministry and celibacy. While the church has no prisons in which to incarcerate people and no dungeons in which to torture them, the judicial processes to which it has subjected and continues to subject dissenters do not stand comparison with those of civilized society, and its sanctions on the guilty (principally deprivation of employment or right to teach) can have devastating economic and psychological consequences.[9]

Many have written about the present papacy's apparent wish to restore the church to its pre-Vatican II condition, at least as far as models of authority and church governance are concerned. As time has gone on, these authors have seemed more and more prescient. If, however, the level of suppression of debate, voice and freedom of the children of God is intensifying, might it not be that this will itself be the necessary catalyst for the emergence of "conscientization" among the laity in the church. Must it not get worse before it gets better? For some, their rising to subjecthood will be a product of the women's ordination controversy; for others it will be celibacy; for others it will be church teaching on some issue of sexual ethics, most likely on homosexuality or sterilization or one of the many irrational avenues down which traditional "physicalist" understandings of natural law carry the official moral teaching of the church. For very many, it will above all be a matter of recognizing the real oppression of women in the church. But whatever the particular occasion, this may be the spark that will ignite the intensely combustible mixture already present: deep love of God and the church, concern for the world, higher education and distaste for cant, from whatever kind of politician it emerges.[10]

How are lay Catholics to be "conscientized," even given the necessary historical catalyst in the experience of each individual? It is axiomatic that the "conscientization" must come from within the lay community. Clerics, however well-meaning, cannot do this, any more than whites can raise the consciousness of African-Americans to their oppression, or men can lead the women's movement. Beyond the symbolic inappropriateness lies the fact that only one who shares the context and experience of the oppressed group is capable of stimulating the process of "conscientization" within the group. Thus, in the case of lay Catholics, there is a need to identify a vanguard of "intellectual workers" from within lay ranks, Gramsci's "organic intellectuals," to stimulate the process of "conscientization." Ada-Maria Isazi-Diaz's concept of the theologian as professional insider, worked out in her recent book,

En la lucha, takes the neo-Marxist sting out of "organic intellectual" but is explicitly indebted to that earlier concept. Gramsci distinguished between the traditional and the organic intellectual. The former is a representative of the dominant hegemony and always argues against the claim that ideological interests are at work in the intellectual life. The latter is distinguished by a critical awareness of ideology and seeks to overcome that ideology through a dialogue between intellectuals and the masses. While it would be simplistic to suggest that Catholics theologians divide into traditional, clerical theologians and organic, lay theologians, it would be true that those theologians, clerical or lay, involved in liberation theologies fall clearly into the ranks of organic intellectuals (Lakeland 1995). Isazi-Diaz's professional insider, moreover, is a textbook example of such a person, from the community, entering into a dialogue with individuals in the community through the ethnographic interview, and working with and in the community to loosen the ideological and hegemonic chains that bind it.

Isazi-Diaz elaborates the notion of the ethnographic interview as a means to capture the directness of the experience of individual Hispanic women. But she adds the metaethnographic concern that these experiences not then be reduced to data and their directness be lost. A similar practice was carried on in Ernesto Cardenal's volumes of *The Gospel in Solentiname,* in which word-for-word transcriptions of debates on the meaning of Scripture passages were preserved intact, not simply used as a basis for theorizing. In their concern for immediacy and in their involvement both of the people and the professional insiders, both these examples suggest the way that lay "conscientization" might proceed. It requires the direct stimulation of the professional insider, but it relies for its efficacy on the hearing and sharing of direct experiences of the non-professional. In the ensuing dialogue, both partners come to name more exactly the true character of their oppression. Indeed, Isasi-Diaz in particular is absolutely adamant that the "grassroots Latinas" *are* as much *mujerista* theologians as their professionally trained sisters are (Isazi-Diaz 176–79).

In one final important respect, Isasi-Diaz's *mujerista* theology has a lesson for lay liberation theology. Throughout this essay I have stressed the role of experience, specifically lay experience, as a resource for theology. Isasi-Diaz points out that the experience that is valuable is not merely everyday experience, but "lived experience," namely, "those experiences in our lives about which we are intentional" [173]. This lived experience of oppression and domination is for *mujeristas* both the site and the source of their theology. In much the same way, we have to say that not just any experience is relevant to the situation of lay Catholics in the doing of a liberation theology. Indeed, for many of them, their everyday experience is anything but oppressive: the white males among them, in particular, experience their secular and their ecclesial reality very differently. So in the doing of lay liberation theology it will be the intentional experience of being lay *within the church* that will be both site and source of the religious reflection. To tie this together to my earlier argument, the intentional experiences of an oppressive church will be the catalysts in the process of "conscientization."

4.

Some years ago I wrote an article for a British journal on "The Lay Theologian in the Church." At that time, I envisaged the importance of lay theologians in the Catholic tradition principally in terms of their greater freedom from ecclesiastical censure and, therefore, as those who could "lead the charge" or "take the heat" in the inbred world of Catholic ecclesial controversy. That role still remains important, but I now believe it to be overshadowed by the requirement that these same lay theologians initiate the process of the "conscientization" of the Catholic laity. Helping the laity to name their oppression is probably the most important thing the theologian can currently do for the church; that lot falls upon lay theologians because only they share the experience of being lay that is a prerequisite for the effective solidarity that must emerge. In that same article on the lay theologian, I quoted one Vatican document that implied there were but two ways to do theology: with the possession of a canonical mission, or as a hobby. I believe I have now named a third way, more important than a mere hobby, but unlikely to be done by a possessor of the canonical mission, or at least by someone likely to retain that mission when word of the work leaks out!

The principal benefit to the church of this new work of the lay theologian is, of course, the "conscientization" of the laity; but there are some additional values of some consequence. For example, characteristic of the reciprocal enlightenment of both partners in the ethnographic interview, there is the "conscientization" of the lay theologian herself or himself. While the professional insider is an insider, sharing the lay condition, he or she is a professional and, to that degree, less oppressed. (Indeed, the secular world's parallel to clergy/lay is precisely professional/lay.) It has always struck me forcibly how much of the oppression of Catholic laypeople, including numerous of my undergraduate students, is partially a self-oppression occasioned by ignorance of the history and theology of the tradition.

A second ancillary value to the church is the reinsertion of the lay theologian into the ordinary worshipping community. Again, I speak from my own experience. I am far less likely than my lay counterparts to imagine my soul or salvation endangered by absences, sometimes prolonged, from participation in a parish, and I am far more likely to shop around for a parish in which the levels of lay oppression are less than in most parishes. In these habits, I am representative, I believe, of most lay theologians. If this suspicion is correct, the result will be a separation of lay theologians from exactly those contexts in which lay oppression is most evident, namely, in the vast majority of Catholic parishes. Life on little islands of liberal sanity is comfortable, but it is not the vocation of the lay theologian, which is to be with and of the people, to stimulate liberation and the emergence of the voice of the laity.

What role might I envisage for lay theologian in parish life that will be at once more productive and — sadly but inevitably — more turbulent? I have already said plenty in the preceding pages about the theologian as professional insider, and about the paramount importance of being a catalyst in the process of lay "conscientization." To identify such activities seems to be rather easier than to find a forum in which these goings-on can take place for, of course, an official space within the structure of parish life would indicate official approval of whatever officialdom imagines would transpire there. On the other hand, courses or talks on "New Structures for the Church" or "The End of Traditional Clerical Power" are not what the lay theologian ought to be envisaging. The professional insider, let it be remembered, helps to create a space within which individuals can articulate and name their own experience in the church. The role of the lay theologian in the pastoral context, then, as opposed to her or his professional career as teacher, scholar and so on, seems to take on more of the character of therapist. The therapist orchestrates a process of self-discovery and self-healing, but the important work is done precisely by those who are not the therapist; and the final value of the therapy is assessed by what goes on outside the therapist's office, after the talking is over.

A final value that I perceive in such a move towards lay liberation relates to a wider context than the Catholic church. Having taught liberation theology now for the past fourteen years on a little academic island of liberal sanity, I have become quite accustomed every semester to the question of the relationship that white, male, heterosexual, relatively affluent people can have to the movements for liberation among the poor, women, African-Americans or Hispanics, gays and lesbians and so on. I have frequently asked myself the same question. While there are things to be said about support and empathy and so on, the truth of the matter is that without the experience of structural oppression, not much real solidarity is possible. But once we recognize that lay Catholics need to come to an awareness that their own religious tradition structurally oppresses laypeople *as* laypeople, then even white, male, heterosexual, middle and upper class men — at least the Catholics — can find a way to become a group which is in solidarity with these other oppressed groups. Their "conscientization" as laity in face of an oppression that is *not* death-dealing can be a first, real but modest, step in expanding the solidarity of oppressed groups. Of course, they will have to be aware of the many experiences of oppression, and of how many of them are much more challenging than their own; and they will have to learn about the double, triple and even quadruple oppressions of some of their fellow-citizens, especially of those in the next pew. But the chances that this will happen are greater when the starting point is the experience of *lay* oppression, and the next step is to recognize that among these laity are many who are articulate about the multiple layers of oppression in their own lives. Just as white feminists grew to appreciate the class and race analysis of their black sister womanists, and Latin American male liberation theologians were made aware of their own sexism, so there is hope for the white middle class, just as far as their openness to their own structural oppression is authentic.

What, finally, of the consequences to the church? I have to confess that I am not much interested myself in novelties like democratic elections for the Pope or plebiscites on proposed new doctrines. These may or may not come, and may or may not be valuable. The first and really only important development from laypeople rejecting their oppression will be to release the experience of 99 percent of the people of the church as a resource for religious reflection on the doctrinal and ethical issues of our time. The validity and representative character of one's experience and the quality of one's reflection upon it then become the experiential basis for a religious reflection that will feed into the formation of authoritative teaching, not the membership of a particular caste or even a professional society of theologians. Lay liberation will not occur in the substitution of the Catholic Theological Society of America for the U.S. Catholic Conference, but only when the conditions exist in which the people can and will speak for themselves, and can and will be heard.

References

Flannery, Austin

1992 *Vatican Council II: The Conciliar and Postconciliar Documents.* Collegeville MN: The Liturgical Press.

Freire, Paolo

1972 *Pedagogy of the Oppressed.* New York: Herder & Herder.

Granfield, Patrick

1987 *The Limits of the Papacy: Authority and Autonomy in the Church.* New York: Crossroad.

Gutierrez, Gustavo

1983 *The Power of the Poor in History.* New York: Orbis Books.

1984 *We Drink from Our Own Wells.* New York: Orbis Books.

Isasi-Diaz, Ada-Maria

1995 *En la lucha: Elaborating a Mujerista Theology.* Minneapolis: Fortress Press.

Kung, Hans
1976 *The Church.* Garden City NY: Image Books.

Lakeland, Paul
1977 *Can Women Be Priests?* Cork: Mercier Press
1986a *Freedom in Christ.* New York: Fordham University Press.
1986b *The Politics of Salvation: Hegel's Idea of the State.* Albany NY: SUNY Press.
1990 *Theology and Critical Theory: The Discourse of the Church.* Nashville TN: Abingdon Press.
1992 "The Lay Theologian in the Church," *The Month* 25, January 1992, pp. 19–25.
1995 "For Whom Do We Write? The Responsibility of the Theologian," in *The Promise of Critical Theology: Essays in Honour of Charles Davis.* Edited by Marc P. Lalonde. Waterloo, Ontario: Wilfrid Laurier Press, pp. 33–48.

Lernoux, Penny
1981 *Cry of the People.* New York: Penguin Books.
1989 *People of God: The Struggle for World Catholicism.* New York: Penguin Books.

Schillebeeckx, E.
1986 *Ministry: Leadership in the Community of Jesus Christ.* New York: Crossroad Books.

Schreiter, Robert
1985 *Constructing Local Theologies.* New York: Orbis Books.

Segundo, Juan Luis
1992 *The Liberation of Theology.*

Swidler, Leonard and Arlene (eds.)
1977 *Women Priests? A Catholic Commentary on the Vatican Declaration.* New York: Paulist Press.

Tavard, George
1973 *Woman in Christian Tradition.* Notre Dame IN: University of Notre Dame Press.

van der Meer, Haye
1973 *Women Priests in the Catholic Church?* Philadelphia: Temple University Press.

Endnotes

1 Consider, for example, the much-quoted statement of the First Vatican Council that "the Church is not a community of equals in which all the faithful have the same rights, " but "a society of unequals." The inequality shows itself to the Council fathers in two ways: first, "some are clerics and some are laymen"; second, and not unrelated, "because there is in the Church the power from God whereby to some it is given to sanctify, teach and govern, and to others not" (quoted in Dulles, 43). The permanent childhood of the laity is thus written into conciliar teaching, if not into divine law.

2 These concerns were at the heart of the conference for which this paper was prepared, and represent leading issues for the conference convener, Michael Warren, whose work on the "material practices of the local church" is so helpful.

3 A recent and notable exception to this judgment is Bernard J. Lee in his *The Future Church of 140 B.C.E.: A Hidden Revolution.*

4 See especially chapters two and four of the Second Vatican Council's Dogmatic Constitution on the Church, *Lumen Gentium* (Flannery 359–69, 388–96) and the Decree on the Apostolate of Laypeople, *Apostolicam Actuositatem* (Flannery 766–98).

5 I am greatly indebted at this point to the insightful critique of Edward Farley, who alerted me to the need to be more precise about the character of the problem.

6 Both Hans Kung and Edward Schillebeeckx deal with this issue at length, particularly in the former's *The Church* and the latter's *Ministry: Leadership in the Community of Jesus Christ.*

7 "All Catholics in and of the Diocese of Lincoln are forbidden to be members of the organizations and groups listed below. Membership in these organizations or groups is always perilous to the Catholic faith and most often is totally incompatible with the Catholic faith.

Planned Parenthood
Society of St. Pius X (Lefebvre group)
Hemlock Society
Call to Action
Call to Action Nebraska
St. Michael the Archangel Chapel
Freemasons
Job's Daughters
DeMolay
Eastern Star
Rainbow Girls
Catholics for a Free Choice

Any Catholics in and of the Diocese of Lincoln who attain or retain membership in any of the above-listed organizations or groups after April 15, 1996, are by that very fact under interdict and are absolutely forbidden to receive holy communion. Contumacious persistence in such membership for one month following the interdict on part of any such Catholics will by that very fact cause them to be excommunicated. Absolution from these ecclesial censures is "reserved to the bishop." Bishop Fabian Bruskewitz, Lincoln, Nebraska, 3/19/96

8 He said this in the mid-seventies in a private, informal conversation that I have never forgotten.

9 Accounts of individuals such as Charles Curran and Leonardo Boff of the process to which they were subjected show how basic rights — to know that an investigation is being conducted, to know the charges, and to presence, participation and counsel in the process — are systematically excluded by the Vatican. On this whole question of authority, see Granfield 1987.

10 Because I have been at some pains to locate oppression in structures rather than in the role of individuals in the church, it is possible to recognize that these structures may truly oppress at least some of those who seem outwardly to be beneficiaries of them. The structures set up a clergy/lay division, but they are set up by a centralized authority that allows little if any real voice to the bishops of the periphery and even less to the priests who have most direct contact with the laity. This may well represent, it seems to me, a re-seizure of power by an essentially bureaucratic organ of the church (the Roman curia) with no theological standing, in face of which even the episcopacy is largely powerless. The precise determination of when this coup d'état occurred is difficult to determine. But it is much easier to recognize that the teachings of the Second Vatican Council represent the (hopefully temporarily) suspended constitution.

Chapter 8

What Does a Local Church Look Like?

Rosemary Luling Haughton

In the previous essay, Paul Lakeland wrote of the need for authentic lay voices in the church. Rosemary Luling Haughton has been one of those voices for over 35 years as a prolific writer and activist. In 1967 she published her influential book, The Transformation of Man: A Study of Conversion and Community *(Springfield IL: Templegate, 1967), connecting psychological concerns with the move to a community of others joined by the Spirit of Jesus: the church. The foreword to this book was written by Daniel Callahan, another lay person who has been an articulate voice in ethics. Haughton's writings have allowed her to speak out for more attention to the experience of lay Christians in all aspects of their lives, including their experience of their sexual relationships.*

In 1974 she co-founded Lothlorian, a therapeutic community in Southwest Scotland, serving the needs of persons with psychological hardships. In 1981 she and a group of lay persons on Massachusetts' North Shore established Wellspring House in Gloucester, a historic fishing town. What they have done since has been a carefully planned and evolving response to the needs of that community of fishing people and others fallen on hard times.

In the following essay Haughton reflects on the localness of the local church and on the particularities of those who people it. They dwell in particular socio-economic locales, are affected by particular environmental and ecological factors and are controlled by decisions of non-elected corporate functionaries. Especially for people at the bottom of the power pyramid, the church might in such situations be an exemplar of what a human community not based on the status quo could be like. She points to two time-honored ways of being local church: one by working for change from within the social structures needing change (the missionary local church), the other by offering an alternative to what needs changing (the "ordinary" local church). Most of her essay is concerned with this second way of being. She offers the ancient, loosely organized Celtic churches as a powerful example of the second way of being a local church.

Haughton's vision of church is not of its inner life alone but of the connectedness of that inner life to the social and environmental conditions within which it lives. As she puts it, "a local, responsible, land-based community is not only a central part of the Christian tradition but is exactly what is demanded of us if a human future is to be sustainable on this planet."

Readers would do well to note how often in her essay Haughton speaks of the importance of the imagination in deciding how to be a local church — and indeed, how to be human is a way that will sustain our planet for the future. Her essay is visionary in the sense of inviting groups of persons to re-vision living the gospel in ways appropriate to our time. She herself has shown such re-visioning can be tailored to the particular needs of particular locales. In the end her essay invites readers to form groups to examine the questions she raises.

In the 1960s Harvey Cox lifted the hearts of many urban Christians in the Western world by suggesting that the "secular city" was a place where God could be encountered, and encouraged Christians to look for the places of divine epiphany in the interactions of urban situations in which close community was a rarity and most of the people with whom one interacted were strangers or known only in a workplace or marketplace situation. This challenge to confront a useless nostalgia for neighborhood closeness and known community was important, but the experience of forty years has made it necessary to take another look at the issue and to ask whether the premise on which such ideas were developed was correct: that the "secular city," in the sense that phrase has been used, is what we have, it is the fact, and therefore it is the "place: — not so much geographically as culturally — where we necessarily have to experience church, in some sense or other.

The experience of forty years — of rising profits and rising crime, of growing wealth and a growing "outer class," of separated and secured neighborhoods for those who can afford them and devastated and dangerous neighborhoods for those who cannot, of rapidly increasing health problems from pollution of air and water and food, of unaccountable, unelected control by huge corporations of decisions about people's lives and the unquestioned acceptance of "market" values as the new infallibility — all these facts of modern life have made many people question whether the secular city is in fact redeemable. Is it, in any sense, a place where "church" can be realized?

My purpose in this essay is to suggest that there are two ways in which "church" can be realized in the secular city: One is as mission. The other — in my view by far the most important — is to look at the goal of the missionaries' efforts toward conversion of the secular city. My proposal is that what a local church looks like is more like a village than a city, not necessarily in a literal sense but in important senses that make the village a useful model in imagining what local church can, should and even occasionally does look like.

The most obvious way in which church can be realized in the secular city, no matter how degraded and immoral such a city may be, is in a missionary capacity. The tradition of mission in the church is an inherent part of its nature; it is the original impulse from the lifetime of Jesus onwards, though in very various and sometimes even disastrous forms. There is certainly a desperate need for mission in the secular city, far more now than when late nineteenth- and early twentieth-century Christians created "settlements" in overcrowded and desperately poor areas of the new industrial cities, in the hope of bringing some element of practical hope, some kind of model of what a human community could be like, to people at the bottom of the heap socially and economically. The settlement movement was a middle class movement, and some of it can be characterized as elitist and not seldom insensitive or self-righteous, but at its best — an inspiring best — it was a missionary movement in the true sense, bringing a gospel vision to people trapped in an oppressive system. There is more and more need for such missionary work now and indeed many groups, such as the Catholic Worker, are engaged in it; but the point about real missionary work, and the kind of local church it creates and requires, is that its intention is to *change* the situation in which it operates.

Missionaries go on mission not in order to melt into a culture but to change it. Even if mission is undertaken with deep respect for the people and the culture among whom and within which missionaries work, the underlying reason for being there is to offer something different from what already exists. This can be seen not so much as "converting" people as offering a long-term vision of unity and wholeness; but if there were no intention of altering the situation there would be no point in being there. The missionary form of church is present in alien and often horrible situations in order to offer, by word or by example, or just by being there, an alternative vision of what life can be like. As soon as the missionaries become part of the situation, in the sense that they no longer see a need for anything other, they are no longer missionaries; they are simply a religious version of whatever the status quo may be. Indeed, given the fact that theology is always hindsight, a great deal of the life of all the mainstream Christian churches has been conducted on the basis of a theology developed in order to justify and "Christianize" the status quo. Even Saint Paul did it, finding ways to spiritualize the patriarchal structures of the day by interpreting them in such a way as to make them appear to be a part of

God's plan of salvation. The requirement of the obedience of slaves and women to their masters, and of all Christians to secular authorities, is just such a theologizing of the status quo as the church has engaged in ever since, including the accommodation of the churches with the systems of slavery, with the death penalty, with the routine subjection of women and even — at least by some church people — with the Nazi system and other totalitarian or oligarchic monstrosities. There is justification for this, if the premise be that the church's primary duty is to survive; but it is not a missionary stance, even though sometimes excused by the statement that unless it survives, the church cannot carry on its mission.

There is a great need for local missionary churches in the secular city, of all kinds. These churches inevitably require a tight-knit, very conscious kind of community, for a missionary church is in some respects inevitably alien. However hard it works to make itself attractive, its nature is to be alien in the sense that it is experientially different: to be different, and to offer different ways of living, thinking and hoping, is what the church is there for. Some churches of this kind can consist of units of small groups within a workplace, in the fashion of the *"Jocistes"* or Young Christian Workers, or it can be more like the settlement houses, an enclave in the vast urban sea but one that is hospitable, available and aware of what it stands for. It can be a whole parish or at least a sizable portion of one, as some parishes were when they took on the work of rescuing and concealing illegal refugees from El Salvador. It can be the work of a single leader — a bishop or advocate for the poor — and those nearest to him or her. In all these forms, and others, there is a strong sense of a shared vision that is needed by those around, whether they know it or not.

A question that arises from such an experience is: What does the missionary vision see? What is offered — whether patiently, respectfully and tactfully or with an intolerant zeal — as an alternative? What do missionaries see as a "normal" way of being church, if the world around clearly is not it?

At this point in the history of Christianity we can no longer assume that the goal of mission work is simply to convert everyone else to

Christianity. We are too aware of the mistakes and crimes of Christians of the past to feel that such a motivation is going to usher in the reign of God, even if mass conversion of that kind were possible. An awareness has developed that the structures of society are the business of the church.

This concept has become accepted by the Roman church and has formed the subject matter of church documents from the encyclicals of Leo XIII to the pastoral letter of the bishops of Appalachia, "This Land Is Home to Me"; it has been true in most churches and has included both more and less radical critiques. There was and is still a tendency to want to preserve a distance between church life and secular life, and to assign to lay-people the job of influencing secular life as a separate category; but this dualism has become increasingly difficult to maintain, either intellectually or in practice, especially when church bodies refuse to their own faithful the civil rights and due process which they demand for others in the name of justice. So if mission is less about converting people to Christianity and more about proposing an alternative to existing secular or religious structures, one that is conceived to be nearer to the vision proclaimed by Jesus, it becomes essential for that vision to be concrete and practical and *visible* — or at least practically imaginable — as well as visionary and prophetic. The "visionary and prophetic" bit means that we propose a way of life that is whole and perfect beyond what we can possibly expect to achieve without miraculous transformation, but the practical part means that what we propose must have a shape, a structure, a dynamic that people can actually imagine living in their daily lives. That is where the other kind of local church comes in.

Mission is, of course, an essential aspect of all church life, and to call what I am discussing "non-missionary" simply means that its way of life as church need not be dictated by the needs of the particular missionary situation but has room to consider "church" as a whole way for believers — that is, human beings — to live, work, play and relate to one another. Local church is where this can or could possibly happen, and mission depends on this for its credibility.

There are always two ways to go about the business of change: one is to work for change from within the structures that need to change, relying for sanity and spiritual support on others engaged in the same subversive activity; the other is to work at providing a visible model of an alternative to what needs changing. The missionary local church is the first; the "ordinary" local church is the other, though, of course, it isn't really ordinary at all but demands a great deal of thought, commitment, hard work and obstinacy.

The creation of "ordinary" local churches that are neither missionary in nature nor too much corrupted by the world in which they live is not a new idea for Christians. For a start, Jesus himself was a villager who, schooled in the prophets of Israel, disliked and denounced the commercial priorities that were destroying the fabric of rural life for the benefit of profiteers — whether Jewish, Greek or Roman — in cities of the empire. Evidence from recent archeological and scriptural research helps to nurture the unexpected (to modern Christians) insight that what Jesus was about was the re-creation of community based in the work patterns of interdependency of an agricultural society. Paradoxically, his missionaries were to be mobile and kin-less solely in order to be free to preach a return to stable, communitarian, non-patriarchal rural communities on the prophetic model, in which the children, the women and the poor would have a place and value that the greedy city culture would never accord them.

The church, as it moved into the urban-centered world of the empire, soon lost sight of the original prophetic context of Jesus' preaching and "spiritualized" it to the point where it lost any practical reference at all. We cannot blame those heroic pioneers for this shift, which hindsight may make us regret but which was scarcely recognized at the time, for people do not recognize the loss of something so familiar that they have never been driven to define it or describe it. It is intriguing to suggest (it can be only a suggestion) that there is a connection between this shift and the extraordinary disappearance from Acts — and therefore presumably from any written or verbal "official" records made available to Luke when he was compiling Acts — of the names of any of the women mentioned in the four gospels, with the exception of Mary, the mother of Jesus, who is mentioned in the first chapter and then disappears. It is likely that a controversy in the Jerusalem church over the role of women (who were a tough, independent-minded and close-knit group) was the cause of a split, and that those women were excluded from the official mission. Is it conceivable that the women, less involved in commercial or power structures, were sensitive to the loss in the developing church structure of some aspects of the good news they had heard, and that this contributed to their banishment from effective ecclesial roles? It is noticeable, and indeed entirely natural given the thrust of the mission thereafter, that the women mentioned in Acts and in the epistles were all urban, and none had known Jesus.

The vision was not entirely lost; it was re-created in a different yet recognizable form in the monastic enterprise. In the Benedictine form this created agricultural communities which, with their many dependents and links to local people, formed stable centers of what might now be called a "holistic" lifestyle. The more fluid Celtic version of monasticism took over from the pre-Christian Celtic model of rural community and was very inclusive to the point where lines between the monks and nuns and the "lay" people who worked and lived with them were often unclear. These monastic centers gave a focus to local life, not only spiritually but commercially. Both cases were responses to a felt need to create a place where people could live by the gospel vision.

Variations of this vision have included medieval Beguines in France and the Netherlands (large communities of unvowed single laywomen living in specially built neighborhoods and supporting themselves by their work), and the seventeenth-century "Diggers" in England and other radical groups who tried to establish practical, self-sufficient alternative communities of believers. Several of the groups of religious immigrants to the New World come into this category — the Amish, the Hutterites, the Shakers, for instance. The first two groups consisted of families, mainly of farmers, and the last — now numbering only a handful of faithful people — of celibate men and women in specially built communal villages.

The Shakers in particular were for over a hundred years extremely successful in creating self-sustaining rural communities combining efficient farming with some innovative commercial projects such as the production of packeted seeds to bring in a cash income. Celibate Shakes men and women lived side by side in separate parts of the same houses and — possibly uniquely — combining absolute equality of the sexes throughout their leadership structure with separation of gender roles. Their model worked, spiritually and practically, in a country where the founding fathers' ideal of the self-sufficient family farm was becoming harder and harder to maintain. The Shakers dwindled in the end for various reasons, among which (apart from the fact that they did not have children) were the competition of factory-produced goods and the improvement in women's legal and social position in the world outside, making the starkly simple, celibate way of life less attractive to women. All of these rural and agriculturally based models, and others, worked to create a real, workable, self-sustaining economic unit, a place where people could live out all aspects of their lives in the context of a commitment to the gospel.

In all of these examples, with one exception, all the people involved were committed to the shared and conscious vision they tried to embody. Otherwise, they would not have been there. Nowadays, some Amish and Hutterite young people do, in fact, leave their communities because, though they may love and respect what that way of life represents, they find it too narrow and perhaps too rigid and patriarchal. Similar or related feelings have made many men and women leave such places of embodied vision, sometimes in a rage, sometimes with sadness and a sense of loss.

The exception, however, is interesting, and that is the Celtic type of local church. The Celtic tradition has recently been much studied by theologians and ecclesiologists because in the history of Catholic Christianity, and indeed of any mainstream Christian traditions, it stands out as peculiar: It doesn't fit. Lasting for roughly a thousand years from its beginning to its final decline, Celtic Christianity had its sources in the missionary work of monks who brought with them the ascetic and eremitic version of monasticism of the African desert fathers. Predating St. Patrick, they went to Ireland and to what is now Scotland, to Wales, Brittany and Cornwall; though they did convert, they went primarily to find places of withdrawal — suitably "desert" locations for their little, intense and severely ascetic communities of prayer. They did not foresee that their preaching would result in drastically curtailing that very monastic remoteness, for in time their reputation for holiness naturally gathered "congregations" around them, in all but the most remote and inhospitable locations, and made them the center of local life. In some ways the monks took over the mystique of the Druids, being regarded as sources of wisdom and divine revelation. While the Celtic local communities continued their ancient matrilocal and hearth-centered patterns, with the women being the holders of the land and of the sense of sacred place and continuity, while the men were cattle raiders and heroes, the monks provided a vision and example of a different kind of spiritual hero-struggle, replacing the hero-tales and exploits of the pagan Celtic past.

There was, in Celtic Christianity, that very strong ascetic strand and the obsessive fear of sexuality among the monks, which led to the fierce "penitentials." In time it led to the gradual erosion of the important role of women in the Celtic church at large and in relation to the role of nuns, who had to some extent taken over the lost leadership roles as hearth-keepers and owners of the land of pagan Celtic women. As Christianity undermined the women's status, yet these losses (from our point of view) somehow managed to continue with a profound sense of joyful interdependence with all of nature. In any case, Celtic monastic centers worked, as a model that enabled self-sustaining local communities for extended periods of time. Where the monks or nuns made their homes there grew up loosely organized settlements, some small and comparatively remote and some quite large and including local markets at the intersection of well-used networks of ways that connected these rural centers of population. The kings still lived in their "castles" (but we should not imagine Norman-type stone castles; these were mainly wooden and small) and bishops, in time, moved around the country and ordained and exhorted, but there were, until the Anglo-Norman invasions of Ireland, no diocesan structures, no feudal system. The churches of Wales and Scotland as well as Ireland long resisted the Roman church structures.

As an example of local church this one is certainly not a working model for contemporary Christians but it is interesting because although it was local — responding to local needs and dependent on local skills and economic viability — it was also linked to larger monastic centers of learning, for instance, that at Whithorn in Galloway in southwest Scotland; and monks and nuns traveled and carried ideas and began new settlements. Such a form of church was influenced by the politics of kings and even more of abbots (who were usually laymen), but the rural dependence on local economy meant that unless they were invaded by the Vikings or the Normans such churches had a freedom to develop their own way of doing things. Out of all this came a wealth of beauty in metalwork and illumination (though little in architecture — churches were simple to the point of starkness) and in poetry, in the bardic tradition. There was a remarkably easygoing community of belief (in spite of those penitentials) and no heresy hunting. Much of the pre-Christian mythology and the pagan divine pantheon were preserved and revered; Christian saints gradually assumed the identity and worship of the old gods and goddesses and adopted their holy wells, mountains and rituals.

There are for us two important aspects of this way of being local church. One is that the people involved were not all, or necessarily, part of the community they lived in by vocation or even strong conviction. They were there because their living was there and most of them felt that the monks or nuns were a source of blessing as well as, often, of teaching and protection. These were churches consisting of all kinds of people of varying virtue, skill or conviction, but who all made up the thing called church.

The other aspect is the fact that these churches were rural. They took the shape they did precisely because they were virtually entirely rural, as well as because the lack of centralized diocesan and feudal authority made it easier and safer for local people to make local decisions according to their needs. At first sight this latter reason might seem to make the Celtic experience less than useful for a highly urbanized society, but I suggest that in fact it provides both a criterion for questioning our assumptions about the inevitability of the secular city as our normal modern habitat and a challenge to ourselves to ask what it is about a rural situation that offers a healthy locus for the growth of local church. This criterion and this challenge, however, though peculiarly well displayed by the idiosyncratic (according to our usual standards) Celtic model, are equally displayed by other situations, not all of them embedded in the distant past.

There were once thousands of small rural churches in Europe which, while at least in theory more controlled by a diocesan hierarchy and a feudal system than the Celtic, continued for centuries to be places where ordinary people identified themselves in relation to their parish, and where the church building and the rituals and laws of the church shaped everyday life. Again, it was the rural separation that made this cohesion possible. Although medieval towns were tiny compared to modern ones, they already made possible a greater degree of anonymity and fostered the tendency to identify one's significant community according to trade or rank rather than by location. A recent book by Richard Critchfield called *The Villagers* is based on twenty years of visiting and studying village life in Europe, Africa, Asia and South America; he discusses in it the pattern of village life in widely separated regions which show an astounding consistency of attitudes and expectations underlying obvious differences. Villagers were — and are still in some places — held together by their economic need for each other, which also encouraged systems of practical help for people in need, and the bond was also at least implicitly a religious one. There was a shared belief system that shaped attitudes, customs and what people expected of one another. This applied even if explicit supernatural beliefs were rejected by some. As in the Celtic model, this religion was less a matter of personally acquired conviction than of something inherited and taken for granted as a description of reality and the basis of hopes and expectations and moral decisions. This "folk" religion was, and is, shaped by a particular belief system (Christian, Islam, etc.) that was in its turn shaped in its expression and its expectations of conduct by the conditions of a particular kind of rural life and an interdependent local community.

Where village life survives now in Europe and even the United States, it is complicated not only by the easy accessibility of alternatives to rural life and the constant pressure of urban expectations via television and schools, but by the fact that few villages now are populated by single denominations. Religion is separated from daily life if only because people go to church in different buildings, as they do in cities. However, it is interesting that people in villages engage in locally centered non-denominational or multi-denominational projects and festivities more easily than do those who in suburbs and cities gather by interests — political, religious, social.

Worldwide, villages have been drastically changed, if not wiped out, in the last fifty years. Agribusiness, that destroys the peasant and small farmer's ability to earn a living, has been the main agent, whether in a collectivized form under communism or in a capitalist corporate form in the West. The consequent need to find other ways to earn a living has depopulated rural areas, even more than the attractiveness of urban lifestyle, which has drawn young people from villages the world over, and the propaganda that equates rural life with stupidity and "backwardness." What we in the United States call "villages" are often really retirement colonies, or housing developments for the well-to-do, or even merely collections of stores, boutiques and restaurants with folksy facades. They are labeled "villages" because that word still carries associations of Old World values and social cohesiveness and can be seen as an alternative to the "faceless" suburbs.

Villages as they used to be were not by any means all good: slaves ("villeins" in feudal Europe) in many places, wife-beating and a narrow-minded "parish pump" mentality have been parts of village life for millennia. Those villages that remain — and there are still hundreds of thousands of them — are having to look for a different basis for their economic survival, and that is being done in many places with radical imagination and a lot of energy, specifically in Finland where a movement to preserve and restore village life has become a national priority.

None of this makes it highly likely that the remaining villages — even the real ones — could, as they stand, be viable models of local church now. Once, villages *were* local church, but that time is long past. My point here is to use the village experience to challenge the notion that the secular city must be accepted as the norm it claims to be and, therefore, as the only real place to form a contemporary ecclesiology. If it is not the norm, if there might be another way that would make the concept of local church more realistically imaginable, then what would be required to make that image a reality? Given the fact that any such alternative possibility is a long-term one, what can local church look like meanwhile?

I have looked briefly at some characteristics of villages historically. To summarize them in relation to a concept of local church: a village is a complex of human population at least partially dependent on the land around it for livelihood, either primarily or secondarily (i.e., farmers grow food but need to buy other things — tools, clothes, etc.). It is linked to other centers of population but has an effective level of internal self-sufficiency socially, economically and often educationally. Even now, it has effective systems of mutual help. As a model of local church, the village expresses inclusiveness, a community of people who are not a spiritual elite but a mixture of levels of spiritual awareness, yet who share in a common system of symbols and rituals that interpret their life-experience.

However, the village concept also makes it clear that a church is not just about the worship and moral conduct of human beings but about behavior of humans as interdependent with other created beings in a community that is, in some ways, a microcosm of the global community of creatures who depend on one another for survival. (At least, human beings depend on other beings; the rest of creation could get by very nicely without us.) Consequently, the life of a local church cannot be complete and healthy without reference to the life-systems that support its existence.

This is the point at which it becomes clear that the attempt to locate local church in the secular city can create no more than a weak and one-sided parody of what church can be. We have become so used to treating the gospels as primarily a moral manual that it is easy to forget that the context of Jesus' words about the reign of God, building on the prophets before him, was a village, as I mentioned earlier: a human community closely and essentially bonded to the land. Because the early mission spread most easily and quickly via big cities along major trade routes, the consequent "spiritualization" of the message to which I have referred was no doubt inevitable, but even the cities of the empire at that date were small by our standards, and city people knew, and took for granted, their dependence on the people who grew the food they ate, even if they often despised them, as urban people easily do. The country people (the *pagani*) remained "pagan" for much longer because of this typically urban assumption that the city is where the important things happen.

With so much history and such clear (and tragically learned) knowledge of our interdependence with all creation and of our dependence on it for health and for healthy earth, water and food, we have not now the excuse of our ancestors in faith, even up to the last generation, for thinking that the self-evaluation of the secular city can be a sane focus of human, let alone Christian, life. We need cities as indispensable centers of culture and learning, places where new ideas can break through the important but limited concerns of the village, where there is room for the strange or the challenging, where people from many places can meet and exchange thought, symbol, technical knowledge and artistic experience. But the vast cities that now imprison millions of the poor, that destroy health and hope (and create wealth for the wealthy to enable them to exploit the rest of creation), are dinosaurs left over from the industrial revolution that required thousands of easily accessible "hands" to run machines. Such cancerous growths are a travesty of what cities can and should be. Now, technology makes it possible to decentralize much of the work we assumed had to be done in huge factories or high-rise office buildings. The secular city as a human ideal is doomed, and in its dying it is killing millions who cannot afford to go anywhere else. The constant efforts at renewing the inner city are well meant, and a lot better than nothing, but they are still based on the demonstrably false premise that huge cities are the normal places for human beings to live.

Such cities are the reality — but we need not dignify them by trying to demonstrate normative status for them. Virtue is, and will be, in them because humans are capable of amazing courage, ingenuity and obstinate hope; but that does not sanctify the reality that evokes those virtues, any more than the undoubted heroism of many soldiers justifies war.

We have to live with this reality but we also need to be imagining alternatives. It is the church as missionary that comes into play in dealing with the reality, but the imagination of the church at large also needs to be reaching out towards some form of church life that expresses more nearly both the gospel vision and the need of the current earthly reality. Can we imagine a decentralized population, with thousands of smaller centers of life and work (including high-tech work) linked visibly and daily and directly with the land on which its life depends? Can we imagine a local church that took that vision as its goal, celebrating God's creative power at work in the whole marvelous complex of lives and respecting all ritualizing the seasons of human and all created life? After all, it is those seasons that have in fact formed the symbols and rituals of the major Christian churches, implicitly reminding us, year after year, that we are one with the earth from which we spring and to which we return. Can we see such a church vitalized by a rediscovery of the profound meaning of those ancient symbols and rituals that grew from experience of life in the land — village life? Can we dare to recognize the way in which differences of history and customs among Christians might seem less important as the deeper symbols, drawn from daily experienced reality, were shared?

That is the vision, and it is one that many people are already working to make a reality, as human beings and as religious people. A few years ago, Robert van de Weyer of Cambridge, England, wrote a remarkable book chronicling the story of a small English village, an imaginary but typical midlands village called "Wickwyn," from the standpoint of an imaginary historian a half century from now. Van de Weyer traced Wickwyn's history from medieval times to a sizable and prosperous community in the nineteenth century and through its decline in the twentieth century to little else than a dormitory for people working in the city; but then he imagined its resurrection into a vital, self-sustaining community in the first half of the twenty-first century. Van de Weyer sees this as a real and practical possibility because of discontent with the city among enterprising people with the will to change, who would, he suggests, be pioneers in (literally) rebuilding the village, living in trailers meanwhile! He sees them working at home with computers or locally at light industry, but also working on plots of land to grow food they would need. He foresees the creation of local schools, clinics, etc. run partly by volunteers, with money raised locally to pay the necessary professionals. He sees other city people attracted to this example and establishing a healthy level of population with links to local towns and (downsized) cities where universities, large hospitals, theatres and government are located, while the village maintains its own local institutions.

It is important that Van de Weyer sees as the heart of this resurrected village the old village church, which, in his vision, is to be used by the whole community for its celebrations and services as well as for denominational services for those that want them.

Echoing this vision, there are some models with similar features. “Tele-villages” are actually being built in a few places, which combine high-tech accessibility for business with life in a rural community that grows food and supports its own institutions. Many architects, planners, ecologists and agriculturalists are designing and have actually created some real-life, full-fledged, village-type neighborhoods in which people can walk to stores, schools, entertainment, churches and at least some gardening and green space. These are, of course, mostly for middle- class or wealthy people, and are likely, as they stand (or could stand), merely to increase the gap between rich and poor, between the possessors and the disenfranchised. The point here is that, while a generation ago the trend was to high-rise apartment or suburban, zoned-for-residence development, newer developments show an awareness that it is better for people to live in places where they can know one another, interact with their physical environment and have local responsibility.

It can be done. But the spiritual aspect of such a vision of practical possibility is less well addressed by the assumptions of contemporary planners.

Perhaps it is time for some pioneering by Christians, who have in their heritage a very good basis for understanding why a local, responsible, land-based community is not only a central part of the Christian tradition (stemming directly from the Hebrew prophetic tradition) but is exactly what is demanded of us if human future is to be sustainable on this planet. If we can pour money into the missionary aspect of the church's work, can we have the vision to devote some to the creation of local churches that could inspire hope and purpose in those confined by the reality of the secular city? Unlike the planners of middle-class professional "villages" (encouraging though that phenomenon may be in some ways), can we envisage a local church that consists of many different kinds of people, drawn together by different motives yet committed to the creation of a sane and just way of life such as Jesus envisaged?

(It is always opportune to remind ourselves, with the power of hindsight, that what Jesus proposed in terms of ways for human beings to relate to each other — in justice, compassion and humility — is not merely a preferable option for the soul's sake but, at this time, the only recipe for ultimate human survival.)

Supposing some pioneering effort of this kind were undertaken, it would not be the first time even in this century; as I have suggested, there are examples old and new of Christians trying to create alternative rural communities, from some early immigrants to this country to Catholic Worker farms and a number of other contemporary Christian rural communities. These have, however, been regarded as necessarily exceptional; because of that, they have attracted only certain kinds of people, and have been viewed as (and often are) escapist. This is not to discount the value of such experiences, which provide a store of valuable knowledge. However, two things make the present needs different. One is that we need not just farms and farmers but integrated communities of many trades, skills and kinds, with realistic and regular links to larger centers for all kinds of purposes. We must have a well-informed and long-range view of the development of non-land-based jobs, as well as, and together with, food production, so as to sustain a viable population. The other is that our awareness of ecological balances, and of the demand for and experiences in food production methods that are *both* intensive *and* "natural," has created a much more sophisticated understanding of how a human population can sustain itself on a particular area of land. All this impels a new and deeper theological awareness as the underpinning of what we can mean by local church.

Having said all this, and supposing a vision of this kind were to inform future development of local churches by creating new ones or calling on new energies in old ones, this leaves us with the immense challenge of the existing urban reality.

This is mission territory, and that is in some ways self-explanatory. But whether the goal is to convert individual people to Christianity or whether it has a wider task, what Christianity proposes as its alternative to the situation where mission is called for must itself naturally shape the methodology of mission. In many places the stark and immediate needs require a mission that concentrates on providing necessities of life — food, shelter, medical care. But where there is scope for more, it becomes important to ask what the priorities are. What is the model of church that is proposed, tacitly or explicitly? It is interesting that projects initiated or supported by urban churches have included housing projects, some quite large and some built with help from the eventual inhabitants, often including space for stores and places of recreation, arts, etc. They have also included city gardening and park projects. In other words, such church projects have tried to create a place for people to live in, neighborhoods that have some characteristics of human and natural community. It becomes possible in such an environment for people to feel sufficiently safe, and motivated, to tackle issues of crime, drugs and city government's normal lack of interest in poor neighborhoods.

People come together with enthusiasm and commitment when they are able to perceive real, practical hope. Whether it be for the improvement of a local school, for cooperative ownership and renovation of neglected housing or for the growing of healthier food, community projects not only achieve a specific purpose but *create the community that pursues it*. In most cases such projects, which can aim as high as the transformation of an entire neighborhood, take many years, involve struggle and disappointment and require the acquisition of a lot of political, technical and organization skills, not to mention fundraising skills. If they survive, projects such as these have — must have — a strong basis of spiritual commitment, a vision and a hope that goes beyond the foreseen practical gains to a different experience of how people can be together.

Is such a community a church? In some sense, perhaps it is, but in any case the existence of such project-originated communities is a challenge to our sense of what a local church can be, and do. City neighborhoods are not villages, and lack the resources of land to develop in an obvious way the full sense of an interdependent community of created beings, but they are places where the vision can actually be realized in spiritual and practical terms, and links to the land provided by direct trading links to both farmers and truck gardeners, outside the city. Investing in community-supported agriculture is now being done in various ways, exchanging labor for food or putting up cash and taking the "interest" in food; city gardens can be, and many already are being, developed in whatever spaces are available, and planning for these frequently goes on whenever new development is in hand.

In ways like these, local churches in "mission territory" are able not only to preach an alternative vision but to take a lead in realizing the vision. It is unlikely that the huge populations of our time will ever be completely decentralized, but it is theoretically possible, given the current development of intensive yet "natural" and biologically sustainable methods of agriculture, such as those taught by the International Permaculture Institute. But it is not unreal to envisage cities that are broken down into neighborhoods, in turn separated by areas of community gardening, park, woodland and wildlife habitats.

The population of the United States leveled off in 1972 and is slowly declining. Richard Critchfield suggests that it is the immigrants from Mexico and other places, people with origins and spiritual roots in villages, who can revitalize the cities, because of their sense of place, of community, of spiritual interdependence with the land. In our own country, could we look to our American "Third

World" in West Virginia and other parts of the rural Appalachia? Whether Critchfield is right or not, this insight suggests that local church, in the sense explored here, is something the churches could study as a main focus of mission.

All over the world, faith communities have been able to mobilize tremendous resources of courage, imagination, ingenuity and patience to confront injustice. What I am suggesting here is that a viable, practical form of local church can emerge from the mobilization of those energies not only to react to injustice but to be proactive by creating what may properly be called "just societies" — small but possibly numerous, interconnected in ways that an international church system makes very possible, and that technology facilitates.

Such churches *have* to be based in what might be called "ecological justice." We know too much now to suppose that a notion of justice that ignores the life-systems on which humans depend can be sustainable in the long term. What was excusable in our forebears is plain idiocy for us. The village image gives us a reference point for working out what a just society, even on a small scale, can look like. We certainly need "real" villages, villages able to sustain a rural life that is actually allowed to grow healthy food and to maintain an integrated and sustainable pattern of wild and cultivated areas. Without them the towns and cities cannot in the long term be healthy in any sense at all. The decline of health in the whole nation — in the whole world — is becoming so obvious, and the reasons for it so clear, that it is harder and harder for interested bodies (agribusinesses and corporate businesses dependent on polluting toxins, and the governments they bully) to deny the links.

Granted the need for "real" villages and what they imply in terms of land use, however, we can take heart and take knowledge even in the great cities from what villages demonstrate. We can build local churches around the need of human beings for a life that is hopeful, accountable, sustainable, safe. It means working *with* people, not *for* them. It means offering a vision and learning the means to make it real. It means drawing community need, hope and vision into worship and bringing the power of faith to the tasks affirmed in prayer. It means mutual caring translated into action and the learning and sharing that action requires — all brought back to prayer and worship and celebration. It is not new, it is happening, it needs to be pointed to and affirmed, because this is local church.

References

In researching this essay I drew on my own previous work, the references for which I often did not preserve. The subject matter of this essay has been and is being written about widely, and many books are available on specific topics, e.g., Celtic culture, Shakers, "humane" town planning, etc. This list simply names a few books I found helpful and relevant, directly or indirectly.

The Celts, Nora Chadwick, Penguin.
The Shaker Adventure, Marguerite Fellow Melcher, The Shaker Museum.
The Land, Walter Brueggemann, Fortress Press.
The Villagers, Richard Critchfield, Anchor Books, Doubleday.
Wickwyn, Robert van de Weyer, Green Books, Bideford, Devon, England
Cities of Tomorrow, Peter Hall, Blackwell
The Health of Nations, Robert van de Weyer, Green Books, Bideford, Devon, England.

Postscript

Since writing this essay I have encountered (there is no other word for it) a book called *Gaviotas: A Village to Reinvent the World*, by Alan Weisman (Chelsea Green Publishing Co., White River Junction, Vermont). I also saw his slide show, which is important because the book has few illustrations, and this is a great loss. I can only recommend that many read it.

The book is about a group of scientists and engineers who, since 1966, together with the few local people, have created a flourishing village community in the most desolate and infertile area of Colombia. They chose this place precisely because it was so unpromising, since if establishing a community could be done there, it could be done anywhere.

By a mixture of scientific knowledge and skill, unbridled imagination, not much money and a lot of luck they found ways not only to feed the community but to develop marketable resources. Almost by accident they discovered how to regenerate thousands of acres of primeval rain forest whose seeds had been dormant for millennia. They developed valuable medicinal crops as alternatives to the coca plants, which are all the indigenous people can usually grow for a living. They made and marketed simple solar devices and violins. They created a community of all ages, comprised of several belief systems and races, which has no weapons, no prison, and is self-governing.

Whether Gaviotas will long survive the combined attentions of the para-militaries and the rebels is an open question. But it raises huge questions about what constitutes a church. Unlike most of the examples in my essay, this is new, without ancient tradition except in the enlightened hearts of its founders. They seem somehow to have used science and ingenuity and belief in human beings to tap into ancient springs of wisdom, and make it all work.

Chapter 9

In Defense of Cultural Christianity

Reflections on Going to Church

Stanley Hauerwas

Stanley Hauerwas's writings focus, in one way or another, on the question of a community of persons standing together around a set of humanizing, religiously empowering understandings and practices. The horizon of his work is the church in the world, but calling it to move away from its worst impulses.

Some miss, I fear, the thoroughly intellectual side of Hauerwas's work. Well-read in contemporary philosophy and in the critique of modernity, he evaluates modernity and post-modernity by the norms of the gospel. Some become frustrated with Hauerwas's almost teasing way of posing counter-questions, avoiding rigidly fixed positions and offering narratives that seem elliptical and open-ended. Academics stumble over his poetry-laced, whimsical prose. (See below, "I have a new law: any time the phrase "X and/or Y and culture" occurs [as in "Christ and culture"], you know a mistake has been made.") His writings are an endless series of clarifications, startling confrontations, refutations and intentional paradoxes. Hauerwas does offer answers, but their most usual form is: Move deeper into the dangerous desert that is God and find there the dilemmas faced only by means of communal fidelity. Often the clearest statement of his own position will be found in a note where he comments on some side issue to his discourse. Behind this skillfully used rhetorical device lies a wider but implicit theory of the nature of discourse. Here, at the start of his essay, he uses this device to question H.R. Niebuhr's approach to culture, so often taken for granted as correct that it has become a piety and, in my view, one needing to be questioned rather than simply rehearsed.

Hauerwas's essay deals with what he calls "that set of cultural habits called church" needed to make Christianity intelligible. He describes his own "going to church" and his encounters with the particulars that coalesce to form a local church. Though his approach is quite different from Marianne Sawicki's, his essay recalls her analysis of "Mary Queen" in the bluegrass area of Kentucky.

Readers may want to tease out of this essay pithy "Hauerwas-isms" useful to guide the local church. There are many, like the need to "discover disciplines necessary for the transformation of our lives." Discovering and employing such disciplined practices is a seminal issue for any local church.

1. Culture, theology and the church

One of the most important questions you can ask theologians is where they go to church.[1] If a theologian does not go to church, they may begin to think their theology is more important than the church. Theology can too easily begin to appear as "ideas," rather than the kind of discourse that must, if it is to be truthful, be embedded in the practices of actual lived communities. That is one of the reasons I do not do "systematic theology." Systems can be beautiful but also easily subject to ideological perversions.

In liberal cultures it is almost impossible to resist the temptation to think of Christianity as a system of beliefs. For example the distinction between the private and the public leads Christians, both liberal and conservative, as well as non-Christians to think of "religious" beliefs as having purchase primarily on our subjectivities. That is why Billy Graham is concerned with our souls and not our money.[2] Christians assume that if we get our "beliefs" right, we will then know how to act right and to know what we should do with our money and possessions.[3]

I have been trying to think and write about Christianity in a manner that does not reproduce Christianity as a set of beliefs that one has. This does not mean, for example, questions about God's trinitarian nature are unimportant. Yet something has gone wrong when questions about trinity have no purchase on how we make as well as what we do with money. I am less interested in what people, including myself, "think." I am much more interested in what is shaping our desires or, if you prefer, our bodies.

Accordingly, I find myself increasingly attracted to cultural Christianity. We were taught in the liberal seminaries of mainline Protestantism in America to be critical of Christians who were Christians because they were Irish or Italian.[4] No book better exemplified this general attitude and stance than H. Richard Niebuhr's *Christ and Culture*.[5] Niebuhr's famous types made invisible the culture that produced the assumption that Christ, or at least "radical monotheism," was itself not a culture. I have a new law: Any time the phrase "X and/or Y and culture" occurs (as in "Christ and culture"), you know a mistake has been made. Such a phrase cannot help but reproduce the presumption of liberal cultures that there is a place to stand free of culture.

Niebuhr's account of "radical monotheism" was an attempt to save theology from sociological reductionism. Given the events of his time, he was also trying to insure that American Christians would not make the mistake of German Christians. But the very means he used to secure "transcendence" ironically provided the theological justification for the spiritualization of Christianity.[6] By "spiritualization," I mean simply he attempted to make Christianity intelligible without that set of cultural habits called church.[7] As a result Niebuhr, like many Protestant liberals, betrays a cultural Christianity in service to a social order that needs "religion" to be "spiritual" and transcendent in order that it not become a challenge to the material practices necessary to sustain a capitalist social order.

This is but a reminder that it is not a question of whether Christianity is culturally embodied but rather what kind of culture Christian practices produce. I am convinced, moreover, that the only way to discover such practices is to try to describe what goes on in actual churches.[8] Put quite simply, I want to ask if individual congregations can sustain a culture able to provide some resistance to the world that threatens to make Christianity "belief." As a way to explore this question, or better, questions, I am going to describe where I go to church.

2. Going to church

I go to church at Aldersgate United Methodist Church in Chapel Hill, North Carolina. I have been a member at Aldersgate for seven years.[9] When I first moved to Durham to teach in the Divinity School at Duke, I attended a number of Methodist churches. Most Sundays I left the services angry not only because the liturgy was so thin but because of the stupidity displayed in the sermon. I am a layman who happens to be a theologian — a dangerous combination. A theologian is tempted to believe your task is to "make Christianity up." I need to be reminded that God thinks me up.

For two years I belonged to a new church begun in Durham as part of the attempt to stem the tide of lost membership. I mistakenly assumed a new church offered the opportunity to "get things right." Yet the church quickly reproduced the habits of mainstream Methodism — it was going to be a place where people found "meaning" for their lives and the men played softball. The church was obviously going to be quite successful attracting upwardly mobile young couples. Realizing there was nothing I could do to stop this church from being successful, I began to look again.

My wife, who is also a Methodist minister besides her work at Duke as Director of Continuing Education and Summer Programs, knew of a church in Chapel Hill that was ministered by a friend she had known in seminary. The church is quite modest but I was struck by the seriousness and integrity of everything the minister, Reverend Susan Allred, did. Moreover, the congregation, usually about 100 members on a "good Sunday," seemed genuinely to care about worship. By that I mean they believe it important to be reminded of the name of the God we worship, confess sin, have three readings of scripture and a psalm, a sermon that attends to the scripture for the day, prayer and thanksgiving in response to the word.

Though we live at some distance from the church, we "liked the church" and sought membership. We were, quite frankly, looking for a church that would not demand much energy or time. We are, after all, busy professionals. But we have found ourselves pulled into the church more than we anticipated, not only because we admire our minister but over the years we have come to know and be known by the people in the church. So, for example, Paula, my wife, simply cannot say "no" when asked to lead worship as part of church's nursing home ministry.

It is important to note that the church is in Chapel Hill. Chapel Hill is a university community, which means the educational level of the church is a bit higher than many Methodist churches. It is also a transient community so our size not only depends on whether the University of North Carolina is in session, but we also constantly lose members who have come to the area universities to study.[10] We have, for example, lost members who failed to receive tenure. Such times never fail to occasion mourning in the congregation.

The church is thirty years old and was once thought to be potentially one of the strong new churches in the district. However, after a promising start, that has proved not to be the case; at least, that does not seem to be the case if you measure success with numbers and money as the Methodist church tends to do. We are a landlocked church and we lack the financial resources to do anything about it. Yet our membership spans generations and includes many of the original members. Over the past ten years, the church has attracted younger members so the church is now filled with children. Our educational space would be considered inadequate, but somehow we continue to make do.

Our worship area is the normal regimented pews with the choir stalls at the front. It is not an attractive sanctuary, but at least its simplicity insures there is no ugliness — e.g., the American flag is nowhere to be seen. Given the simplicity of our space it makes all the difference who is and is not present on any Sunday morning. We need everyone we can get. A missing body is not overlooked, particularly if it is the member who is 96 years old. The congregation is largely white and middle-class, but there are wide differences in age. Though we appear homogeneous, there is a great tolerance, or better, enjoyment of our differences. For example, it is a small but, I think, telling matter that some of us do not "dress up" to come to church because we do not dress up to go anywhere.

The congregation probably tends to be on the liberal side. Many of the members are involved in AIDS ministries or serving meals at the Community Shelter, and we support the North Carolina Council of Churches. The latter is quite significant since the Methodist Conference of North Carolina withdrew support from the Council because the Council accepted two churches whose membership is largely gay. Though little is made of it, Aldersgate has quite prominent gay members who are valued by almost everyone in the congregation. They are valued because they are "just like us" — that is, they work with the kids, sing in the choir, play softball (our team has both men and women) and lead worship.

As I indicated, we have been increasingly drawn into the congregational life, but in truth we were first attracted to the church by

Reverend Allred. She never does anything for which God does not matter, and as Christians we worship God. She would not describe herself as theologically sophisticated, but she has something much more important than theological sophistication — that is, she has a wonderful appreciation for the seriousness of theological speech and in particular the importance of how that speech is shaped by worship. She never fails to remind us where we are in the Christian year, calling attention to the difference "church time" does and should make in our lives. Her preaching is always scriptural and she has a wonderful way of narrating our lives together as Christians by the scriptural texts.

Like most Methodist churches we celebrate the Eucharist once a month. Reverend Allred usually celebrates the Eucharist at the beginning of Advent or Lent, but these are not sufficient to make us think something is odd when we do not celebrate. I use every opportunity to urge the church to move to more frequent eucharistic practice, and I am not without hope that some day I will prevail. I am also trying to convince the church that putting up Stations of the Cross could not hurt our sanctuary.[11]

I assume Aldersgate is a typical example of a mainline Christian church. It is a "Sunday church," as most of us seldom see one another through the week. We do business at various committee meetings and find other times to get together. But Sunday morning remains the central event for us as a people. We cannot claim to know one another well, though there are some very close friendships within the church. It has certainly been the case that Paula and I have come to know many members in a manner that we feel claimed by them as I hope they feel how important they have become for us.

In fact, one of the high points of our liturgy is always the prayers of the people. There we learn of one another's lives as through our prayers we reveal our sufferings and our joys. This person is having an operation, that person's mother has just died, a couple has just separated, and so on. Through the prayers we learn to have our lives lifted up to God and, thus, to one another. That is how slowly we learn of and from one another's stories.

Aldersgate is not a distinctive church. We are not the kind of church where one would expect to find "Resident Aliens." Most of us are there because in some way what we do on Sunday morning "pleases us." In other words, we are there because we have selected Aldersgate as a "good church," a "church with a warm heart," as our motto reads — a motto, I might add, that I particularly dislike.

So I go to church at Aldersgate because I like the church, which, of course, bothers me. No matter what its peculiar attractions, it is finally part of a capitalist economy, which means my involvement at Aldersgate is but another consumer choice. Therefore, in my own ecclesial life I reproduce the kind of church shopping I otherwise wish to defeat. As a result the practices that sustain our worship of God at Aldersgate are too easily undermined by the alleged voluntary culture that forms our lives separate from worship. I will argue, however, that this description of my membership at Aldersgate does not do justice to the complexity of my — and I believe most of the congregation's — involvement with the church. We voluntarily join the church, but such a "joining" is finally inadequately understood as a "choice." The difficulty of how to understand how that happens — that is, how our "choice" becomes something that happens to us — is what I want to try to describe.

3. The church as a non-voluntary community

In order to try to name the complexity, the culture-shaping potential of a church such as Aldersgate, I suggest we think of such a church as non-voluntary. By "non-voluntary," I am attempting to name a set of practices that offers an alternative to the assumption that our membership in the church must be either voluntary or determined. Because we have assumed these descriptions are the only alternative, Protestants in particular have put far too great a weight on our "true" participation in the church. As a result, we lose the resources to name the disciplines necessary to resist the church's becoming a "life option," another consumer preference, because we fail to note how we became Christians in spite of ourselves. That is, we lack the means to learn we were chosen before we chose.

By employing the notion of "non-voluntary," I hope to name how we might think of an alternative to the unhappy choice between voluntary or coerced behavior.[12] Elsewhere I argue that Christianity is extended training meant to help us discover and name those practices and narratives that hold us captive, but that we fail to see how they do so exactly because we think we have chosen them.[13] In other words, the great task before Christians today is to unmask the invisibility of those stories that constitute our lives which we assume wrongly are commensurate with our being Christian. How, for example, can churches maintain disciplined forms of examination of people who wish us to witness their marriages when the same people can easily be married at a church that does not require they be so examined.[14] Even more pressing, how can we witness marriages when we assume that divorce is for many of them inevitable?

I confess one of the reasons I probably over-romanticize Catholicism as an option to mainstream Protestantism is that Catholicism still maintains at least some habits I assume are characteristic of cultural Christianity.[15] In many of its settings Catholicism is not "a church" but a culture which formed — and forms — bodies to inhabit the world in a distinctive fashion.[16] Such formation was materialist to the core since it was never a matter of whether one had all the beliefs right but rather whether one prayed, obeyed, paid and died rightly.[17] Salvation was not some set of ideas but being part of a people constituted by material practices that shaped one's life in a manner that made one part of God's great communion.

Of course, Protestants learned to critique Catholic cultural formation primarily for its alleged perversions. Such a church was and is called authoritarian and alleged to underwrite the worst forms of oppression. Catholic Christianity allegedly failed to challenge the status quo and accepted far too readily the structures of power written into a feudal social order. When the church enjoyed such cultural power, when people had no choice not to be Christian, the church far too easily became an end in itself, confusing what was good for the church with what is good for God's kingdom.

I have no stake in denying that such perversions may well have taken place and in practice continue to take place, but I think such a critique provides a far too comforting narrative for those of us who assume that Protestantism constitutes a strong alternative. The so-called voluntary church nicely underwrites patterns of domination characteristic of capitalist social orders with much less basis for critique than was provided by the Catholic Church. At least that church had an account of the just wage and usury that could challenge corrupt economic practices. Given the voluntarism of mainstream Protestantism, we have no such resources other than vague calls for something called social justice. Accordingly, the gospel in mainstream Protestantism becomes an "ideal" that lacks any material specification.

I am of course aware that Catholicism, particularly in America, has increasingly come to look like mainstream Protestantism. Catholics now think they too ought to "choose" to be Catholic, so they think of it as simply that form of religious life they prefer, perhaps because of their upbringing. Yet there remains in Catholicism a sense that Christianity is finally not something that I get to make up my mind about, but rather a set of practices to which I submit my life. Again, this can lead to unhappy results, but it also remains a resource for the constitution of disciplined communities that have power of resistance against that order of necessity called freedom.

The problem in the mainline Protestant churches is that we no longer can imagine what it would mean to obey. Laity and ministry alike think they can be Christians without training. They think it is their duty to think for themselves even in matters religious. Such a view underwrites the presumption that "religious" names their personal relationship with God. Accordingly, mainstream churches are not able to maintain any account of authority that would sustain the formation of those who have come to the church as a self-selection process but who must, if we are to live faithful to the gospel, discover disciplines needed for the transformation of our lives.

I am aware that the "voluntary character" of being a member of the church seems intrinsic to the very character of Christianity. The church is God's promise to the Jews sent to the Gentiles. Intrinsic to the character of the church, therefore, is witness and conversion. We have learned to describe conversion as the making of a voluntary commitment, but such a description fails to do justice to the complex character of Christian conversion. Christians discover that what they thought they had done voluntarily has in fact been done to them since they could not have known what they were doing by being baptized when they were baptized. That is why Christianity is an extended set of skills learned through imitating others that is meant to help us make our baptisms our own over a lifetime. Such skills can become virtues sufficient to help us resist the powers that would otherwise determine our lives. The challenge is how to maintain that process, a process for becoming holy, without the process being perverted by the presumption that I am doing what I have chosen to do.

I do not pretend I have an adequate response to the challenge. Will Willimon and I call for Christians to rediscover their alien status,[18] which of course invites the question, "Where is this church that you and Will Willimon talk about?" "Where did it ever exist in Christian history?" "Where does it exist today?" "How can it exist today?" Given my own theological commitments, I cannot respond to such questions by underwriting the distinction between visible and invisible churches. That is exactly the kind of spiritualization I am trying to avoid.[19] Nor can I put off the question by suggesting that because I am a theologian I can talk about what the church ought to be, not what it is. The "is" has to exist for me. It must exist at Aldersgate United Methodist Church, even though those of us who attend there believe we are there because we have chosen to be there and yet by being there we are made more than our choice.

4. Returning to Aldersgate: a sermon with commentary

I believe that God's church does exist at Aldersgate United Methodist Church in Chapel Hill, North Carolina. I believe, moreover, that Aldersgate United Methodist Church embodies material practices that I hope can force me to live faithfully, to be faithful to ways of life I have not chosen. Moreover, I believe that Aldersgate makes me at least something of a Christian by teaching me how to speak Christian speech by listening to other Christians speak.[20] After all, few activities are more physical than speech.

In order to exemplify such speech, I offer a sermon preached by Reverend Allred at Aldersgate on March 17, 1966.[21] There was nothing "special" about this particular Sunday or the sermon other than its being preached while I was trying to think through this paper. When I heard it, all I could think was, "Well, that says it all." I will, therefore, interrupt her sermon with short commentaries on why I find her sermon so hopeful. That such a sermon was preached after all suggests much about the body of people who must exist to make such a sermon possible.

Sermon by Reverend Susan L. Allred
Aldersgate United Methodist Church, Chapel Hill
March 17, 1996

My dear friends in Christ, have you ever seen such a full plate of scripture readings in your entire life — a banquet of the rich food that seems to last forever. There were thirteen verses from 1 Samuel (on the anointing of King David by Samuel), the reading of one of our favorite psalms, the Twenty-Third, a great passage about light from Ephesians, and then 51 verses from John's gospel, the entire ninth chapter. What has happened to our minister! These are the readings for the Fourth Sunday of Lent in Year A.

What's going on! It's Lent — it's mid-Lent; the church's pilgrimage to Jerusalem to experience again Christ's death and resurrection continues and intensifies! Three weeks from today is Easter! As Christians we are baptized into Christ's death and resurrection and Easter means baptismal renewal. It is a time to celebrate anew that through baptism we have been anointed (just like biblical kings) to be part of a royal priesthood, a sign of our being chosen by God. We have been chosen and adopted as God's own people so that we may proclaim God's

> mighty acts. We believe that at the early church's first baptisms a song was sung whose words are recorded for us in 1 Peter 2:9–10: "But you are a chosen race, a royal priesthood, a holy nation, God's own people, in order that you may proclaim the mighty acts of him who called you out of darkness into his marvelous light. Once you were not a people, but now you are God's people; once you had not received mercy, but now you have received mercy." Do we know how to proclaim God's mighty acts today?
>
> Since we worshipped together a week ago, a member of our congregation has died. Those of you who could rearrange your work schedules and other commitments gathered in this worship space on Friday for a Service of Death and Resurrection for Ray Moore. Ray's body was cremated and we brought his ashes into the sanctuary in a box and we placed them on a table in this central aisle and covered them with a beautiful white satin cloth with an embroidered gold cross, the colors of Easter, and we said these words in the service: "As in baptism Ray put on Christ so in Christ may Ray be clothed in glory."

Reverend Allred begins noting the lengthy passages of scripture we have taken the time to read. This obviously means the service is going to "run over," be longer than an hour. Yet she does not apologize but rather reminds us that this is what you would expect a royal people to do. We have all the time in the world because we are a people who have been baptized into Christ's death and resurrection. We are no longer a people lost in time but rather a people who can take time in a lost world to enjoy what God has done for us. Taking time shapes our bodies. We can be at rest. It is, therefore, particularly appropriate that Reverend Allred reminds us that one of our members died during the week. Notice we did not have a funeral, but a "Service of Death and Resurrection." This is the church's language that narrates our lives, names who we are as the baptized, reminds us whose time we are in. We can take the time to hear the scripture, worship God and care for one another because our death and our body have been shaped by our baptism.

When the blind man in the gospel lesson was anointed, he received sight. A study of baptismal practices in the church's early history reminds us that anointing was a familiar practice. We also know that baptism was often referred to as illumination. At an early date in the church, we know that the newly baptized one was given a lighted candle and these words were spoken: "You are the light of the world. Let your light shine." At your baptism you were anointed and set apart so that you may declare the wonderful deeds of him who called you out of darkness into his marvelous light.

When God called us Gentiles to be grafted into God's family, he made of us a royal nation — "Once we were no people, but now we are God's people." Once we had not received mercy but now we have received mercy. We have been called out of darkness into God's marvelous light! It is appropriate for us as Christians because of our baptisms to consider ourselves as royalty, but do we often think of ourselves in that way? One writer expresses our claim to royalty with these words: "The Queen of England, at her coronation, was dressed in priestly garments and anointed with oil. We are not less royalty and priests because of our baptism, our coronation as Christians."[22] But there are also "risks of baptism." There are "consequences of commitment."

The healing of the blind man in John's gospel is about learning to see what God is doing in the world. The fact that the story *begins* with Jesus taking clay from the earth and placing it on the eyes of the blind man reminds us from the beginning that this is a story about God's creative work in the world — just as God formed clay to create humanity so Jesus makes mud. From the dust of the earth we were formed and God continues to be a creative God in our lives. Through Jesus God helps us to see what life is intended to be. Jesus came to make God known in the world.

> The blindness in chapter nine of John's gospel is about people who can technically see but can only see what is literally and simply before them. The story is about sight and non-sight, especially those who are blind to God's work in Jesus. To make them see who Jesus was truly constituted a *miracle*, a divine healing! One commentary on the text rightly recalls Paul's experience on the Damascus Road when he was suddenly blinded. "When the scales drop from his eyes, he who thought he saw everything now sees for the very first time. We speak of this as a conversion experience, a turning around, not so much a second chance but rather as the first time to get it right."[23]
>
> How fortunate that God has called us to live in community! We do not have to travel the road of discipleship alone. God calls us to live in community with one another and to show each other the light. We are called to be priests to one another and to the world, walking together in the light.

Clay that sees — that is what we are reminded we are: clay that sees! We can now see and in our seeing we become God's light for the world. Heady claims to be made about this modest group of people at Aldersgate United Methodist Church in Chapel Hill, North Carolina. But Reverend Allred reminds us that God — miracle of miracles! — God has made us royalty in a town that does not believe anyone does or should rule. To see God's rule requires nothing less than miracle, which turns out to be us.

Which turns out to mean we are certainly going to need one another. To be God's light means darkness is revealed as darkness that has no use for the light. If we are going to survive we will need one another. As bodies, as clay that sees, we are not called to be heroines or heroes, but to "live in community." As we learn to minister to one another, to be bodily present to one another, we become God's witness to the world of the salvation wrought in Christ. How good it is to need one another.

Having said all these things which we believe about our priesthood as baptized Christians, I remind you again of the consequences of our commitment.

This congregation is filled with many faithful disciples of Jesus Christ, but it still isn't easy living together. At a recent meeting of the Administrative Board we focused on the ways we as a congregation can do a better job with financial stewardship. We are all baptized Christians — named and anointed — but aware that planning for a faithful ministry brings up differences of opinions. We do not all think alike. We have different personality styles and we have to learn to *talk* to one another.

We all know the membership vows by heart. I will be loyal to the United Methodist Church and uphold it by my *Prayers*, *Presence*, *Gifts* and *Service*. (We have those four words memorized.) We promised to support the church in those ways. We *want* to support our missionary family in Liberia, to support our ministries at the Shelter for the Homeless, Willow Springs Nursing Home, activities of our United Methodist Women, the Reconciling Church Movement; and today thirteen members of our congregation, having finished an intensive training program, will receive the name of an AIDS patient who will become our "Care Partner."

It is never easy to talk about money in the church. As a community, our vision of what God is calling us to do in outreach ministries beyond ourselves and increasing our own programs has outgrown our pocketbooks. God has given us a vision but our pledges continue to stay the same. We must increase our pledges in order to support this vision that God has given us. These are hard discussions but we must work through them as a congregation! These are difficult discussions but they are necessary. Can those who are pledging pledge more? Will persons who have not pledged find a way to make a pledge to this year's budget? Will those who thought a gift from a grad-

> uate student was so small it would not make a difference now be able to see that *all* sizes of gifts are needed for the ministry of Christ's church?

Money! I thought the sermon was about important theological issues — baptism, death, light — but it turns out it is about money. But what could be more appropriate than to be reminded that God wants our money? — that our money is not "ours" but rather a mode of service to one another and to the world? Money, particularly in a capitalist economy, becomes one of our most determinative spiritual realities. The task is to demythologize money's mythic power by making it a mode of service. The simple reminder that we are behind in our budget at least puts us on that road.

Moreover, note Reverend Allred's realism. She knows we do not agree, that we have to learn to talk to one another. She knows that some who support our ministry at Willow Springs Nursing Home have serious reservations about "homosexuality," yet she makes us more than we are individually by reminding us that all the ministries of the church make up the one body of Christ. We do not get to withhold our money in support of those ministries with which we do not agree. This is no democratic institution. It is a community of Christ's body through which we are made subservient to one another. We are not called on to be agreeable but to expose our differences, believing as we do that we are constituted by a unity made possible by God.

> What does it mean to be faithful disciples? I like the increasing feeling we have that it's OK to ask for the church to pray for us when we experience times of discernment. We are learning to listen to God's wisdom and the wisdom of the church on our decisions. In addition to the supportive community we experience through worship, confession, praying for one another and listening together to God's word, we have in the United Methodist Church a special process called "candidacy" for persons who believe that God is calling them into the ordained ministry of the church. All of us are ordained by our baptisms to be in the ministry of Jesus Christ, but there

> is a process for persons to seek discernment as to whether they are being set aside by God for an ordination of word, sacrament and order.
>
> In recent months, a member of our own church, Joy McVane, has invited us into a period of discernment in her life concerning God's call to ordained ministry. We have entered into some early stages of this process with Joy. She has met with the Staff-Parish Committee and the Charge Conference and was unanimously approved. Recently she was approved before the District Committee on Ordained Ministry and was certified as a candidate for ministry in our denomination. In the fall she plans to enter Duke Divinity School for a minimum of three years of study. It is our privilege and honor to continue to be companions and Christian friends for Joy as she continues this journey. We will pray for her family and for our life together with them here at Aldersgate.

By holding up Joy McVane, Reverend Allred moves us from money to ministry. In some churches that move may seem a stretch, but not at Aldersgate. Because Sunday after Sunday we are reminded what it means to be God's people, we know that money and ministry cannot be separated. Accordingly, Joy McVane placed herself under our care and was appropriately examined by the Staff-Parish Committee. As a member of that committee I can testify that she was seriously examined not just for her own self-understanding but, more importantly, for how her sense of ministry was confirmed by how her life contributed to the upbuilding of the church at Aldersgate. We recall that our examination of Joy was but part of the process of our learning to share our lives with one another through prayer.

Our joy concerning Joy, however, was tempered by Reverend Allred's next reading us a letter from a former member of the church. He had also decided to enter the ministry as a so-called "late vocation." He discerned, however, that serving put too great a strain on him and his family. The letter was addressed to his current congregation but was also meant to be read to us, announcing his decision to discontinue. That he thought it right to share his decision with us was a wonderful testimony that he felt he could trust us. Just as we had supported his decision to enter the ministry, so he knew we would support his decision to leave the ministry. He knows, moreover, that he would be welcome to return to us. That was made unmistakable by the last two paragraphs of the sermon:

> In view of Joy's newly announced candidacy and David's announced changes, let us continue to open ourselves to God's love and grace through Jesus Christ so that we may have eyes to see how God is working in our community. God will show us how we are to support and love one another. God will continue to shape us by the story of his great love for us through Jesus.
>
> God is continuing to work in our midst. We know this to be true *because* this is God's church! It was not our idea that all of us would end up here at Aldersgate Church to share our lives so deeply with one another. The promise is clear: God through Christ will lead us to Easter to renew our baptisms and will help us to see more clearly what God has yet to teach us about God's story. Long before we went in search of God, God came in search of us. While we were yet sinners Christ died for us. On that day of crucifixion we became God's royal people through Christ!

5. One sermon does not make a culture, but it is a good place to start.

I am aware that this sermon is insufficient evidence that Aldersgate United Methodist Church is a culture capable of resisting the culture of choice. But neither is the sermon the product of Reverend Allred's peculiar genius. If Ray Moore, Joy McVane and David did not exist, this sermon could not be preached. Yet in the preaching, their lives, all our lives, receive specification as part of the church's life and, thus, part of Christ's life. The sermon may sound like "ideas," but from beginning to end the sermon is as unapologetically material and bodily as was Ray's cremated body on the table in the central aisle on Friday.

Of course, most of us at Aldersgate continue to think "our bodies are our own." Most of us at best remain about half-Christian, possessed as we are by practices that give us the illusion we control our lives.[24] But Aldersgate remains for me a sign of hope, a small island of cultural Christianity, where we get hints of what it means to be part of God's salvation, God's church. For as Reverend Allred often reminds us, the church is not some idea she has had; it is God's church.[25]

Endnotes

1 I make this claim in *In Good Company: The Church as Polis* (Notre Dame: University of Notre Dame Press, 1995) 223.

2 Chris Ayers, "When is the last time you wanted to kill your preacher," *Charlotte Observer* (forthcoming). Reverend Ayers, a Southern Baptist preacher in Charlotte, North Carolina, asks in his editorial why Billy Graham is so popular when Jeremiah, Jesus and Peter were not. He ends his quite courageous editorial — "Billy Graham is Charlotte" — by asking, "Have we organized our churches so that prophetic preaching is highly unlikely?"

3 The assumption that my money is "mine" is of course a reflection of capitalist practice. Capitalism names those material practices that make Christianity appear first as belief and only secondarily as embodied. What I am attempting in this paper is similar to Robert Inchausti's project exemplified in his *The Ignorant Perfection of Ordinary People* (Albany: State University Press of New York, 1991). Inchausti narrates the lives of Gandhi, Solzhenitsyn, Wiesel, Mother Teresa, King and Walesa in an effort to describe a form of resistance he calls "plebeian postmodernism." One who represents such a view "honors the concrete deed before the abstract stance and the claims of the family before the fictions of the state. It [Such a view] judges the quality of one's practice by the good it concretely accomplishes rather than by the party it serves, the money it makes, or the coherence of the theory upon which it is based." (13)

4 Such views were not explicitly anti-Catholic though such sentiments were often close to the surface. Less obvious was the class bias against "cultural Christianity." I will have more to say about these matters in the next section.

5 H. Richard Niebuhr, *Christ and Culture* (New York: Harper Torchbooks, 1951). I realize this way of understanding Niebuhr's work is contentious, but Niebuhr's understanding of "Christ" reflects the displacement of Christian practice capable of cultural embodiment. Niebuhr exemplifies the attempt of Protestant liberalism to save some "meaning" for Christianity in the aftermath of the loss of the church's social power. With his usual insight and candor John Dewey observed that the greatest change in Christianity has not been due to the challenge of science, though that has been the focus of attention, but rather:

"the change in the social center of religion has gone on so steadily and is now so generally accomplished that it has faded from the thought of most persons, save the historians, and even they are especially aware of it only in its political aspect.

. . . There are even now persons who are born into a particular church, that of their parents, and who take membership in it almost as a matter of course; indeed, the fact of such membership may be an important, even a determining factor in an individual's whole career. But the thing new in history, the thing once unheard of, is that the organization in question is a *special* institution, within a secular community. Even where there are established churches, these are constituted by the state and may be unmade by the state. Not only the national state but other forms of organizations among groups have grown in power and influence at the expense of organizations built upon and about a religion. The correlative of this fact is that membership in associations of the latter type is more and more a matter of the voluntary choice of individuals. who may tend to accept responsibilities imposed by the church but who accept them of their own volition." *A Common Faith* (New Haven: Yale University Press, 1960) 61. Niebuhr's *Christ and Culture* simply accepts this displacement as a *fait accompli*. I do not think it possible or desirable to return to a Christendom model of the church. What may be possible, and it is the strategy behind this paper, is to now use some of the leftovers of Christendom as resources for a church capable of saving us from "our own volition." That is, we may discover that we have been more shaped by what we "chose" than what was present in the initial choice. So "cultural Christianity," which once named the way Christians made a home for themselves, now becomes a way for Christians to know how to survive without a home.

6 "Ironically" because H. Richard Niebuhr, unlike his brother Reinhold, had, at least in his early work, a quite impressive sense of the importance of the materiality of the church. This is particularly apparent in his "Toward the Independence of the Church" in *The Church Against the World* (Chicago: Willett, Clark, and Co., 1935) 123–56. In that essay he continued to challenge the capitalist betrayal of the church he had begun in *The Social Sources of Denominationalism* (New York: Meridian, 1972), which was first published in 1929. From my perspective, *The Kingdom of God in America* (New York: Harper, 1959) represents a reactionary development just to the extent that Niebuhr's increasing "idealism" (that is, the stress on transcendence) makes the church less necessary to his theology.

7 I am indebted to Raymond Williams's analyses of culture in his *Key Words: A Vocabulary of Culture and Society* (New York: Oxford University Press, 1976) 76–82. Williams developed through his wide-ranging work an account of the materiality of culture that avoids the unsatisfactory base/superstructure distinction of Marxism. Williams helps us see that all forms of signification must be analyzed within the actual means and conditions of their production and reproduction. For a discussion of Williams on this point, see John Eldridge and Lizzie Eldridge, *Raymond Williams: Making Connections* (New York: Routledge, 1994) 45–75.

For one of the most discerning discussions of these matters in a Christian perspective, see Nicholas Lash, *A Matter of Hope: A Theologian's Reflections on the Thought of Karl Marx* (Notre Dame: University of Notre Dame Press, 1982). Lash argues that Christian materialism is required because our relation to God is mediated. Such mediation frees history from necessity based on cause and effect. So the Christian stance toward the future cannot be "to wait and see what happens" (p. 137). Christian hope names the conviction that in Christ we find our lives narratable, that is to say, hopeful.

8 "Description" is, of course, anything but innocent. The methodological assumptions that often shape the "sociology" that governs such descriptions reproduce the kind of "spiritualization" of the church for which I am trying to provide an alternative. The following description will seem quite naive as that is exactly what I want it to be.

9 It is interesting how language functions in this context. I claim to be a member of Aldersgate. One can also say that we belong to such and such church. I prefer "member" because such language is more physical, as in "bodily member." There is nothing wrong with the language of belonging, but one can belong to many organizations without being a member.

10 The church consists of people loyal to the University of North Carolina. Since Paula and I are "Duke people," we have to endure a good deal of friendly abuse.

11 My graduate assistant, Kelly Johnson (in critiquing a first draft of this paper) asked, "If we had such Stations, would you use them?" — a good question that could come only from a Roman Catholic. All I can respond is that, if they were there, if we only looked at them, that would begin to challenge the rationalism of Protestant worship. The materiality of medieval Catholicism could lead to abuse but it also served to remind Christians that Christianity is about the formation of the body. As Miri Rubin observes in her wonderful *Corpus Christi: The Eucharist in Late Medieval Culture* (Cambridge, Cambridge University Press, 1991), the whole structure of the church,

the approval of secular authorities, the very naturalness of being the only place of worship and of a comprehensive world view preached and taught frequently, was empowered in the claim of sacramentality and in the practice of an exclusive right of mediation. A Christian narrative of sacramentality was the dominant tale that embraced man, the supernatural, order and hierarchy, sin and forgiveness — it punctuated life, marriage, birth and death." (pp. 8–9) Stations of the Cross might at least remind Protestants that Jesus' death was not the result of "a difference of opinion" or an example of a "failure to communicate."

12 The notion of "non-voluntary" action raises fascinating issues in philosophy of action and moral psychology. Such issues go back to Aristotle's account of "choice," in his *Nicomachean Ethics,* that is still unsurpassed. For my recent reflection on these matters, see my "Going Forward by Looking Back: On Agency," in *Theology and Ethics*, eds., Lisa Cahill and James Childress (Cleveland: Pilgrim Press, forthcoming).

13 In particular, see my *Dispatches from the Front: Theological Engagements with the Secular* (Durham: Duke University Press, 1994)164–76; and *Where Resident Aliens Live: Exercises for Christians* (Nashville: Abingdon Press, 1996).

14 That such a discipline is required is due to the presumption that Christian marriage is a commitment to lifelong monogamous fidelity. How would you ever know what you were doing when you made such a promise? That is why the church insists we must know, we must examine, who you are before we are willing to witness your making such a promise. For it will be the church's duty to hold you to a promise you could have not known what you were doing when you made it. We must have some sense that the habits of your baptism have shaped your life so that you will find our mutual support for the keeping of such promises a joy.

15 See, for example, my *In Good Company: The Church as Polis* (Notre Dame: University of Notre Dame Press, 1995) 19-31.

16 I do not mean to suggest that mainstream Protestantism does not reflect a culture, but that is just the problem — Protestantism more reflects a culture than creates a culture. In this respect it is interesting to compare Catholic and Protestant *kitsch*. Catholic catalogues sell, for example, "egg rosaries, moulded

1 1/4" diameter egg (plastic) contains a delightful moulded cord rosary. Comes in an assortment of pink and blue rosaries, sold 36 eggs per box, 39 cents" (*Autom*, March 1996, p. 33). How wonderfully material! As my colleague Professor Brett Webb-Mitchell points out, Catholics in New York during the Pope's visit were selling "Pope on a rope" shower soaps. Protestants just do not have that kind of possibility. For example, people at the Methodist General conference would be surprised if Cokesbury were selling "General Conference on a rope" or even "Bishop on a rope." I am indebted to Dr. Mary Collins for calling my attention to the wonders of the *Autom* catalogue. (I confess I ordered a wonderful chasuble from the catalogue for my wife because she often presides at Eucharist.)

I suspect that Catholic *kitsch* continues to draw on the habits of the body correlative to the Christian understanding of the resurrection of the body. For example, Caroline Walker Bynum argues in her *The Resurrection of the Body in Western Christianity, 200–336* (New York: Columbia University Press, 1995), "for most of Western history body was understood primarily as the locus of biological process. Christians clung to a very literal notion of resurrection despite repeated attempts by theologians and philosophers to spiritualize the idea. So important indeed was literal, material body that by the fourteenth century not only were spiritualized interpretations firmly rejected; soul itself was depicted as embodied. Body was emphasized in all its particularity and physicality both because of the enormous importance attached to proper burial and because of the need to preserve difference (including gender, social status, and personal experience) for all eternity. But the 'other' encountered in body by preachers and theologians, storytellers, philosophers and artists, was not the 'other' of sex or gender, social position or ethnic group, belief or culture; it was death." (p. xviii) Bynum's book is a wonderful account of the interaction of piety and theology and, in particular, how the piety of the "simple" was often more profound than the theology of the day. I am sure little hangs on rosaries in plastic eggs, but that Catholic hospitals continue to bury fetuses of early miscarriages is a practice that I suspect, if lost, would change the character of Catholic theology.

[17] What could be more important than "dying rightly"? That Christian bodies are no longer shaped by baptism results in the medicalization of our deaths. No longer able to make our deaths our own, "assisted suicide" begins to sound like good news.

[18] Stanley Hauerwas and William Willimon, *Resident Aliens: Life in the Christian Colony* (Nashville: Abingdon, 1989). I am indebted to Will Willimon for helping me learn how to write for Christians. That theologians now write primarily for other theologians in the universities is an indication of the material malformation of Christian practices. I am not in the least critical of those who try to write for a "popular audience." I simply wish I were better able to so write.

[19] David Yeago attributes the "spiritualization" of Christian practice to a misreading of Luther's understanding of justification, the distinction between the law and the gospel, and the articulation of the so-called "Protestant Principle." See his "Gnosticism, Antinomianism and Reformation Theology: Reflections on the Costs of a Construal," *Pro Ecclesia* 2,1(Winter, 1993) 37–49.

[20] I am often struck by the prayers of my fellow lay members. Recently at a staff-parish meeting in which we were trying to discern with our minister whether she should seek reappointment to Aldersgate for another year, I was stunned when the chair of the meeting simply announced that this was something we ought to pray about. The chair, a woman in her late fifties who works for H&R Block, began to pray eloquently and directly. I was literally in tears, moved by her unapologetic presumption that God could be asked to help us. What a wonderful gift for a theologian to learn that such speech is possible and perhaps to begin learning to imitate it.

[21] Reverend Allred graciously gave me permission to use her sermon. In the first draft of this paper I reproduced the sermon without commentary. I am indebted to Tex Sample for suggesting why it is important to indicate how I heard the sermon.

[22] Soards, Dozeman, McCabe, "Preaching the Revised Common Lectionary" (Nashville: Abingdon Press, 1992) 71.

[23] Peter J. Gomes, *Proclamation* 6, Series A, Lent (New York: Fortress Press, 1995) 50.

[24] Since Reverend Allred is now more the author of this paper than I am, I told her the only thing I could do is give the stipend I receive for the paper to the church. After all, the church needs the money and I need examples if the argument of the paper is to make sense of a material practice. It is a frightening thing when working on an essay requires me to live differently. I am not sure I like that it does so.

[25] I am indebted to Ms. Kelly Johnson and Mr. David Cloutier, and especially to Tex Sample, for reading and critiquing earlier drafts of this paper. Ms. Sarah Freedman, surely one of the most theologically sophisticated secretaries in the world, patiently put the paper in readable shape.

Chapter 10

Liturgy, Preaching and Justice

John J. Barrett

A university-trained ethicist, John Barrett brings focused concern for "right doing" to his full-time pastoral work as a parish priest on Long Island. Here he deals with a key piece of the puzzle of congregational transformation: preaching God's word the context of the eucharist. Two initial assumptions frame his essay: first, that individual and social transformation is the ongoing task of the church and, second, that disagreement about the form our gospel response should take can itself be creative and transformational.

In his search for wise procedural advice for those who seek to preach the just word, Barrett relies on the writing about homiletics by the well-known Jesuit Walter Burghardt. Burghardt advises homilists to stay with biblical justice as their foundation rather than ethical or legal justice cut off from biblical justice. Biblical justice offers listeners a basic perspective of God's call needing to be embodied in individual, communal and social life. The overall goal of such preaching is awareness of justice issues and the need to address them through study and action.

Barrett looks to virtue ethics for insight into how progress toward wise action works. He seeks to get inside those situations where concrete action may be hesitant, unsure, even fearful. Preachers do well to reflect wisely on these matters. Casually brushing them aside could split a community, defeat any kind of action and even imperil the call to transformation. One becomes a moral subject through the discipline of enhanced listening and reflection, a step at a time. Barrett encourages preachers to learn and foster this discipline and the action that can result from it.

Introduction

I wish to explore the challenges facing pastoral ministers in their efforts to assist the Sunday Liturgy in its role as a communal locus of individual and social transformation. In particular, I will focus on the Sunday homily.[1]

I will approach these challenges from two points of view: that of a presiding minister and homilist at the Sunday Liturgy and that of a student of social ethics. As a guide to this exploration I will use the ongoing reflection of Walter Burghardt, S.J., and his project, *Preaching the Just Word.* My contention will be that the interrelation of l;iturgy and justice exhibited in homilies can benefit from perspectives about the moral subject and justice available from the study of contemporary moral philosophy.

I heard the following story from a member of the peace and justice committee in the parish I joined as a pastoral staff member:

With the advent of preparations for the Persian Gulf War, the parish peace and justice committee met to discuss how the ethical issues raised by this conflict could be addressed by the members of our community at the Sunday eucharist. Discussion ensued, and members of the committee found themselves divided not only by their understanding of the ethical issues involved, but also by the knowledge that several members of the parish soon would be called up to serve in combat roles in the conflict. At the end, the chair adjourned the meeting and asked members to pray and reflect on the discussion and return in several days prepared to work on plans to involve parishioners in prayer, discussion and action about the ethical questions raised by the conflict.

The committee members returned for the next meeting and found themselves even more sharply divided than before about the question of raising the issue at Sunday eucharist. Some felt that if the peace and justice committee itself was so divided, then there was great risk of dividing the parish, especially since members of several families would be participating in the war. A suggestion was made by a committee member to consider some action that all could agree upon and present this idea to the parish. Subsequently, a plan to establish a soup kitchen was endorsed by the committee and accepted by the parish.

To this day, several years later, two things have resulted from this decision: 1) The soup kitchen has continued every Sunday evening in its mission of offering food, companionship and support for over 250 people. It is staffed by an equal number of parishioners and representatives from other religious communities and local organizations. 2) The issues of the Gulf War and other subsequent armed conflicts have never been publicly raised in a homily at the parish Sunday liturgy.

The Liturgical Question

If I might use this story as a metaphor, I think it illustrates both how far we have come and how far we must yet travel in considering the interrelation of the liturgy and justice in a Sunday homily. In a former generation, requests for incorporation in homilies at the Sunday liturgy would ordinarily be mostly provincial, that is, focusing on the interior life of the church (vocations, missions, Catholic education). Occasionally there would be forays into local social issues (St. Vincent de Paul Society, movie ratings and collections to assist those in need). As a result, when the Vietnam War became a matter of serious moral debate, Catholic parishes were unprepared for this type of liturgical reflection. In some cases, mention of the war in prayer or homilies caused great conflict. But for the most part, Catholic homilies and liturgies largely avoided the issues and remained silent.

Perhaps in response to this experience, it seems, there is not a week that goes by where there are not requests for liturgical incorporation that reflect more widely comprehensive moral concerns. For example, last year in this same parish, liturgical planners and homilists were asked to focus on the following issues at the Sunday liturgy: abortion, domestic violence, homelessness, capital punishment, marital commitment and, of course, our local soup kitchen. In one sense, this shift is most encouraging. It appears that an understanding of the sacramental life of local communities is expanding to reflect the interplay of the personal and the social dimensions of faith. In addition, and most importantly, this process is taking place at the heart of the community's life — the Sunday liturgy.

But as the above story indicates, all is not encouraging here. In addition to issues of armed conflict, there was little or no mention of other pressing moral concerns facing this community such as gender, racial and sexual orientation discrimination, HIV/AIDS, divorce and economic justice. In attempting to assess these gaps several lines of inquiry could be fruitfully undertaken. Among these are: the religious identity and sociology of suburban upper middle-class communities such as this one, the different models for understanding the relationship of religion and morality, the complexity of current Catholic church attempts to address these issues and even the persistence and resourcefulness of certain advocacy groups in bringing these issues to public attention. However, for all the insights to be gleaned from these perspectives, I think the question pastoral ministers face is basically a liturgical and theological one.

I adopt this position for three important reasons. First, the liturgy is central to the nature of the Christian life.[2] As the liturgical theologian Louis-Marie Chauvet, states, the liturgy is "the symbolic place of the on-going transition between Scripture and Ethics, from the letter to the body."[3] Second, as a result of this understanding, I think that the discussions about parish life should always begin with the liturgy and not end with it as usually seems to occur. For example, as Karl Rahner reminds us, preaching precedes and grounds teaching.[4] Third, unless we have a clearer understanding of the interrelation of the liturgy and justice, the transformative possibilities of the liturgy for action in the world will be lost and the liturgy will end up supporting the status quo.

The Work of Walter Burghardt

Fortunately, we have an impressive recent body of reflection on the interrelationship of liturgy and justice. For Catholics, the impetus of the Second Vatican Council and the limitations of past experience have taught us Catholics well.[5] When it comes to focusing this question on homiletic preparation we can find a wise and experienced guide in the work of Walter Burghardt, S.J. In his writings, and specifically in his program entitled *Preaching the Just Word*,[6] Burghardt has spent over a decade exploring the homiletic contribution to this relationship of liturgy and justice.

Early in his reflection Burghardt focused his efforts on what he labeled, "the neuralgic problem" for homilists. As both a practitioner and listener of homilies, Burghardt initially recognized the difficulty of treating certain issues. As he put it, the question "How concrete dare I get?"[7] usually arose in homiletic preparation. In guiding the search for a response, he advised the avoidance of two extremes: on the one hand, manipulation of the Mass in the interests of ideologies; on the other, a perilous conservatism that makes the liturgy utterly inoffensive, a peaceful Sunday service where oppressed and oppressor escape from the furies and passions of the week and simply praise God for his wonderful works.[8]

In his more recent reflection, Burghardt has refined the question of concreteness into a distinction between biblical and ethical justice. Many homilies, he states, at best reflect ethical or legal justice, that is, giving people what is due them because it is written into law or can be proven from philosophy. He recognizes that this approach can often be a source of conflict in the parish because of its focus on theoretical principles and strategies for carrying them out. In addition, he cautions that statements of principle and strategy do not always engage the listener in a faithful and imaginative response. As a result, for him, this notion of justice is important but not primary for homiletic exposition.

Alternately, he suggests that the justice we must preach is biblical justice, that is, fidelity to relationships, to responsibilities, that stem from the covenant with God in the Christ. Biblical justice, he observes, conditions the listener's response in light of God's justice and the search for ways to embody that justice in individual and social life. With the use of this distinction he states that two things can follow: homilies reflecting "social" justice do not have to remain the bone in the preacher's throat (i.e., the question "How concrete dare I get?"), and it is difficult if not impossible to preach a good homily that is not a justice homily in the biblical sense.[9]

This review of Burghardt's efforts clearly shows that it contains many important points. His work is deeply conversant with theological reflection in several crucial areas. There is an understanding of the relationship of the homily to the liturgy as a whole, and a structured call for prior collective discernment on the part of preacher and listener. Additionally, as he says, there is a recognition of communal worship's power to change hearts and refocus concern from self to others. Most important, he reflects admirably the insights of Catholic and Protestant biblical scholars who state that in most biblical texts, indicative precedes imperative: we learn who we are and who God is before we learn the behavioral consequences of this knowledge.[10]

Having made this distinction, however, Burghardt does not shy away from concrete issues. He liberally draws from the patristic tradition to show examples of homilies that confronted the justice issues of the day. In surveying the present scene, however, he acknowledges that the justice issues are complex and opinions are often sharply divided. As a consequence, he proposes another distinction. He states that homilies do not solve complicated social issues, but attempt to raise awareness and consciousness. This attentiveness is then focused on the local justice issues, the resources available to address them and concrete steps to begin.[11] In this, he parallels current teaching in the Catholic church, which has relinquished the practice of handing down solutions to specific questions and now freely admits the lack of ready-made alternatives to present political and economic systems.[12]

Well said. But is this enough? Can the distinction that Burghardt offers between biblical and legal justice and the description he offers of homilies raising awareness and consciousness adequately face the challenge of concreteness about a specific issue? The above story about the Persian Gulf War or the example of the lack of advocacy regarding issues of discrimination, HIV/AIDS, divorce and economic justice illustrates the difficulties encountered in this effort.

I think the answer to the question is yes, especially if Burghardt's distinctions are recognized and applied. In speaking of "biblical" justice and "legal (ethical)" justice, Burghardt is creatively adapting what the theological tradition described as the relation between the order of charity and the order of justice.[13] He rightly places emphasis on the transcendental dimension of the relationship (biblical justice). He also seems to imply that extended discussions of justice issues should be continued in other parish forums.[14]

But I think to be even more helpful to pastoral ministers, Burghardt's distinction between biblical justice and legal justice has to be expanded in two ways. First, I think that the description of legal justice needs to be elaborated. Second, based on a wider notion of legal justice, I think more can be said about the response that a listener can make to a homily. Here a brief inquiry into what recent moral philosophy has learned about the nature of justice and the individual as the moral subject can, I propose, profitably supplement Burghardt's helpful theological analysis.

Legal Justice

Daniel Mark Nelson remarks that in most contemporary discussions "justice . . . is regarded almost exclusively as an attribute of legal systems and social structures."[15] David K. O'Connor adds that "We are much more likely to commend a policy than a person for being just."[16] Simply put this means that most discussions about justice are "procedural" or "distributive," that is, they reflect studies of how different theories go about insuring a fair distribution of goods, services and benefits to those who have rights to them. Examples of this understanding are the legal system, the tax structure or governmental aid programs. This description reflects Burghardt's use of the term "legal" justice.

As Nelson, O'Connor and others have also argued, however, this view of justice as related to systems and structures is a relatively new perspective, at least since the Enlightenment. Scholars such as these are drawing our attention to a previous description of justice. This description is related to persons, and reflected in the ancient thought of Aristotle and the medieval synthesis of Thomas Aquinas. Here justice pertains not first to the external actions of individuals and groups, but rather to an interior quality of mind and focus that directs these external actions.

For example, as Normand J. Paulhus notes, when Thomas Aquinas speaks of justice he does so both in a general and a particular sense.[17] Justice in the general sense (known traditionally as "legal" justice and more contemporarily as "social" justice) orients a person towards the common good. It is determined by what is called a *medium rationis*, which is reflective of the interior creative capacities of reason. Justice in the particular sense (known commonly as "distributive" justice, although also present in a "commutative" form) orients a person in her or his dealings with other individuals or groups. It is determined by what is called a *medium rei*, which is reflective of an external objective reality. Simply put, this expanded understanding of justice takes into account not only principles and procedures but, more importantly, the individuals involved in this process.

The Moral Subject

Corresponding to this retrieval of an enlarged account of justice has been an equally important reappraisal of moral activity. This account includes not only a description of moral acts but also, and again more importantly, a wider appreciation of the subject of these acts. Modern morality (taking the form of either deontology or consequentialism), it is charged, "makes minimal demands upon the intelligence and developed moral character of moral agents, requiring little or nothing of them in the way of wisdom, courage or integrity." It is also minimal in the sense that it limits the arena of moral choice to a small sector of human experience.[18] Often, it is confined to particular roles such as professional ethics. With the focus on acts, critics argue, these approaches do not take into primary account the moral agent's history or concentrate on developing patterns of moral activity in the agent's life. Once again, the suggestion being made here is to attempt a retrieval of the ancient and medieval accounts of justice from Aristotle and Thomas Aquinas.[19]

For example, James Keenan suggests that most current approaches to moral evaluation focus on determining which particular act bears the best value in fulfilling the demands of an objective situation. The advantage, he states, of a different approach is that it engages the person more directly. When prescribing right action it asks which type of activity will make the agent a better or more prudent agent in the future. It presupposes that the moral subject becomes the agent of the actions he or she performs and that therefore the self-understanding of the agent is necessary for determining the course of action. The focus of this approach is broader than either deontology or consequentialism in that it includes not simply the acts as bearing value and the states in life as warranting particular demands, but also the agent's own personal strengths and weaknesses.[20]

This new approach, often referred to as virtue ethics, reinterprets the span of decision-making on the part of the moral subject through a retrieval of the virtue of prudence. The role of prudence is expanded beyond the purely motivational or the correct application of principles previously decided. Prudence is the virtue by which one becomes a moral subject able both to anticipate the immediate present and to shape the course of the future. Through prudence not only does one make choices, one also articulates the more distant ends or goals which one seeks. In the practice of this virtue one is not a reactor to one's history, but an agent transforming the world.[21]

It should be noted at this point that discussions such as these about the moral subject, especially when they take place within the context of exploring virtue ethics, often make those who are working for justice nervous. It seems that descriptions of moral character and of the personal nature of justice lack a communal dimension and are simply another manifestation of the individualism that many are working to transform; yet such an evaluation, although sometimes warranted by the contemporary use of terms, misses the wider context of this discussion.[22] Undergirding the discussion of justice is the relationship of the common good and the good of the individual. In fact, an approach to these questions that relies on Aquinas and Aristotle even goes so far as to maintain that the common good takes precedence over the good of the individual![23] This claim flows from the Thomistic and Aristotelian recognition that human beings are, as Porter describes, "intrinsically social beings who can exist and flourish only within the context of a community."[24] Space does not permit a further elaboration of this point other than to again quote Porter, who interprets Aquinas as saying, "The well-being of individual and community are interrelated in such a way that what promotes one promotes the other, and what harms one harms the other as well."[25]

A Return to Burghardt

To repeat, Burghardt's approach to preaching about justice could be expanded with a wider description of both legal justice and the understanding of the listener so that it can be of even more assistance than it already is. This review of contemporary discussions in moral philosophy, I propose, offers two helpful insights. The first assists in the struggle with the question of concreteness. In making the distinction between general (legal) justice and particular (distributive and commutative) justice, Aquinas suggests that each has a different but interrelated focus. As Paulhus observes the concepts of distributive and commutative justice offer guidance to the construction of a just economic order. Legal justice, however, is identified with issues related to the common good. Moreover, he states that it is legal justice that orients and directs the efforts of distributive justice to the preservation of the common good.[26] Recognizing this distinction can aid homilists in fulfilling Burghardt's goal of raising awareness and consciousness as well as being concrete. A homily reflecting this understanding of legal justice can be concrete in its recognition of the overall commitment of biblical justice to the common good and service to all, especially those in need (legal justice). It could also be factual in naming those attitudes and systems that block this commitment. At the same time, and quite possibly in the same homily, the understanding of particular justice could acknowledge the plurality of possible responses to this commitment, while accommodating the differing competencies of the listeners.[27]

The second insight concerns the renewed appreciation of the dimensions of the moral subject. This insight again reflects the question of concreteness, but now focuses on the context of listening and the pattern of listener response. With an emphasis on just people who do just acts, preaching can become more direct and better engage those listening. This is so because the category of moral subjects allows more attention to be paid to the context of listening. Listening occurs within the integrated horizons of individual Christians and particular communities of faith, both of whom have histories, strengths and weaknesses and measurable potentialities of growth. Preaching about the obligations of justice (here again in its legal form) can be directed toward these individuals and this particular community of faith. Cognizance can also be made of past attempts, present struggles and future possibilities because homilist and community are in the continuing process together of prayer, reflection and action. In addition, this approach recognizes that Christian life aims not at singular acts of justice but at becoming a just person, able to visualize a just world and continually struggles to bring that vision to birth within a community of faith. As Jean Porter reminds us, "To live a humanly good life, we must maintain a course of activity of a certain sort over time, indeed, over the course of our whole lives."[28] In the gospels, Jesus calls his disciples to an openness of heart to the inbreaking of the Kingdom. This openness is displayed in the stories he told. For example, in both the parables of the unmerciful servant (Matthew 18:23–35) and the laborers in vineyard (Matthew 20:1–16), the biblical text is used to play against the routine patterns of thinking. In them the listener is invited to recognize the transformation of accepted standards of justice into mercy and to participate in like actions.[29] This participation is not to be limited to individual acts, but to the development of a "certain habit of mind" in facing the questions of everyday existence.[30]

The question of concreteness is also reflected in the pattern of listener response. In addition to a recognition of the particularities of individuals and communities, this understanding of legal justice is not first directed toward the straightforward implementation of social strategies, however inspired or required. It is rather an engagement of the imaginative faculties of the mind through the virtue of prudence. In the intersection of prudence and justice, as Keenan states, the immediate present is anticipated and the course of the future is shaped. Again as Paulhus observes, both the common good and social justice are not already existing realities. They are not a magical formula waiting to be applied automatically to concrete situations. Instead, they are characterized as a *medium rationis.* The common good and social justice must be constantly worked for and created.[31] In this understanding, as Burghardt stresses, the energy of the listeners is directed toward exploring the struggles and the possibilities of embodying justice in their lives.

In elaborating this understanding of legal justice, one final point needs also to be kept in mind. Even in an expanded appreciation, legal justice in a homily would still fall under Burghardt's initial criticism of homilies that fail to reflect the rich understanding of biblical justice. In placing my emphasis on exploring the further dimensions of legal justice, I am not unmindful of this proper focus on biblical justice. In Catholic theology, reflection on the order of justice has been related to the order of charity. In the same way, the questions of legal justice have to be related to those of biblical justice. As Porter observes, the virtues of faith, hope and love add something to justice that is beyond motivation for right behavior. They are transformative of the individual's horizon of reflection and action while at the same time leaving intact their rational structure.[32] In attempting a wider description of the rational structure of legal justice and the moral subject, I also have in mind the transformation of this understanding. Biblical justice, concerned about the poor, is not identical with legal justice, which has as its focus the common good. Biblical justice argues for prioritizing concern for the poor in attempting to address the requirements of the common good.[33]

Conclusion

The above discussion by itself does not qualify as a comprehensive theological reflection on the nature of homilies, nor is it even a complete description of the interrelationship of the liturgy and justice in the praxis of a homily. Rather, it has been an attempt, largely indebted to the work of Walter Burghardt, to assist in the process of homiletic preparation at least in two ways. First, as Mary Catherine Hilkert notes, "The preacher listens with attentiveness to human experience because he or she is convinced that revelation is located in human history — in the depths of human experience."[34] Second, as the American bishops have stated, homilists use the scriptures to interpret human experience to show how God is present and active in our lives today.[35]

The use of the expanded understanding of the moral subject and justice from moral philosophy can be of some service to homilists and communities as they seek to follow Burghardt's sage advice in facing our collective reticence to wrestle with moral issues in preaching. As a homilist and member of the above community for several years, I can testify to the continuing difficulties in applying this understanding. But I have also found that these distinctions have helped to make progress in the preaching of justice along the path that Walter Burghardt has so ably laid out.

Endnotes

1 In focusing on the Sunday homily I am very conscious of two important qualifications: 1) that in Catholic liturgical understanding the homily is an act of worship and is not to be understood as separate from other acts of worship within the liturgy; and 2) that the focus of the entire liturgy, not just the homily, is on transformation. In addition, and most importantly, homilies are not topical but rather flow from the scriptures read at the eucharist.

2 Bernard Häring holds that there are two basic and inseparable forms of human response to God's self-offering: worship and moral living. (See Mark O'Keefe, "Catholic Moral Theology and Christian Spirituality," *New Theology Review* 7:2 (May 1994) 66.

3 See his *Symbol and Sacrament: A Sacramental Reinterpretation of Christian Existence* (Collegeville: Pueblo/Liturgical Press, 1995) 265.

4 He writes, "Because there is preaching — for that reason there is theology; not vice-versa. "Priest and Poet," *Theological Investigations* 3, trans. Karl H. and Boniface Kruger (Baltimore: Helicon Press, 1967) 303.

5 Two important and useful guides for pastoral ministers reflecting in this area are: *Living No Longer for Ourselves: Liturgy and Justice in the Nineties*, ed. Kathleen Hughes and Mark R. Francis (Collegeville: Liturgical Press, 1991), and *Liturgy and Spirituality in Context*, ed. Eleanor Bernstein, C.S.J. (Collegeville: Liturgical Press, 1990).

6 Through a weeklong workshop this program offers an extended opportunity for homilists to join in a period of prayer, learning and practice dedicated to exploring the interrelationship of liturgy and justice. Burghardt also collaborates with David H.C. Read in an ecumenical monthly journal, *Living Pulpit*, which serves as a continuing resource for homiletic preparation.

7 Walter Burghardt, *Preaching: The Art and the Craft* (New York: Paulist Press, 1987) 134.

8 Ibid., 131.

9 Walter Burghardt, "Preaching: Twenty-Five Tips," *Church* 12:4 (Winter 1996) 23. For a fuller exposition, see his "Characteristics of Social Justice Spirituality," *Origins* 24:9 (July 21, 1994) 157, 159–64.

10 See also *Fulfilled in Your Hearing: The Homily in the Sunday Assembly,* (Washington, D.C.: United States Catholic Conference, 1982) 18. This is an official statement of the National Conference of Catholic Bishops on preaching. It suggests that the purpose of a homily is to lead a congregation to thanksgiving and praise by enabling those assembled to celebrate the liturgy more deeply and thus be formed for Christian witness in the world.

11 Burghardt, *Preaching* 23. See Avery Dulles's earlier exposition of these points. "Preaching: The Dilemmas," *Origins* 4:47 (May 15, 1975) 746–50.

12 Marie-Dominique Chenu writes, "It is no longer the case of 'social doctrine' taught with a view to application to changing situations but of these situations themselves becoming the theological 'loci' of the discernment to be effected through the reading of the signs of the times." "The Church's 'Social Doctrine' Christian Ethics and Economics: The North–South Conflict," *Concilium* 140 (1980) ed. Dietmar Mieth and Jacques Pohier (New York: Seabury Press, 1980) 73.

13 See Paul Wadell's helpful discussion of the relationship of charity and justice in his "Confronting the Sin of Racism: How God's Dream for the World Can Be Restored," *New Theology Review* 9:2 (May 1996) 11–16.

14 See George Higgins's earlier suggestion about the location of these discussions. "Politics: What Place In Church?" *Origins* 2 (April 1973) 211–16.

15 *The Priority of Prudence: Virtue and Natural Law in Thomas Aquinas and the Implications for Modern Ethics* (Pennsylvania: Pennsylvania State University Press) 149.

16 "Aristotelian Justice as a Personal Virtue," *Midwest Studies in Philosophy* 13, *Ethical Theory: Character and Virtue*, ed. Peter A. French (Notre Dame: University of Notre Dame Press, 1988) 417.

17 Normand Paulhus, "Uses and Misuses of the Term 'Social Justice' in the Roman Catholic Tradition," *Journal of Religious Ethics* 15:22 (Fall 1987) 266–67.

18 David L. Norton. "Moral Minimalism and the Development of Moral Character," *Midwest Studies in Philosophy* 13, *Ethical Theory: Character and Virtue,* ed. Peter A. French (Notre Dame: University of Notre Dame Press, 1988) 183.

19 For a helpful guide to these attempts see Jean Porter, *The Recovery of Virtue: the Relevance of Aquinas for Christian Ethics* (Louisville: Westminster/John Knox Press, 1990).

20 James Keenan, "Virtue Ethics: Making a Case as It Comes of Age," *Thought* 67:265 (June 1992) 116–17.

21 Ibid.

22 See Paulhus, op. cit., 263, for his helpful discussion of how the common good began to be seen as an "alien good," thus changing the Thomistic synthesis of the common good and the good of the individual into the tension between person and society.

23 Porter, op. cit., 125.

24 Ibid., 126.

25 Ibid., 127.

26 Paulhus, op. cit., 264, 267.

27 The larger point here is the balance between the both aspects of justice in a homily. This balance, of course, is not simply one of composition. It is more importantly a reflection of the homilist's life and prayer with a particular community. I find an interesting parallel to this question in Dulles's discussion of the grounds for specificity in church teaching, especially in his recognition of urgent situations and the charismatic guidance of the Spirit ("The Gospel, Church and Politics," 644–45).

28 Porter, op.cit., 100. She further suggests, "While that course of activity will include discrete actions and will also be characterized by the absence of other sorts of discrete actions, it will not be possible to describe it in those terms alone. Much less will we be able to carry out such a course of activity solely by setting ourselves to choose correct actions and to avoid incorrect actions over and over again."

29 John Donohue, *The Gospel in Parable*, (Philadelphia: Fortress Press, 1991) 84–85.

30 Francis Greenwood Peabody, *Jesus Christ and the Social Question: An Examination of the Teaching of Jesus in Its Relation to Some of the Problems of Modern Social Life* (London: MacMillan & Co., Ltd., 1904) 82.

31 Paulhus, op. cit., 277.

32 Porter, op. cit., 66–67.

33 Joseph Kotva, *The Christian Case for Virtue Ethics* (Washington, D.C.: Georgetown University Press) 148–51.

34 Mary Catherine Hilkert, "Preaching and Theology: Rethinking the Relationship," *Worship* 65:5 (September 1991) 400.

35 *Fulfilled in Your Hearing*, 24.

Chapter 11

Christian Practices and Congregational Education in Faith

Dorothy C. Bass and Craig Dykstra

Craig Dykstra has been working on the phenomenon of "practice," in an effort to reclaim a neglected category for understanding church transformation. Note his thoughtful 1991 essay, "Reconceiving Practice," in Farley and Wheeler, eds. Shifting Boundaries *(Richmond VA: John Knox Press). A version of it had previously been published in* Theology Today. *The seeds of Dykstra's ideas on practice can be found in Vision and Character (Mahwah NJ: Paulist Press), his critique of Kohlberg's approach to ethics. Currently Craig Dykstra is Vice-President for Religion at the Lilly Endowment in Indianapolis.*

In early 1997 Craig Dykstra collaborated with Dorothy C. Bass, a church historian who directs the Project on the Education and Formation of People in Faith, at Valparaiso University in Valparaiso, Indiana, who co-wrote with him two important summary essays in Practicing Our Faith: A Way of Life for a Searching People. *This book, edited by Bass and published by Jossey-Bass of San Francisco, lucidly lays out the practices that might be embodied in a Christian ecclesia. My suspicion is that time may show that book to be a breakthrough in conceptualizing the specifics of discipleship. The following essay represents another look by these two writers at their important project. Indeed, not only does the piece speak for itself, but it caps this volume with a wonderful final essay that clearly deals with "the particulars of the specifics."*

Readers will also want to know Dorothy Bass's essay on congregations as the bearers of traditions, one of the multidisciplinary pieces in Volume 2 of American Congregations, *ed. James P. Wind and James W. Lewis (Chicago: The University of Chicago Press, 1994).*

Ours is a time of widespread spiritual hunger. People seem to be searching for something, though they often have a hard time articulating exactly what it is. Sometimes it seems that the search is for meaning, sometimes for worth or belonging. Sometimes this elusive something is called "spirituality." Whatever they call it, many people feel that something is missing from their lives. Yet it is clearly not some *thing* that they are lacking. This search is not for *more* but for *kind*, for a qualitative dimension. It is for a kind of life, a way of living, a way of being and doing that is truly alive to God, neighbor and self — a way of life that, to use a biblical phrase, chooses life.

Helping people to see and grow stronger in such a way of life is what education and formation in Christian faith are all about, too.

Though they can sometimes seem remote from the hungers of contemporary culture, faithful education and formation at their best involve Christians in a lifelong process of learning to choose life in all its fullness. Within this process, however, our hunger is transformed: We discover that full, rich and meaningful ways of living take on patterns that are in accord with what is true and good.

This essay arises from our conviction that worshiping Christian communities *know* something about such patterns. Their knowledge appears not only in their written or spoken affirmations, however. It is also embedded in "Christian practices," in the *things Christian people do together over time to address fundamental human needs in response to and in the light of God's active presence for the life of the world.*[1] As the bearers of such practices, congregations are places where Christian people, as individuals and as communities, can take on the patterns of a way of life that chooses life. In the pages ahead, we shall explore this claim, suggest its usefulness to interpreters of congregational life and propose a practices-focused approach to education and formation in Christian faith.

Let us begin with the example of a single practice: the practice of *hospitality to strangers.*[2] This practice has been embodied in such places as the monasteries that have sheltered travelers in late antiquity and still do today; the urban soup kitchens run by Catholic Workers; and the French village of LeChambon, where Huguenots protected thousands of Jews from the Nazis during World War II. These communities' acts of kindness — often done at great risk and always at considerable cost — were remarkable. But *random* they were not. Each act was sustained by a way of life. Years of "practicing" prepared the members of these communities to answer a knock at their doors in a certain way. There was room in their lives and in their hearts for hospitable acts — not infinite, unboundaried room, but a certain kind of open space. In these places, hospitality has been grounded in a way of life made up of very real, everyday elements done in certain ways instead of other ways — elements like handshakes and words of greeting and food and furniture and the use of time.

This sort of profound participation in the practice of hospitality to strangers does not emerge naturally. It is taught and learned. Good hosts learn stories that frame the practice; they enact rituals that include words and gestures of hospitality; they reflect deliberately on the shape and limits of the practice in their community. In the course of all these, the how and why of the practice is implicated in some of the deepest affirmations of the tradition that shapes their way of life. The practice of hospitality becomes a response to God's own hospitality in preparing creation as our dwelling place. It is instructed by the glad surprise that came when Abraham welcomed three strangers to his tent and by the obligation of a people who had wandered in the wilderness always henceforth to welcome strangers, for they had been strangers themselves. It is empowered by seeing the practice in the life of Jesus, who accepted the hospitality of sinners and preached about a banquet to which people would come from east and west, from north and south. It continues within a centuries-long process of formation and reformation, as successive generations of Christians seek, in ever new contexts, to shape ways of life that show forth the love of God and the love of neighbor in the very concrete practice of hospitality to strangers.

At our own moment in history, when millions of people around the world and near at hand are displaced from their homes, it is easy to see that hospitality is a practice that addresses a fundamental human need. Also evident, however, is the fact that fitting and gracious responses are often absent, overcome by the widespread human fear of strangers. Where people are able to resist such fear, they do so most readily through a social practice that is shared by the members of a hospitable community. Hospitality is made up of hard work accomplished under risky conditions; without structures and commitments for welcoming strangers, fear crowds out what needs to be done. Hospitable places where guests can disclose the gifts they bear come into being only when people take up this practice and grow wise, by experience, in doing it well.

Christian tradition makes normative claims about what truths shape this practice and mark its enactments as theologically and ethically sound. Using the term "hospitality" is not enough to mark the offering of shelter as an embodiment of this practice; even though there are fundamental human linkages between what is called "the hospitality industry" and a Catholic Worker House of Hospitality, these two forms of sheltering strangers arise from different motives and pursue different aims. When a practice such as hospitality to strangers takes shape in continuity with the narrative and content of Christian tradition, it embodies some of the wisdom of that tradition; and when that happens, living the practice shapes not only the behavior but also the spirits of the practitioners.

Often it is ritual that makes these connections manifest, crystallizing the meaning of the practice and holding it up in normative form for all to contemplate and enter, renewed. In the Hispanic community, for example, the ritual of *Las Posadas* provides a liturgical setting in which the whole community takes part in celebrating and affirming the practice of hospitality to strangers. In the days before Christmas Eve, community members reenact the drama of Joseph and Mary's search for a place to stay as the birth of their baby draws near; going from house to house, they sing their request for shelter, only to be turned away. When, on Christmas Eve, they are finally taken in, the community rejoices with a feast, having learned once again the goodness of receiving the stranger.

Today, as shared ways of life capable of sustaining hospitality change all around us, our culture is experiencing a crisis in this practice. Not only are most American Christians unlikely to risk the radical hospitality of the monk or the Chambonais, we retreat also from policies that would address homelessness or give decent welcome to immigrants. We turn away from the faces of those who are strange to us, and we rarely break bread with those from whom we are estranged. In fact, as *life style* replaces *way of life*, even the basic hospitality of the family table seems imperiled.

Change is also rocking most of the other activities that address fundamental human needs in our society. Such change affects the most basic things people do, things like getting dressed, caring for the sick, playing games, resolving disputes and forming households. Some of the change is good, insofar as it breaks ancient patterns of oppression; some is bad, insofar as it destroys communities; some we can't judge yet. In any case, rapid change heightens the urgency of thinking together about and growing stronger in the practices through which Christian communities over time characteristically address these needs in ways that respond to and reflect the light of God's active presence for the life of the world.

Hospitality is only one of the practices to which we need to attend. Many other shared Christian activities also cry out for reflection and strengthening. As a starting point, we propose a set of twelve: honoring the body, hospitality, household economics, saying yes and saying no, keeping sabbath, testimony, discernment, shaping communities, forgiveness, healing, dying well and singing our lives.[3] Each is fundamental to human well being and informed by the wisdom of Christian tradition; each is also, sadly, in danger in our time.

We shall argue that Christian congregations are crucial places for teaching and learning practices such as these. First, however, we must explore more fully what Christian social practices are — and thus what we mean when we say that practices are *things Christian people do together over time to address fundamental human needs, in response to and in the light of God's active presence for the life of the world*. Key features include the following.

1. Practices address fundamental human needs and conditions. They are not trivial; they matter deeply to human well being. In practices, a basic, often inarticulate, understanding of the human condition finds its fitting response in concrete, practical human acts. A fundamental human condition is that we all have bodies; a fundamental human need is that our bodies be honored — not violated, not ridiculed, not murdered. A fundamental human condition is that we are all mortal; a fundamental human need is to die with a sense of being upheld by the One who is the source of life itself and knowing that our life has somehow mattered to ourselves, to others and to God. A fundamental human condition is our vulnerability to being cast upon the mercy of strangers; a fundamental human need is for hospitality. Practices are thus congruent with the necessities of human existence.

2. Practices involve us in God's activities in the world. They are the human activities in and through which people cooperate with God in doing what needs to be done, given the fact of our humanness. Thus needy travelers are beckoned inside, given some supper and shown where to sleep. The hosts may or may not be able to explain why they do these things, but in fact they are engaging in a practice that is informed by ancient wisdom: they are practicing hospitality to strangers. The other practices are like this, providing concrete help for human flourishing. In doing so they become the means of human participation in God's own care and redemption of the world.

3. Practices involve a profound awareness, a deep knowing: they are activities imbued with thinking — imbued, in fact, with the knowledge of God. Moreover, participation in these practices is precisely how we come to such knowledge and awareness. To understand this point, we can take a lesson from Rabbi Samuel H. Dresner's explication of a central Jewish practice, the observance of the sabbath: "One can never truly know the inward feeling of the Sabbath without the outward form. The Sabbath is not a theory to be contemplated, a concept to be debated, or an idea to be toyed with. It is a day, a day filled with hours and minutes and seconds, all of which are hallowed by the wonderful pattern of living that the nobility of the human spirit has fashioned over the course of the centuries."[4] In a similar way, the Christian practices we are describing are not abstract obligations, rules or ideas; rather, they are patterns of living that are full of meaning. Each practice carries particular convictions about what is good and true, embodying these convictions in physical, down-to-earth forms.

4. Practices are social and historical. Practices are activities people do with and for one another over time. Since each of us is mortal, only corporate, social action can be extended over long periods of time and in a wide variety of social and cultural circumstances. Practices are patterned, human activities carried on by whole communities of people, not just in one particular location but across nations and generations. Even when we do them alone — praying silently in our own rooms, for example — we do them after learning them from, and in continuity with, those who have done them in the past and who do them around the world today. The specific forms are flexible, taking on the contours of many societies and cultures; but something about the Christian *way* of forgiving or resting or testifying ties the separate instances together. The Christian practices of a contemporary Christian congregation are intricately, though mysteriously, linked to the practices of communities long ago. At the same time, they are also oriented toward the future, as communities today search for ways to give full expression to the good purposes of the practices in the contemporary context.

5. Each practice can — indeed, must — be crafted in varied ways and forms, depending on the specific cultural and social situations in which it is manifest. In a sense, practices sweep through history, seeming somehow larger than any person or specific community. But when a practice is vital and authentic, it is also very concrete and particular, very here-and-now. It is made up of many apparently small gestures and words and images and objects, taking fresh form each day as it subtly adapts to find expression in each neighborhood or cultural group. The particular elements that compose it change from time to time and place to place; some of them, indeed, have yet to be imagined. And yet they are recognizably appropriate to and part of a discernible, historical Christian practice. The content of Christian practices resists those features of contemporaneous cultural practices that are not congruent with human well being; but at the same time, practices that are explicitly identified as Christian practices often overlap and merge with good activities arising from other traditions.

6. Practices pursue the good, involving us in life patterns that reflect God's grace and love. When a teenager knows with certainty that her parents honor her body, she begins to understand her God-given strength and beauty. When the bereaved are surrounded by mourners who sing and pray, they become able to thank God for the life of their beloved. When an overstressed worker takes one day every week to worship, feast and play, he is renewed in relation to God, other people and the work that he does on the other days of the week. In all these things, people share in the practices of God, who has also honored the human body, embraced death and rested, calling creation good.

7. At the same time, there is no denying that actual communities rarely if ever attain transparent participation in Christian practices. Both our individual failings and the wrongs embedded in economic or political structures set obstacles in the way of practices that are good for all people. Indeed, any given practice can become so distorted that its outcome becomes evil rather than good. Thus much of the thinking we need to do about practices is critical thinking, thinking that can disclose how destructively the basic activities of human life can actually be organized — globally, in American society, in our churches and in our homes. If we are willing to risk further change, however, this kind of thinking can also guide us into renewed ways of life.

8. Participating in practices shapes people in certain ways, developing in them certain habits, virtues and capacities of mind and spirit. Communities become hospitable — and so do individuals — as they move from fear to openness. Such becoming involves an increasing generosity that can stretch not only the purse but also the heart. The content of each practice challenges, lures, coaxes and sometimes drags its practitioners into new capacities and ways of being that are commensurate with that practice. It is easy to see how singers acquire skills in their practice, taking a pitch from others, developing a repertoire and learning when to stand, when to breathe and when to boost or diminish the volume. Sometimes — often, we hope — music even happens! Though harder to recognize, other practices — practices like forgiving, discerning, healing and sabbath keeping — develop capacities in their practitioners as well.

9. All of the practices of daily life come to a focus in worship. As the community gathers to share words, gestures, images and material things that make manifest the presence of God, each of the Christian practices is rendered more visible, more articulate, more pure. Worshipers glimpse what Christian hospitality or forgiveness or healing can more fully be, encountering them afresh in the rich thickness of song and scripture, greeting and giving. In one sense, we learn something about the practices by participating in their liturgical expressions. In a deeper sense this process is not didactic, for at worship both we and our practices encounter the *mystery* of God. Sacraments, after all, are not practices but gifts, gifts greater than our own power to conceive them, gifts greater even than the power of death. Receiving them together in worship, we receive anew the way of life we have entered, now not as task but as gift.

Honoring the body, hospitality, household economics, saying yes and saying no, keeping sabbath, testimony, discernment, shaping communities, forgiveness, healing, dying well, singing our lives — woven together, these constitute a *way of life*. Each of these practices could be found somewhere in the life of every Christian congregation. Sometimes one practice, or more, might be so frail that detecting it would be quite a job, while finding distortions at many points would be easy. Yet sometimes a certain congregation knows a certain practice by heart, and we can see the practice taking shape with great profundity in that concrete setting. Reading the practices as they take shape in the life of a particular congregation can help us to discern what knowledge of God's active presence in the world these little bands of human beings bear.

Viewing congregations in this way, we would see the practices not only in the activities done in or by the congregation officially acting as congregation, however. We would also see practices in the activities of members in their homes and schools, in their places of work and play, sometimes conflicting and sometimes congruent with those of the congregation. And in this doubleness would lie a dimension of challenge and complexity, not only for those who look *at* congregations but, more importantly, for those who seek to live faithfully under their guidance.

So it has been since Christian congregations came into being. In *The Origins of Christian Morality*, the New Testament scholar Wayne Meeks examines early Christian congregations as communities of shared practices. Practices, he argues, shaped and reinforced the moral sensibilities of the earliest Christians and defined the tensions they experienced in daily life beyond their communities. Upon entering the church, Christians took up a set of specific communal activities that taught them the way of life they were entering: baptism, eucharist, hours of prayer, and certain patterns of eating, hospitality, giving, admonition and healing. Belief and behavior, action and thought were integrally related in these activities; theological convictions were woven into the social forms of community life. But when these Christians went home from their communal meetings, these clear patterns frayed. Meeks continues, "One way of thinking about the great monastic movements that developed in the fourth century and later is as an attempt to resolve the tension between the practices of 'the world' and the practices of the Christian community, by renouncing the former to the maximum extent possible. For most Christians, however, . . . the Christian life was an amphibian life, life at the same time in the old world that was passing away and in the new world that was coming."[5]

Anyone who has studied even a little church history and Christian ethics — or looked closely at the contemporary religious scene — is aware that the tensions Meeks describes are enduring ones. But it is precisely this "amphibian" quality of Christian life that makes the combination of practices and congregations so generative, for practices are inextricably tied to God and to the gathered life of the church *and also* thoroughly entangled in the stuff of everyday living. The twelve practices we have named do not happen only within the gathered Christian community; they also become manifest in the daily lives of practitioners in other spheres. Moreover, in the public realm Christian practitioners find themselves working with the members of many different communities of practice to address fundamental human needs or to resist the cultural, economic and social forces that erode such practices and leave fundamental human needs unmet. They move from one context of practice to another, in other words, like amphibians, though perhaps not conscious that they are doing so.

More than any other places, however, congregations are the settings where people look for the resources to bridge these contexts — the places where they hope to learn about life-giving patterns of life suited to the multiple complex contexts in which they now live. Joining a congregation is not the same as going into the desert — it leaves one an amphibian — but congregations do resemble monasteries in aspiring to model the way things are supposed to be in their own internal life; they aim to develop shared internal practices that are theologically sound and, indeed, in continuity with communal practices of early Christianity. Yet congregations are also significantly different from monasteries, for they are perpetually and unavoidably open to what Meeks calls "the practices of 'the world.'" They do not draw only highly dedicated adherents, nor do their members usually journey great distances for the sake of joining. Rather, congregations are deeply embedded in very specific localities, where members live always elbow-to-elbow with nonmembers. They are much more porous than monasteries; the members, and the surrounding culture, seep in and out all the time, mixing the worlds of home, school, work, the media, a city, and the congregation willy-nilly every day.

Congregations are brilliantly adaptive institutions in that they become immersed in their own unique local settings. Critical theologians are aware that this can be a liability, as congregations lose their theological distinctiveness over/against the surrounding culture; but this peril is only one side of the story of congregational adaptiveness. At the same time, congregations are also, remarkably, the places where people encounter Christian practices that more or less resist the social forms through which the surrounding culture addresses fundamental human needs. Indeed, congregations are among the few places where people deliberately expose themselves to that which is strange to both local cultures and the mass media. Sometimes, as at LeChambon, the resultant call to participate in the startling practices of God is sharp and clear, while in other settings it may be barely perceptible. But the strangeness is there nonetheless, in the biblical text and the liturgy.

Such qualities make congregations places where the patterns of people's daily lives beyond the church can encounter the critical challenge, the gracious help and the transforming power of Christian faith over long periods of time. They are places where members can *practice* the practices of Christian faith.

What foundation does this way of thinking provide for education and formation in Christian faith, particularly in a time when many people are searching for something they can barely name?

To act with and for other people over time in response to fundamental human needs and in the light of God's active presence is to have a *way of life* that adds up to something, and not merely a *life style*. It is a way that can draw on the wisdom and testimony of past generations while also being alert to the urgent needs of contemporary people. Educating and forming one another in this way is a guiding purpose of Christian education.

Yet obstacles arise — and one of these is the problem we might call "the problem of the too big and the too small." The problem of the too big is that our purposes as Christian educators are rightly and necessarily large: they have to do ultimately with learning a whole way of life. But that kind of purpose is too large, too grand, too big to be of much directly useful guidance. Something that large is impossible to get your mind around. It's too big to do.

The problem of the too small is the opposite. In our actual work of educating we do a little of this and a little of that and a little of something else. But too often it doesn't seem to add up to much. We can't tell what larger wholes these smaller pieces are parts of. The connections get lost, and we lose any sense of the significance and import of particular educational activities and projects and events. That's the problem of the too small.

Part of the educational significance of the idea and social reality of Christian practices is that this concept provides a good answer to the problem of the too big and the too small. It breaks down a way of life into a set of constructive practices. At the same time, it draws together the shards and pieces of particular events, behaviors, actions, relationships, inquiries and skills into large enough wholes to show how they might add up to a way of life.

In the present cultural context, Christian educators need to think about how to lead people beyond a reliance on "random acts of kindness" into shared patterns of life that are informed by the deepest insights of our tradition, and about how to lead people beyond privatized spiritualities into more thoughtful participation in God's activity in the world. In the mainstream Protestant communions to which the two of us belong, large numbers of members — and even some leaders — often seem to be unaware of the rich insights and strong help the Christian tradition can bring to today's concerns. Thinking about our *way of life* as standing in dynamic continuity with our Christian heritage and with the world-wide church today opens fresh sources of insight into how the practices that pattern our days can shape our lives in ways that respond to the active presence of God for the life of the world. Reflecting together on the shared activities we are calling "Christian practices" can help us learn from the generous spirituality of historic Christian faith even while we walk the unfamiliar path that lies ahead, through the surprising realities of each new context.

Thus the practical theological assessment and transformation of practices can be a generative focus for congregation-based efforts in Christian education, as Christians try to assist one another and the larger society towards a future whose patterns of life are wholesome and just. What is required is thoughtful attention to practices and Christian mindfulness of them as we encounter them in church and society in times of rapid social reconfiguration.

Let us once again consider as an example the practice of hospitality to strangers. Many congregations have already come to closer attention to this practice in response to specific challenges. An urban Presbyterian church was forced to consider this, for example, when homeless people came into the after-service coffee hour and swept all the cookies off the platters into their shopping bags. After considerable debate over how to respond, the congregation founded Rosie's Place, which now serves lunches to homeless women several days a week. In this same congregation, meanwhile, some of the other hospitable events by which they had welcomed newcomers over the years were dying out; as the generations turned, fewer members had time to prepare casseroles for potluck suppers, and a gap was opening in the communal patterns of the congregation. Some of the gap was filled by small groups formed around special interests; several of these became warm friendship circles, small enough to meet in a member's home or to fit around a restaurant table and open enough to absorb new members at an appropriate pace.

Through these new patterns of shared life, this congregation was responding to fundamental human needs in ways that were both informed by the Christian tradition and alert to the concrete possibilities of its own context. Reflection on these new patterns as aspects of a single Christian practice might lead them to consider other aspects of congregational life as well. Does the congregation's worship life bespeak hospitality? Has it taken seriously the eschatological hospitality celebrated in its primary meal, the Lord's Supper? How is it helping children and other newcomers to learn this practice? What does Christian mindfulness about hospitality suggest for families or friendship groups in the congregation? What insights might the members' experience of practicing hospitality as a congregation enable them to contribute to the larger society's debate over the practice of hospitality? Questions such as these will not be easy to answer. It will be fruitful to take them up, however, not as a way of imposing abstract ethical norms but for the sake of strengthening a *practice* in which the congregation is already active.

Christian practices appear in slightly different forms in each unique local congregation and surrounding community. Deliberate and ordered thinking, observing and participating could enable people to notice, analyze, renew and publicly explain the practices in their own situations.[6] The concreteness of practices and their grounding in the Bible and theology make them an excellent way to focus on many dimensions of a congregation's life, both as they are and as we yearn for them to be. An exploration of this sort could focus on any of the twelve practices we have named, as well as on other practices identified in particular communities. They would include attention to questions such as these:

a) How is this congregation already participating in each practice in its life together? What would an analysis of a week's schedule disclose about how various church activities embody specific practices? What practices are provided with room and resources within the church building itself? Where in the church building do people participate in specific practices?

b) How does this congregation's participation in the practices prepare members to engage in the practices in their daily lives, at home and at work? Conversely, how does their participation in the practices in those places influence what happens among the people gathered as church?

c) Are some of the practices done especially well here? Certain congregations have a gift for a certain practice, such as singing our lives or surrounding one another with care when death comes. Similarly, certain denominational or cultural streams within Christianity are more closely attuned to a certain practice, such as testimony, forgiveness or sabbath keeping. Congregations can be helped by this way of thinking to identify the gifts they bear.

d) Where are the practices missing or broken in this congregation? Is there evidence of pain or yearning that suggests that a certain practice is in trouble? With what practice does this congregation need help? What biblical, theological, historical and practical resources can help to cleanse and amplify their participation in the practice?

e) How are the practices related to one another in this congregation? How does participating in one of them lead people into the others? Or does it?

f) How does what happens in Sunday morning worship help the gathered people to understand and grow in Christian practices? Do the words, gestures, images, sounds and feel of the liturgy vividly manifest the active presence of God in and for the life of the world and warmly invite worshipers to offer response?

If, as we claim, worshiping Christian congregations know something about a way of life that is in accord with what is good and true, the explicit exploration of Christian practices can provide a means of articulating, amplifying and clarifying that knowledge, so that each unique congregation might grow stronger in that way and better able to invite others to walk it as well. Such an exploration would make an important contribution alongside the everyday learning and growth that take place within the ordinary flow of congregational and daily life, as members enter into the practices with and for one another and the world. This is of great importance, particularly in a fast-paced, divided and violent society where fundamental human needs often go unmet and where the patterns of life even of Christian congregations and individuals are too often misshapen. Alert to Christian practices, we may learn in our congregations to comprehend more fully the knowledge they bear and to embody more wholly the divine grace and love they reflect.

Endnotes

1 We originally developed this definition as part of the working group that produced *Practicing Our Faith*, ed. Dorothy C. Bass (San Francisco: Jossey-Bass Publishers, 1997). The idea of "practices" has received much attention from philosophers and social scientists in recent years. Our use of the term is loosely based on the work of the moral philosopher Alasdair MacIntyre (see *After Virtue: A Study in Moral Theory*, 2d ed. [Notre Dame IN: University of Notre Dame Press, 1984], 187–88). Craig Dykstra led the way in exploring how this idea can helpfully address our yearning for a Christian way of life; see *Growing in the Life of Faith: Education in Christian Practice* (Louisville KY: Geneva Press, 1999) and "Reconceiving Practice," in *Shifting Boundaries: Contextual Approaches to the Structure of Theological Education*, ed. Barbara G. Wheeler and Edward Farley (Louisville KY: Westminster John Knox Press, 1991).

2 A brilliant exposition of the Christian practice of hospitality to strangers in Christine D. Pohl, *Making Room: Recovering Hospitality as a Christian Tradition* (Grand Rapids: Eerdmans, 1999).

3 *Practicing Our Faith* includes an essay on each of these twelve.

4 Samuel H. Dresner, *The Sabbath* (New York: Burning Bush Press, 1970), 21.

5 Wayne Meeks, *The Origins of Christian Morality: The First Two Centuries* (New Haven CT: Yale University Press, 1993), 109.

6 Suggestions for this process are in Dorothy C. Bass et al., *Practicing Our Faith: A Guide for Learning, Conversation and Growth* (San Francisco: Jossey-Bass Publishers, 1997). The questions in the next few paragraphs are adapted from this source.